AF587879

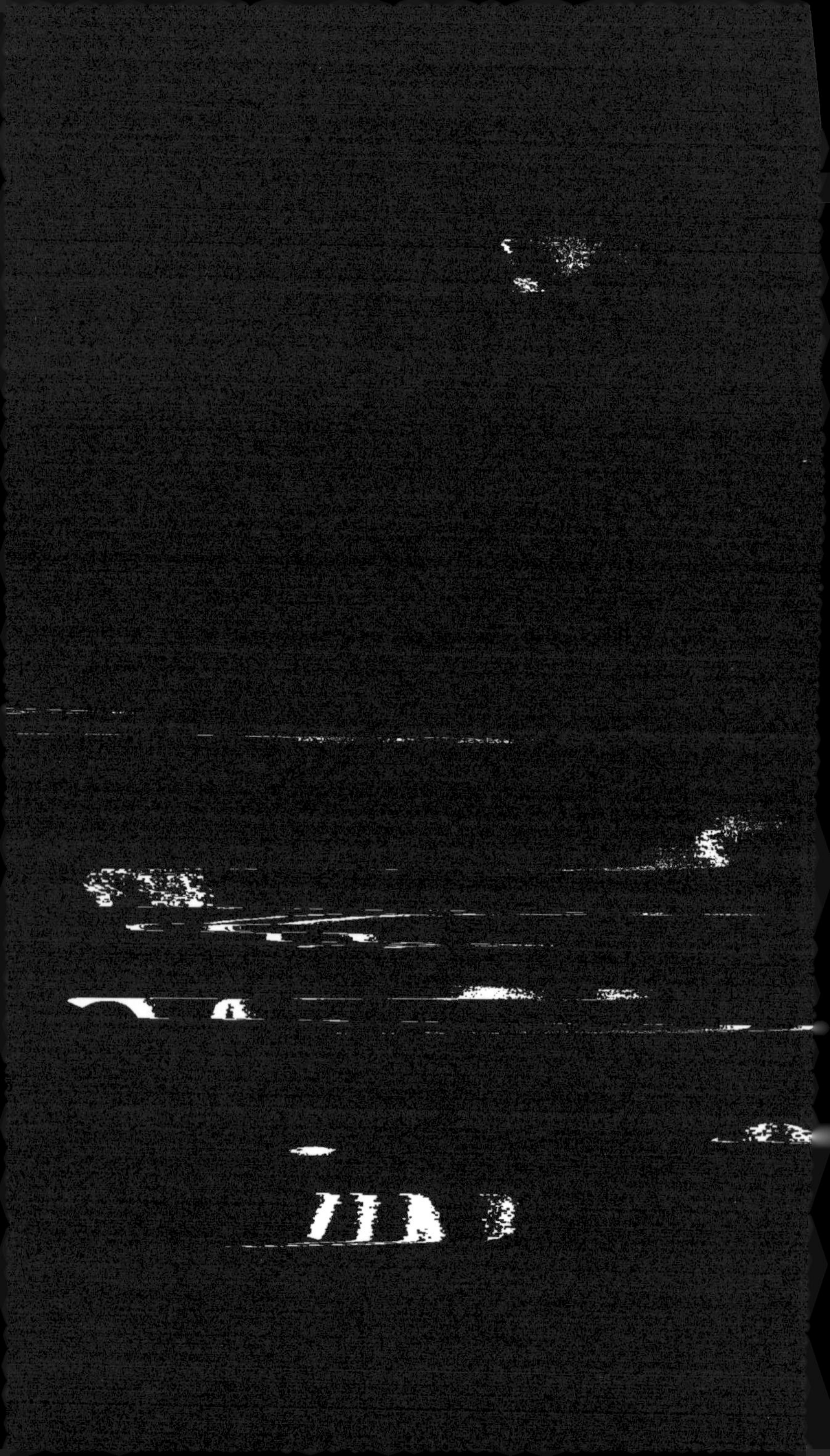

WATCH THIS SPACE FRANCESCA GAVIN

WATCH THIS SPACE

FRAN
CESCA
GAVIN

CONTENTS

CONTENTS

VIDEODROME

There seems to be a disconnection between our experiences of the screen in daily life and how it is represented in film, television and fiction. It is almost as if other mediums are unable to express the speed and tactility of the relationship of the swipe, the button press or the hyperlink. Most often the screen is reduced to a blue glow on an actor's face.

There are exceptions. The Nokia 8110 phone was intertwined with the entire narrative of the film *The Matrix*. On screen, it had a flip-open element that was added specifically as a dramatic element to its usage. (Samsung followed up by placing their SPH-N270 in the sequel, *The Matrix: Reloaded* with less fanfare.) The mobile phone was an incredibly important part of the narrative. The phone set characters free from locations and dimensions. The screen in *The Matrix* represents freedom: a link between the dream world and gritty, bitter reality. As a Nokia promo text put it at the time, "The heroes of the movie could not do their job and save the world without the seamless connectivity provided by Nokia's mobile phones."

There are other examples where screens are central to narratives. The unintentionally hilarious horror movie *Cell* (2006) is based on a novel by Stephen King. Starring John Cusack, the apocalyptic story is based around a mobile phone network gone wrong. Graphic novelist, Cusack, is on a landline in an airport, when he witnesses everyone on his or her mobile phones transformed into murderous zombies through a corrupt message takeover. They foam at the mouth, eat dogs and throw each other out of windows. They wander in packs on the street, covered in blood, mobile phones in hand. When they are out of signal, they collapse, unable to function. It is a wonderful metaphor for the zombie-like behaviour we present when engaged with our screens.

There is innate cultural discomfort about the phone, something that emerges in the work of David Lynch. In *Twin Peaks: The Return* (2017), receptionist Lucy is talking to Sheriff on the phone, assuming he is away fishing. When he appears in front of her, she is so discombobulated by his presence in life and on the phone to her simultaneously, that she passes out. Lynch's film *Lost Highway* (1997) addresses the same issue in a less comedic way. The protagonist of the film, Pullman, is approached by a strange white-faced man at a party. This strange man insists they have met before. He claims that he is in Pullman's home at the same time he is present at the party. The proof is a mobile phone call. The horror comes from the sudden realisation that the white-faced man is in two places at once, an innately uncanny realisation.

Why is technology so duplicitous and disturbing? The screen repels representation, echoing the way vampires cannot be reflected in mirrors in horror literature. This is in fact a physical problem that fiction fails to camouflage. The radiation emanating from laptop and LCD screens is so much that they become unreadable when viewed through another camera.

Professional filmmakers have a number of solutions to this problem. A computer playback supervisor's entire job is to look at the complex representation of screens.

One way to represent the screen, on screen, is to just turn the thing off or use green screen technology and add fake content afterwards in post production. Another option involves camera operators using special video monitors that run at 24 FPS in sync to the film camera. Most computer monitors run at 60 Hz; if the moving image camera is adjusted to correspond to the same speed of the monitor it should look OK. For something so common place and almost banal, it is interesting how hard the screen is to depict or incorporate into cultural narrative. It is far easier to insert the screen into a narrative of fear and horror.

Mary Shelley's *Frankenstein* (1818) is the classic blueprint for the manifestation of our fears of technological progress and its impact on the human body. The monster made of human body parts, sewn together into a new, uncanny hybrid, reflects tropes around industrialisation and scientific experimentation. The villain in Shelley's novel is both the victim and the source of fear. He is created by humanity, in the form of the doctor. What we are afraid of here is the modernist project of progress. Gothic narratives aimed to reaffirm the norms of sexuality, morality and social placement in the eighteenth and nineteenth century. The genre's excessive, hysteric vision of progress was reimagined in twentieth and twenty-first century science fiction. Yet today, in our era of instability, with economic, social and political turmoil now the norm, there is little to soothe our fears. Things are changing too fast.

We worry about the loss of the boundaries around ourselves. How do we define our identity as it becomes increasingly manipulated, muted and morphed by screens attached to our hands? We now inhabit a world similar to William Gibson's *Neuromancer* (1984) where life is controlled by large corporations through computers. However, this breakdown between state and self, power and the individual, manifests not just as a political friction. It also leads to trauma. "The spiller of the private into the public, the overflowing of inside into outside, is itself pornography (sex in public) and pollution (shit in public)," Mark Seltzer writes in *The Serial Killer As A Type of Person*.

This is a book that attempts to dissect and come to terms with the screen, and how it is affecting society, the self and culture. It is an amalgam of questions around what the screen is, how it functions, how it dominates our experiences, our eyes, our emotions. It is an examination into the politics of objects. The screen is the item that defines the twenty-first century. It's about time we worked out why.

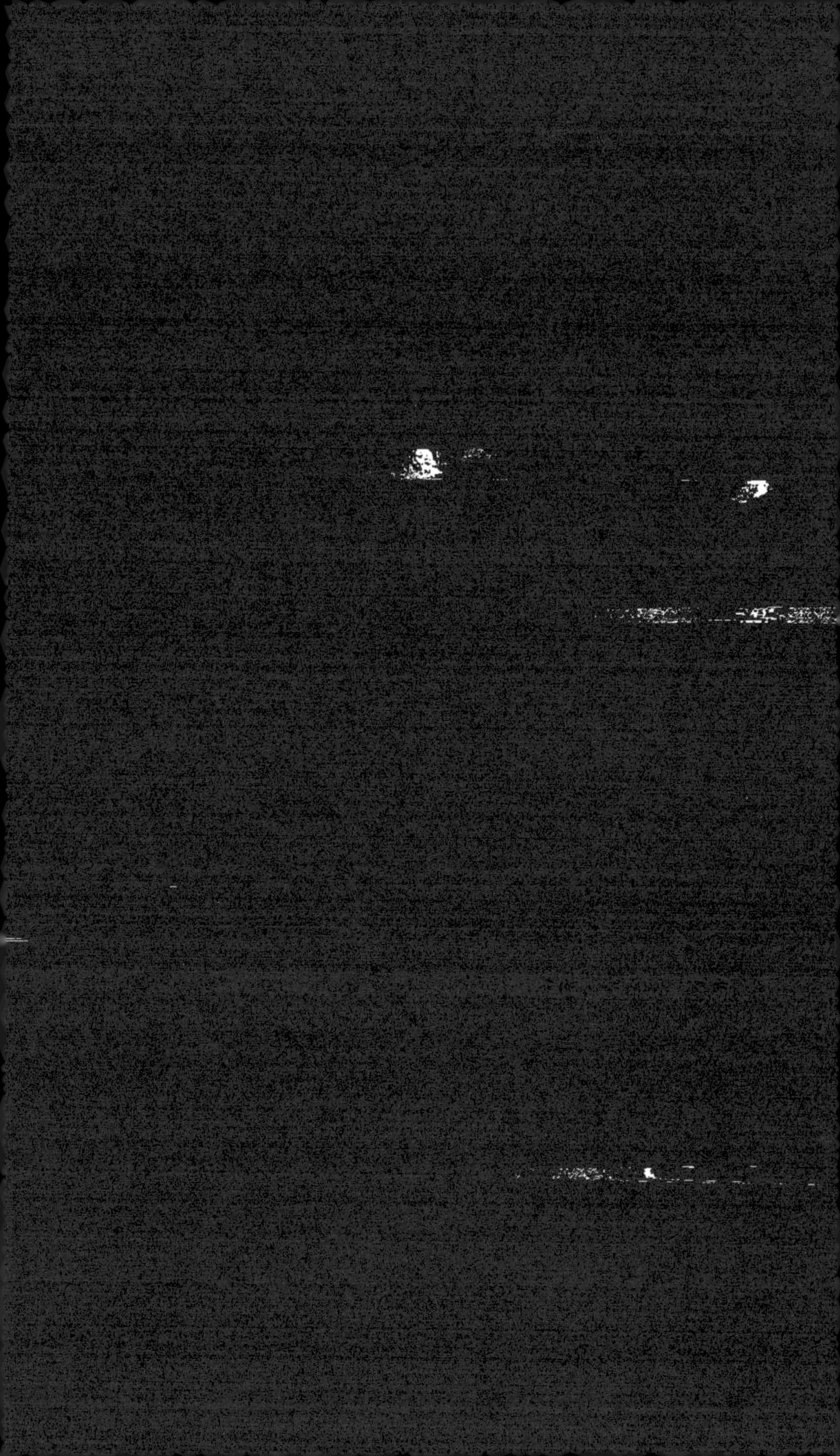

YOU LOOKING AT ME?

A friend recommended an app to me over coffee in Berlin. It had an inviting name, Moment, and recorded how often you use your phone each day. After a few days I discovered my screen use was average. I used my screen device for four hours a day. This did not include time on my computer. I spent 240 minutes each day staring at my phone screen, swiping, pressing, checking, texting. It raised an obvious question. What the hell was I looking at?

The screen is the one of the most present surfaces in modern life. We use screens to pay for things, to communicate, to be entertained. The screen has changed our daily experience, our ways of thinking, our ways of looking. The phone is the most intimate example of our relationship to technology; it is the screen-object we carry with us everyday. If you search 'looking at phone' on the Internet, what comes up is a YouTube clip of people staring at their phones. The voiceover in the video describes "an epidemic of texting while walking" and positions this as something seriously dangerous.

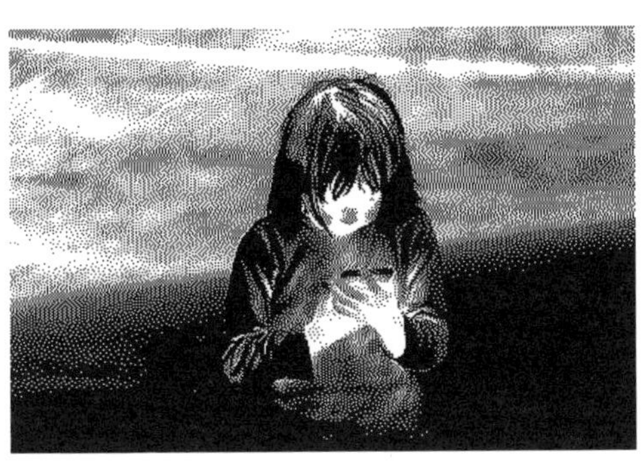

Illustrated by funny amateur footage, this humorous news excerpt is a perfect example of our relationship with our phones. How we fall into our focus on the screen, forgetting the physical space around us. We forget our own physicality. The narrator uses the phrase "inattention blindness." But in reality it is the opposite. The people featured are consumed with attention—they are just looking down at the object in their hands not at their 'real' surroundings.

There are screens around us at all times. We wake up and check our screens for messages. If we travel to work on public transport, more than half of us are on our phones. We stare at screens for work, communication, play and diversion throughout the day. At home, we watch a screen again for entertainment, or swipe it to hook up. Sometimes with a second screen on our lap. Then we go to sleep with our screens next to our beds. We experience screens in advertising, moving alongside us on the escalator, blown up on the sides of buildings. At music gigs or exhibitions or cultural experiences, everyone is watching things through their screens, capturing the moment in some form. Amateur mobile screen footage is now normal on the news. As James Bridle in his essay *The New Aesthetic and Its Politics* writes, "protest, repression, revolt and schism are framed not through the lens of critique, but the lens of iPhones and iPads held aloft."

It is easy to join the choir of criticism to the screen. There is enough of it and the effect on life in the past two decades is visceral. My own feelings are ambivalent—a midpoint between horror and fascination, admiration and addiction. Before you can even get to grips with screen content, you need to first focus on the screen as a medium.

WHAT IS A SCREEN?

When I first started thinking about the subject, the screen seemed easy to define. It was something that grew directly out of the construction and composition of painting, referencing the dimensions and constructions of the canvas. The modern screen was an extension of the cinema screen and the television. It developed into the computer monitor, the laptop screen, the phone screen and the flat screen. Yet, as the academic and writer Peter Lunenfeld pointed out to me, my conception was perhaps limited. “The newest screens really are sort of pseudo-screens,” he explained. The screen today is no longer necessarily a black rectangle or square. It is also an Oculus Rift headset or a projected surface with moving imagery, such as the blank tunnels on the London tube system that are transformed into screens between trains. The screen has moved beyond the confines of the screen.

Scale is also changing. We no longer have big screens or small ones but a variety of sizes for different purposes, for example, the ‘phablet’, a phone with a bigger space to watch films or play games. We are seeing a move away from mid-range ‘human’ sized towards the tiny or the supersized. The same applies to narrative itself. “The classic Aristotelian dramatic unity of the 90 to the 120-minute theatrical presentation, which moves from Greek theatre into medieval passion plays, into narrative length films—that just disappears in favour of the Vine at six seconds and Game of Thrones at 28 hours," Lunenfeld observes. There is a strong connection between what we watch and how and what we watch it on.

The contemporary screen has its own texture, colour and illumination. It has its own physicality. The screen exudes warmth, releases high-pitched buzzes and squeaks. The screen makes itself feel present. When we look at images on a screen they appear stable, but in reality they often fall apart, get stuck, fail to emerge or disintegrate. Laura Marks in *Touch: Sensuous Theory and Multisensory Media* argues that digital media is in fact analogue. Screen technology is unpredictable. Connections cut out and errors occur. These are all things that remind us of technology's physicality rather than its transcendence. Failure is inbuilt into screen design. As Marks puts it, "technologies age and die just as people do." It is just manufacturers and techno evangelists with vested interest that make us want to imagine that technology is superhuman.

In the past three decades, the LCD screen has become the most prevalent model. The materiality and aesthetics of liquid crystals is something at the heart of the work of the British author and lecturer, Esther Leslie. For Leslie, the ability of LCD and plasma screens to be flicker-free, still at any moment and negate the time progression of narratives, is influencing creative content.

Liquid crystals were first recorded in the 1880s. The discovery that crystals could be electrified, melt and exude colour and fluorescence was something concurrent with the nineteenth century fad for science-based entertainment. It echoed the spectacular aspect of magic lantern shows, dioramas and zoetropes. George Heilmeier began research around liquid crystals at the Royal College of Art in 1964. He combined them with dyes and electrified and created colour changes in the crystals under polarised light. By 1966, a prototype liquid crystal display was made and unveiled to the public two years later. Artist Gustav Metzger was also working with liquid crystal installations at the time, on Polaroid film. He would heat them and then project them in destructive, psychadelic light shows.

The RCA research department discovered that patterns could appear on the crystals at the flick of a switch, when they were sandwiched between glass. The college sold the research to Timex in 1976, who wanted to experiment with its use in watches. Seiko, Hitachi and Sharp licensed the process and in 1977 Hitachi presented the first prototype LCD television. By the 1990s, LCDs had overtaken cathode ray TVs, resulting in ever-skinnier boxes with glowing blue surfaces.

The thinness of LCD screens has created new experiences. We want to enter the screen. As we touch screen surfaces, we are constantly trying to move beyond their boundaries, to get inside the material somehow. The screen exists in a zone between the human and the machine. Its workings are invisible, almost magical. We do not see the processes that mediate our experience between the social and the technological.

The interface influences how we view the screen, how we absorb information and imagery. This gateway is impossible to enter without its own language of swipes, touches, taps, buttons and clicks. Before we even begin, our interaction is being determined and formed by an 'other'. Our swipes, taps and pushes imply we have agency, but the design of our phones and computers are very regimented. We are far more passive than we think. As Branden Hookway describes in *Interface* (2014), "Even at the moment human and machine come into contact, their encounter has already been subject to a mediation."

We think of the screen as inert until activated by our actions. How phones function is decided by outside forces, designers, companies, and 'choice architects'. What are their intentions? Are we always choosing to look at the screen or is the interface so addictive, the moving image so manipulative, that we have no choice? You could argue screens have an autonomous intelligence and sense of control over us. Or perhaps agency is something bouncing between us and the screen. There is a struggle for power or ownership that the screen space will always win. The interface has come to define human agency. "There is no political power exerted through the interface that is not also some form of admixture or hybrid, whether material, technological, or human," Hookway notes. The interface is not technology itself. It is not the tool; it is how control is exerted.

The word 'interface' itself was invented in the late 19th century for the field of fluid dynamics. It describes a kind of transaction. An interface looks inwards, even if its display is on the outside. 'To interface' can also be a verb to describe our communication with the screen, with technology. The passive and the active, the outer and the inner are all intertwined in this relationship. The screen is no longer a place for content but a space that invites you in—or at least implies depth and contribution. But how much contribution is truly there? Surface is a vital element to the screen. The shiny blackness; the flatness where depth is always implied and projected. Rather than a window, it is a void we fall into. More like *Alice's Adventures Underground* than a scene through a window. The screen surface is also superficial and illusory, a fake smile. Maybe its falseness is what makes it so apt in the world today? Or have we become more fake as we replicate the screen?

THINKING BODIES

What happens when we touch the screen? There is something important about the haptic element of interaction. Touch is a vital aspect in the creation of emotional response. We think through our bodies; perception is bound with action.

The history of art is bound up with the imitation of nature, or in its professional Latin term *mimesis*. Today's photorealistic 3D animation attempts to do the same thing—to make the fictional feel faultless. Yet digitisation is not a thing itself, but a simulation of something. A computer transforms an image into pixels, code, a language—the result is a version of something.

The idea of static perspective does not apply to tablet or phone images. There is no single point of view in contemporary screens. When images are placed together they form a kind of narrative flow. When we swipe or touch screen images, in a sense they move. Our viewpoint is always shifting.

The marketing around technology is less about function and more about a desirable experience, as Melanie Swalwell observes in the 2012 essay 'A critique of the Hyper State: Aesthetics, Technology and Experience'. Focusing on the idea of hyperstimulation, she documents the "valorising of hyper states" and how screen manufacturers describe their products as "explosive" experiences that will "blow you away". They promise intense, immediate visceral excitement. It is less about engagement and more about novel effect.

When Apple chief executive Steve Jobs unveiled the iPhone in 2007, his aim was to present a button-free giant screen. What a perfect way to appeal to his audience's desires—a screen that could be tilted, pinched and pulled. The image covered the entire surface. There was no distraction created by the edges, the keyboard, the mouse or the button. This was the screen, and nothing but the screen. Jobs was selling humanity its own reflection.

What could be more uncomfortable or disturbing than the cracked or smudged screen, a rupture in the perfection of the interface and the surface? Screens are becoming increasingly large and increasingly thin, but always faultless, perfect and tactile. The word 'ergonomic' was a buzz term at the turn of the millennium, indicating design made to fit with the human body.

Now it is us who work around the screen. Its resolution, its shape and its clarity dictate our experience.

Have you ever noticed that when you truly need to make a call or see an email, your phone dies or the computer screen freezes? What happens when the screen fails? When we cannot connect? When the screen crashes? "Technology always fails eventually," Martin Dixon correctly points out in *The Horror of Disconnection*. "Failure is a face of technological functions and counteracting or containing failure is routinely incorporated in product design." The Utopian dreamy possibility of the screen fails, the aura is gone. Instead we are left with a blank book cover and no way to open it to access the information inside.

50 million iPods were sold in the five years after its launch in 2001. At this point, the technological object moved the intimate experience of listening to music on a walkman or headphones into something social and public. Wearing white headphones had social meaning. New gestures were created to interact with the technology. Music itself became socially networked and accessible. A white cube to curate, reflecting our own interests back at us. The iPod was the first object that defined contemporary immersion. Tactile, aural and visual, yet impossible to truly enter. A new category of cyborgian thing.

We don't really want to be controlled by our objects, but we want choice removed from our hands. For Freudians, you could see this as the release of the death drive. A broken thing means we have no options. Martin Dixon raises Jean Baudrillard's ideas: "Do we even want technology that is infallible... Infallibility brings with it an anxiety no less acute than the event of our bodies being abandoned by it?"

Everything in the world that is not of the screen is falling away—paper media, modes of communication, entertainment spaces. Aesthetics increasingly have to adapt to the screen; still images, TV shows, films, artwork, even individuals have to fit its dimensions.

Research into gambling machines, in the context of addiction, has highlighted how speed of interaction and screen content is something we quickly have become accustomed to and find pacifying, almost like tranquilisers. Casinos insulate players physically so they become more absorbed in the playing, unaware of their bodies, passive under the control of the flow of the game. Money itself is irrelevant. To a lesser extent it is the same sensation produced by phone flash games or even scrolling social media streams. We override our instincts, our physicality and instead become so hypnotised we dissolve. This sensation is heightened even further by virtual reality headsets, which have established a radical new relationship to the screen. We are immobile yet have to move. Strapped in, trapped by the image but turning our heads. We feel active but are, in fact, passive.

US AND IT

What in the thing is thingly? Martin Heidegger's question is apt when we consider how we connect to the 'objectness' of the screen. We know it's a thing, but project so much more onto it. The screen functions somewhere between an office, a lover, a mirror and a pet.

Its thinglyness emerged from broadcast media. Radio and television were transmitted through electromagnetic waves. They were part of domestic homes. Private yet, to an extent, social. Immediate, live and transformative. VHS and tape allowed people to manipulate the medium's innate authenticity, and record, edit and rework moving imagery. Video recorders were sold to the general public from 1971 but didn't catch on until a decade later. By the early 1980s, there was a rise in aggression towards the television and its control on the social mind. Video became a way to breakdown the economic control of advertisers and broadcasters. The rise of VHS was a way to record programmes, skip commercials and interact with film material directly. Interaction meant democracy, and for the first time viewers were able to curate and manage their own cultural experiences rather than watch what was presented to them by someone else. It provided choice—something that tuned in perfectly with the rising individual-led Reagan-era thinking of the self.

Video art was innately connected to this era. This was when Nam June Paik emerged with sculptural artworks incorporating switched-on TV sets. Artists began to claim video as a way to highlight the materiality of film, the inequality of representation, and show how what we watched was structured and controlled. Artists working with the medium included Vito Acconci, Susan Hiller, John Baldessari, Joan Jonas, General Idea and a notable number of Japanese artists including Kyoko Michishitz and Fluxus names like Wolf Vostell. This was a special moment of screen resistance, where there seemed to be a possibility of agency and action. This morphed into public access television, the DIY, and even the narrative of *Sex, Lies and Videotape* (1989).

At the same time, Hollywood began to fear its loss of power. A group of film companies sued Sony in 1976 for selling a device enabling the audience to record movies, and lobbied Congress intensely in the early 1980s to impose royalties on blank video cassettes and VCRs that would lead to revenue losses. These attempts feel futile and almost comedic now in the wake of the video revolution that redefined the decades that followed. Watching entertainment at home created a whole new market, a sense of ownership. The spread of digital access took the same process and propelled it to another level. Now we all 'Netflix and chill'.

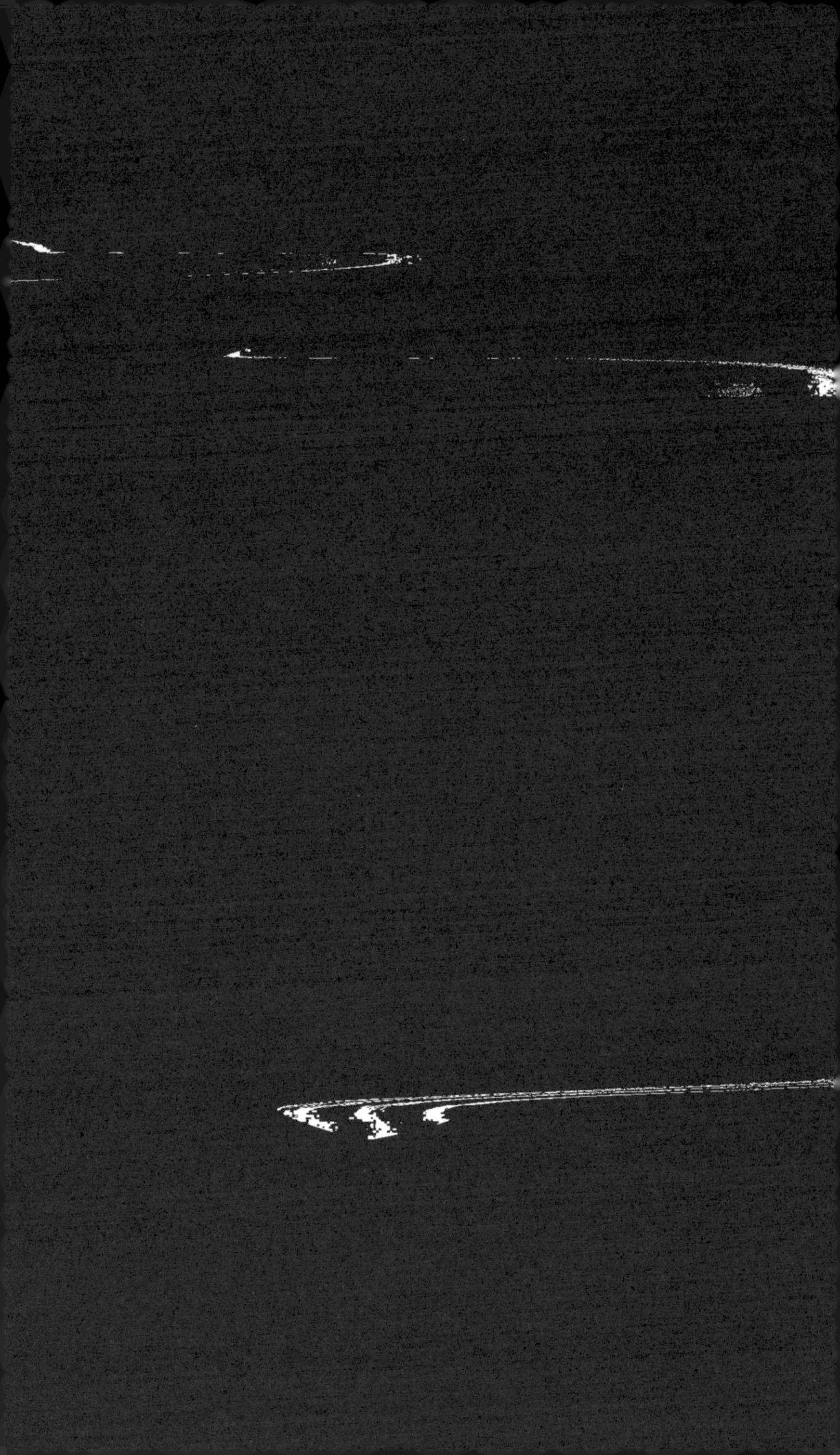

The screen lives on our bodies. It sits in our pockets and our bags. We often touch it or look at it for reassurance numerous times per hour. The content of the screen soothes us. This emotional connection to the screen is a major difference to older media such as the telephone or television. "Distance is abolished... between stage and auditorium, between subject and object, between the real and its double," the postmodern French sociologist and philosopher Jean Baudrillard writes in his essay *Screened Out* in 1996. "There is no separation any longer, no empty space, no absence: you enter the screen and the visual image unhindered." We are connected in an almost umbilical way. Our addiction to the screen is fuelled partly by a desire for self-immolation—the desire to disappear and dissolve "oneself into a phantom of conviviality."

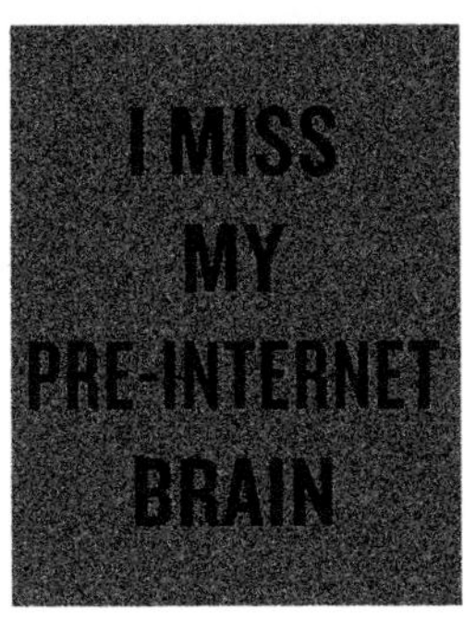

Screens have a bad reputation. They are blamed for eye strain, sleep damage, brain rewiring and social isolation. A recent Norwegian study observed teens slept less when they used computer screens more. The artificial light activated wakefulness and suppressed melatonin. Charles Arthur, in his 2008 article "It's the screens, not the Internet, that are making us stupid" wrote in *The Guardian*, "Low resolution monitors (including all computer screens until now) have poor readability: people read about 25% slower from computer screens than from printed paper."

A study from Manchester University found reading on paper 10-30% faster than on screens. The screen is often positioned in contrast to the book page—a throw back to the work of Marshall McLuhan. His book *The Medium is the Massage* focused on the television, yet his ideas could easily be applied to the modern screen. "In television there occurs an extension of the sense of active, exploratory touch which involves all the senses simultaneously, rather than that of sight phenomena, the visual is only one component in a complex interplay... Television demands participation," he wrote in 1967. "It will not work as background. It engages you. Perhaps this is why so many people feel their identity has been threatened." It is amusing to think anyone would feel this way about TV after so much more invasive technology has been developed. The demand for participation is much harder to ignore today.

TAKING PART

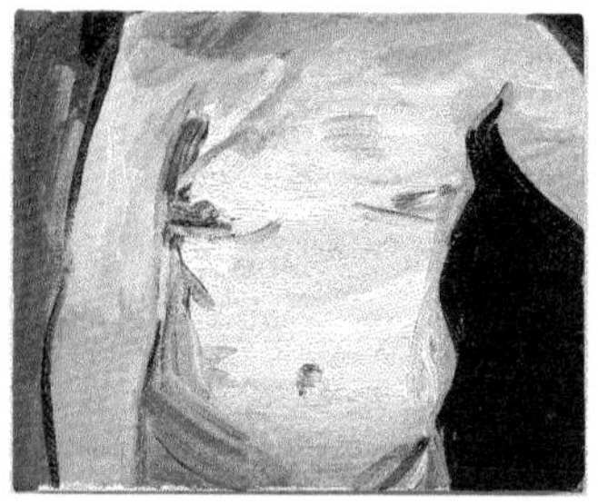

Last week I signed up for *My Invisible Boyfriend*. For a monthly fee, the online service provides you with a text message relationship. Some unknown (and probably poorly paid)

individual sends you messages as if they were your other half. I sat in a café and created my fictional boyfriend. He looked like Jeff Goldblum, had a witty and intelligent personality, and we met on a plane. I invented a DIY ideal to provide daily dopamine rushes and daydreaming.

I quickly received my first text. "Ooo, he's keen," my mother joked. I replied and then heard nothing in response all day. I realised I was filled with the same sense of projected expectation and impatience I had when sending someone who I liked and knew a text. We always know when things are delivered, so any delay of response is a choice, not an accident. The expected response is always implicit in any text.

As the days progressed, I was deeply unimpressed with my faux beau. He could barely put a sentence together. We talked about the weather and Netflix. It felt like I was writing to a bad pen pal. I began to complain to him. "I expected a bit more inspired conversation. Just a bit disappointed really," I lamented. "You didn't really make sense in your replies." He responded sympathetically and asked me how my day was going. The conversation continued to be dull. I tried to tell him how to act—after all I was paying for a service. "Ask me about myself but in a real way. Tell me anything you find culturally exciting. Have depth. Is that a weird desire? I want a screen to have emotional and intellectual depth? Ha." He sidestepped and I dumped him.

Our experience of technology is essentially internal. We may touch a button or a screen, but the experience is rarely solely physical. It is about how we interpret what we see. It is logical that our responses to screen interactions are emotional. The screen is often the only link between ourselves and others. This, however, is not always a joyful or connective exchange.

The screen has become a space for human psychological expression, dissolution or distrust. André Nusselder's *Interface Fantasy: A Lacanian Cyborg Onotology* argues that the computer functions in cyberspace as a psychological fantasy space. At one point he mentions the work of MIT professor Jozeph Weizenbaum, who wrote the first computer psychotherapy programme ELIZA in 1966, which fascinated the philosopher and psychologist Lacan. The programme would rephrase questions presented to it in a way that resembled a curious, human therapist. People became enthralled. "Lacan acknowledged that ELIZA appears to produce some sort of transference relation. People find something (of themselves) in the machine; they unconsciously transfer (phantasmically) the object of their desire onto it," Nusselder writes. "Computers may appear as fellow 'humans': you can talk to them, they can ask you questions, you can play and cooperate with them." We think of our screens as sentient.

Psychologist Sherry Turkle has been strongly critical of the changing emotional fallout from technological developments. "We are moving towards a culture of simulation in which people are increasingly uncomfortable with substituting representations of reality for the real," she laments in *Life on Screen* (1995). In a more recent 2012 TED talk, Turkle highlights the opportunity for self-editing and distance that technology allows us. "Texting, emailing, posting lets us present the self as we want it to be. We get to retouch. Human relationships are messy. We clean them up with technology. We sacrifice conversation for connection." The phone presents the fantasy that we are never alone, will always be heard. As Turkle notes, "Being alone feels like a problem that needs to be solved. I share therefore I am." That repeated desire for validation or acknowledgment—the 'I exist' we search to have confirmed on our screens—can be very obsessive. Are we addicted to the hormone rush of self-acknowledgement in the same way as a substance such as nicotine or alcohol?

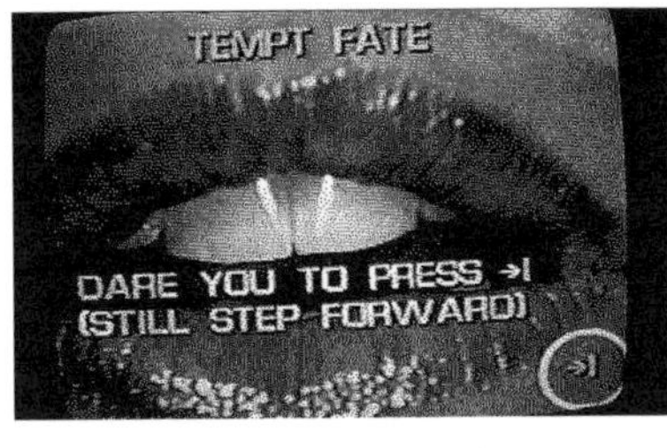

TOTALLY DEVOTED TO YOU

Psychology is based on the idea of knowing oneself. Clinically, this manifests in therapy in relation to another individual. What happens, however, when that therapist becomes virtual; when the voice becomes a screen? Can we only open up when the screen is inserted between ourselves and our emotions? Online therapy is something increasingly sold to an unhappy public. This is essentially an instant message relationship with an invisible, trained therapist often living on the other side of the world. The success of this form of therapy is debatable. Anonymity means spilling our guts is easy but there is a mediated process happening here. It gives patients the ability to rephrase and edit their feelings. This safety net has large holes.

There are positive uses of the screen in therapy. Turkle brings attention to a senior child psychiatrist who uses discussions of how adolescent boys use the Internet and virtual lives as a way to connect. Here, the online is seen as a space to help them develop feelings of appropriate masculinity. “In my offices, these young men are withdrawn and hard to reach. But many have active virtual lives in which they are energetic and forthcoming. These virtual lives represent an opportunity for the patient and for the clinician,” she quotes. The Internet becomes a fantasy space for representations or explorations of gender roles.

Our screen self is innately part of our conception of identity. This is a worrying thought in an age of consumer imagery. Are we our social media feeds? Where is the ‘me’ in screen-scape? How does the idea of me form? Matthew Crawford in *The World Beyond Your Head: How to Flourish in an Age of Distraction* (2016) dissects how our experience is highly mediated through the largely commercial representations we are surrounded by. It is a bleak environment. He depicts individuals surrounded by a fog of choices, in need of ever more stimulation. Our mental lives are becoming more susceptible to the orchestrated machinations of the marketing world. Life with our phone is like being in a department store with really loud music on a Saturday afternoon—you become so disorientated that you buy ill-fitting jeans because you can’t think straight.

The owners and promoters of products are predatory, battling for our attention with highly orchestrated imagery. We cannot help but look at screens around us, which employ attention-getting technologies that are "directing us away from one another and toward a manufactured reality." Advertisements are increasingly inserted into emotional space. Products and services pop up between profiles on dating apps like Happn or Tinder, between songs on Spotify or Soundcloud, and before you can watch YouTube videos. Pay a subscription fee and often the advertising goes away. Luxury is a life on demand a la Netflix. Freedom is to give in and buy so we can step away from being sold to.

Do we really want autonomy? I doubt it. Perhaps that's why BDSM fantasies like *Fifty Shades of Grey* are so popular at this moment. We're so exhausted we want to be told what to do. Our personal desires have become the same as corporate goals. We are happier being ruled by something alien without the burden of self-regulation and the constant failure implicit in our attempts. The screen world which we are absorbed into can tell us what to emulate.

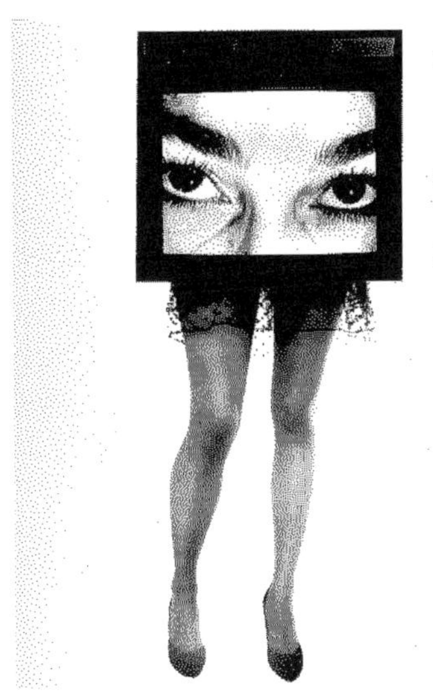

Sugar is an apt metaphor for our screen relationships. Sugar is one of the most common additives in prepared food and is increasingly being presented as addictive a substance as cocaine. We try to avoid reading the ingredient lists for its presence, and instead are easily manipulated by strap lines like 'low fat' or 'healthy'. In this context, if you're fat or poor it's your fault, because it is a result of your choices. Fighting for control takes the discipline of a football team trying not to be relegated to a lower league.

TOUCH ME, FEEL ME

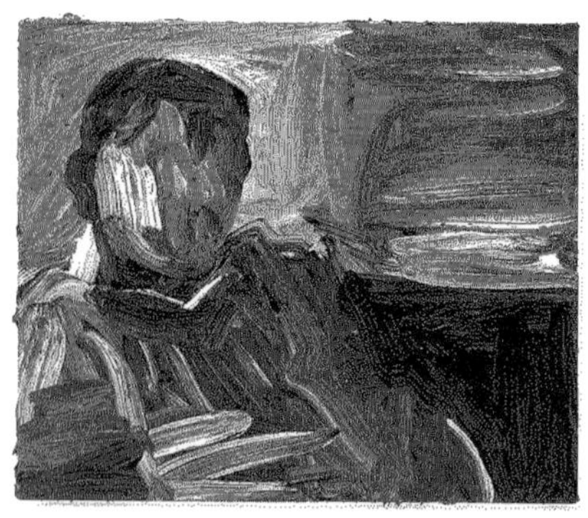

The screen has insinuated itself into our ideas, relationships and practises, like a really large hi-res digital condom. The pornographication of the Internet has entirely changing how sex is performed. In fact it has emphasised the idea of performance itself. It has transformed how intimacy is being created.

The percentage of single people who have experimented with online dating apps and sites has trebled since 2013. These sites and apps present us with a never-ending glut of people, creating the impression that something better may constantly appear at the next swipe. Nick Paumgarten in *The New Yorker* wrote, "Internet dating can be a sport, an end in itself." There are so many things to hate about Internet dating—the speed, the superficiality, the lack of engagement. On apps in particular, where profile content is negligible, the images of faces and bodies could easily be replaced with a stream of commodities from Amazon. One of the few differences between Tinder and eBay is there is no ratings system. (I give this date two out of five stars…)

Paul Oyer picked up on this well in *Everything I Ever Needed to Know About Economics I Learned from Online Dating* (2013). As a newly single economist, he had quickly realised the relationship between online dating and the market. “Match.com, eHarmony and OkCupid it turns out, are no different from eBay or Monster.com,” he writes. “On all these sites, people come together trying to find matches.” He compares how the modern economy works and applies this to our personal lives—focusing on the themes of “search, signalling, adverse selection, cheap talk, statistical discrimination, thick markets and network externalities.”

In order to succeed in online dating, you need ‘top click prominence.’ Cheap talk, or rather exaggerating information to present your ‘product’ well, is the norm. Research has found most men exaggerate their height, most people understate their weight, and about one-fifth of people lie about their age. This process directly echoes the techniques of deceptive advertising, the hyperbole of political campaigns and behaviour of stock analysts at investment banks. The market assumes exaggeration.

Rebecca D Heino, Nicole B Ellison and Jennifer L. Gibbs in their article ‘Relationshopping: Investigating the market metaphor in online dating’ (*Journal of Social and Personal Relationships*, 2010) found more than half of the people they interviewed called online dating sites 'supermarkets' or 'catalogues' and compared the process to economic transaction. Compiling a profile was like presenting a CV, "a promotional tool that market's one's 'best self' rather than a complete or accurate representation." Yet people criticised the shopping mentality for its 'lack of magic'. We hate it for dehumanising us.

The process of reaffirming one's positive characteristics when presenting oneself for the 'market' gives daters an increased sense of their own desirability. Online dating creates inflated egos. Perhaps that, alongside the ever-growing catalogue of faces to choose from, is part of the attraction. 'Look how hot I seem. Are any of you really worthy?' How ideal for the individualist present. We look for others but really emphasise the role of the self.

Popular culture doesn't quite know how to represent online dating in a way that is engaging. How can you show the incessant repetition of swipes with any drama? Online dating lacks narrative. It is a continuous search rarely with a fulfilling outcome. *You've Got Mail* (1998) is a deeply outdated representation of a romantic screen interaction—closer to an epistolary screwball comedy than anything that reflects how contemporary screen-led interactions work. Dating disaster blogs, such as soontobecatlady.com or whytheyaresingle.com, and books on dating failures have proliferated, appealing to equally hapless readers. Part of the pleasure of these bad date stories is to see how the idealisation of the screen is false. How underneath a nice blurb and set of pictures are human beings with all their faults and failures.

The phone screen has made everything intimate. Text and image messaging—in particular the increased speed of instant messaging—have changed our idea of communication. There are now new rules of communication, which are constantly being reformed and are platform-dependent. Social media technology has supplanted other forms of communication—including emails, chat rooms and websites, let alone phone calls. Our relationship status is often displayed or online to be deciphered or implied. Public and private space do not exist in the same way. We are always intimate with our screens. The greater sense of control that comes from slower responses, well-chosen words and anonymity also leads to intense focus. This focus stimulates our pleasure centres and creates connection.

The use of ellipses and emojis as emotional signifiers are notable here. When messaging someone, a 'dot dot dot' appears on screen, indicating that the other recipient is typing a response. This process has an innately emotional aspect. The longer the time we see the 'typing' in progress, the more considered we feel the reply is. The ellipses keep us on our toes—expectant, a little excited and unsure. Using ellipses in text conversation also adds a sense of nuance—an indication of something unsaid. Emojis and emoticons, with their replacement of the textual with the visual, do a similar thing. We are left to interpret the variance of different smileys or the meaning of a small purple aubergine. The meaning behind this screen symbolism is fluid, personal and unstable.

This instability built into online romantic communication is both attractive and repulsive. The screen presents the coexistence of distance and immediacy, anonymity and disclosure, the real and the false. The transitory dynamic of screen space can make us feel more intensely because we don't know when or how change will hit us next.

HOT OR NOT

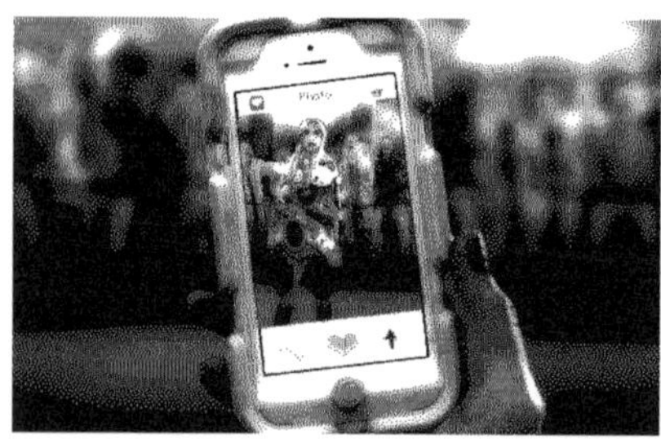

Network-led social media strengthens emotional ties between people at a long distance. Yet it is also blamed for a decrease in genuine bonds. The screen encourages friendship and intimacy alongside a constant social pressure of self-presentation. Many online dating apps, notably Tinder, cannot be activated without being connected to social media platforms. Thus, the representation of the self on these sites is deeply intertwined with the search for a match. Exclusive dating app Raya approves paying members based on the number of their Instagram followers (among other factors). How we present and display our physical self and promote it is intertwined with sexual intimacy. The body here becomes a gift—a possible reward. Swipe here and you might win the prize of the six-pack or well-filled bikini.

According to research, people tend to exaggerate and idealise people they meet online. Limited cues about a person's real personality and background can lead to a tighter focus, a greater intensity of imaginative input by the viewer. It is not unlike how individuals view idealised cinema screen figures as erotic objects, "the scopophilic instinct" Laura Mulvey discusses in *Visual Pleasure and Narrative Cinema* (1975). The screen reduces us to fragmented bodies bound to live out visual fantasies.

What is perceived as sexually attractive is increasingly influenced by these screen-mediated presentations. For decades there have been connections made between unrealistic advertising images of the body and the rise of eating disorders and body dysmorphia. Susie Orbach's *Bodies* (2009) explores how contemporary body is subjected to pressures and constraints from beyond the self. "Brands invest heavily in marketing. Their spending works. Where once religious iconography penetrated the consciousness of the people, brand iconography conveyed by particular kinds of bodies does that today," she writes. Desire is something formed in relation to our world—exhibiting and literally embodied by our forms. The screen spreads particular, commodified ideas of desire.

We are now ever more responsible for our representation. The language of positivity, the well-angled selfie, the display of curated interests and tastes, the presentation of our politics. As the world is focused on the self not the other, in order to engage with society we are encouraged to 'work on ourselves'; to constantly perfect out bodies, our appetites, our ethics. Like a computer, the subject is constantly updating itself.

ME ME ME

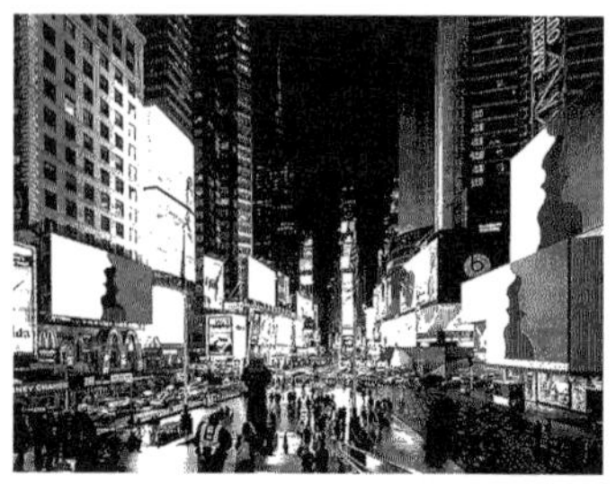

As such a large number of us are on social media, it would be ridiculous to assume we are all insecure narcissists staring into the abyss of our own reflections. Perhaps the problem is that, optimistic or pessimistic, all discussion of the screen is media-centric. Technology and digital communication is often described as something leading social change that we must adapt to. Instead, we need to question how can we create a new relationship to media that works for us.

The success of girl-gang television programmes like *Girls* or the series *The Real Housewives*, or bromance films such as *The Hangover* or *21 Jump Street*, emphasise a new positioning of groups of friends as an ideal beyond romantic or familial relationships.This focus on the 'friend' is something encouraged and exploited by social media designers. Hence Facebook's readymade videos which place friendship histories in narrative packages to easily reinsert into your current feed. Social media thrives on a sense of benign connection and positivity, yet has increasingly become an exploitative network serving marketing and advertising firms. (Facebook makes $5.11 per user per year. There are currently 1.86 billion monthly active users.) Real friends, however, are still differentiated from 'Facebook friends.' Privacy levels and the ability to compartmentalise what is viewed in social media and communication threads in WhatsApp or Snapchat mean friends are increasingly managed.

As our browsing patterns, and buying practices, tastes and movements are observed, social media companies have increasingly tailored or manipulated the information that reaches audiences. We are beginning to rebel. Users are becoming too conscious of privacy and trust issues. Product placement and endorsements with influencers on Instagram are increasingly transparent—and do not necessarily lead to the increased sales brands hope for. There is a desire to return to spaces that are truly social and ephemeral—hence the rise in the popularity for transitory posts that are not archived, such as Instagram Stories or Snapchat. The results feel less mediated and more intimate, rather than hyper-constructed.

IT'S JUST HORMONES

Dopamine is the hormone most cited as a response to our screen engagement. It is released when we get a text, a like, a little bleep of recognition. Susan Greenfield in *Mind Change: How digital technologies are leaving their mark on our brains* (2014) references Dr. Susan Weinschenk, who emphasises that small pieces of information such as a like or a tweet have a specific relationship to dopamine stimulation. The "information coming in is modest enough not to satisfy entirely." The more unpredictable, anticipatory and immediate the triggers are, the more likely we are to get a rush.

Cortisol is another hormone that is often cited in recent technological debate. The hormone is secreted in response to stress, fear and anxiety. Originally created as a way for the body to respond to danger, stress is making cortisol release constant. It leads to everything from anorexia to burnout, dementia to weight gain. Multitasking, something built into the way we engage with screens, also increases cortisol. Even being lonely—something that the screen creates despite its alleged best intentions—can enhance cortisol levels. Emotional upheaval is one of the hormone's first symptoms. With all this screen based hormonal stimulus how can we not feel like we are on an emotional rollercoaster?

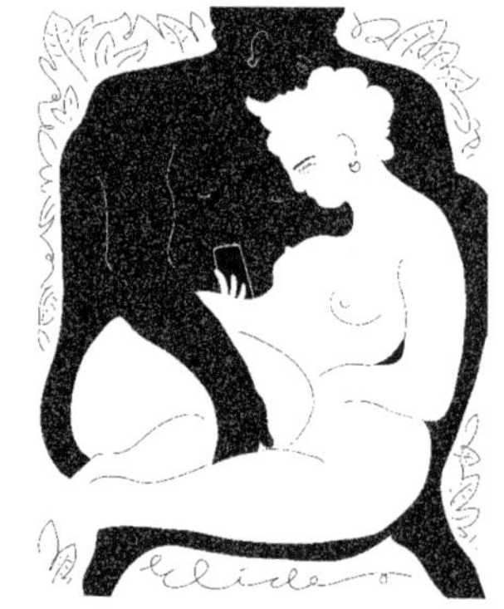

In 2016, the web magazine *Real Life* published an article 'Time Capsules' by New York based anonymous author Fuck Theory that had a very interesting take on our relationship to stimulus, productivity and drugs. 'FT' questioned why the widespread use of substances such as coffee and alcohol are seemingly banal. They are encouraged because they help us conform to social order—to work faster and stay awake. "In late capitalism, what it means to be an individual thinking entity is first and foremost existence as a labouring body exploited for its productive capacities," Fuck Theory notes. "The prescription drugs that are most socially acceptable are also those that maximise our ability to live on time." This is production at a symbolic, not necessarily physical, level. Today, time is about always being on, available, ready to respond —getting to work on time, meeting your deadlines, answering your emails.

Human beings are limited. The stream of information is not. Everything we do is about an attempt to keep up with a dysfunctional sense of time. This also relates to the substances we put in our bodies. Fuck Theory quotes Deleuze, "all drugs involve speeds, modifications of speeds, thresholds of perception, forms and movements."

Roughly 500 million tweets are sent each day. Nearly 300 hours of footage is uploaded to YouTube each minute, in up to 76 different languages. 300 million photos are uploaded to Facebook every day. We constantly attempt to keep up with our streams of information, despite the limits of our ability to absorb what surrounds us. We attempt to understand something incomprehensible. It is an almost liquid experience, like swimming through information. Media, like water, is relentless. We are now always on, in a continuous flow of action, bouncing from one dramatic episode to the next without respite. Time does not stop.

The undercurrent of stress, fear and addiction that we feel looking at the screen is increasingly positioned as our fault. The buck seems to repeatedly return to the individual to gauge technology's role in their life. It has entered the world of self-help. The *WW Club*, an online networking group of working women, created an inspirational blog post entitled 'Rethinking your Relationship with Technology'. It questioned "Which of your technology habits most frequently creates anxiety for you?", "When was the last time you regretted oversharing some aspect of your personal life online? What led you to do that?", "How much time (honestly!) do you spend looking at the phone each day?" The WW suggested new rules to 'look less,' including turning off notifications, scheduling specific times to check email and social media, call more and text less, and avoid sleeping next to your phone. Their conclusion: "Set your own rules. Then live by them." As valiant as their efforts are, one wonders how capable human beings are of resisting things that trigger their hormones. Screens are just as addictive as smoking or sugar.

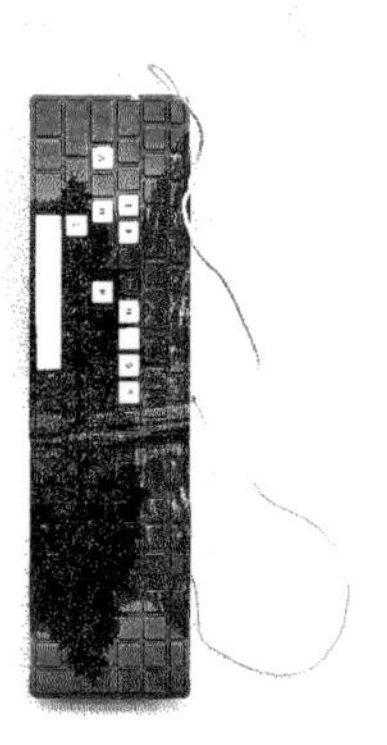

Obsessively checking and responding to work emails out of work hours is a default experience. "Flexible employment systems were once sold to us as a path to more time off and greater autonomy," wrote Peter Fleming in *The Guardian*. "The way to a better work-life balance? Unions, not self-help." As he continues, "The trick is to see the ritual of overwork as societal pressure, not an individual fault. And much of this pressure stems from the disempowerment of the workforce that has occurred over the last 20 years. Insecurity, real or imagined, naturally makes it more likely that people will sacrifice everything for their job... Want a healthier work-life balance? Join a union. Or better still, create your own."

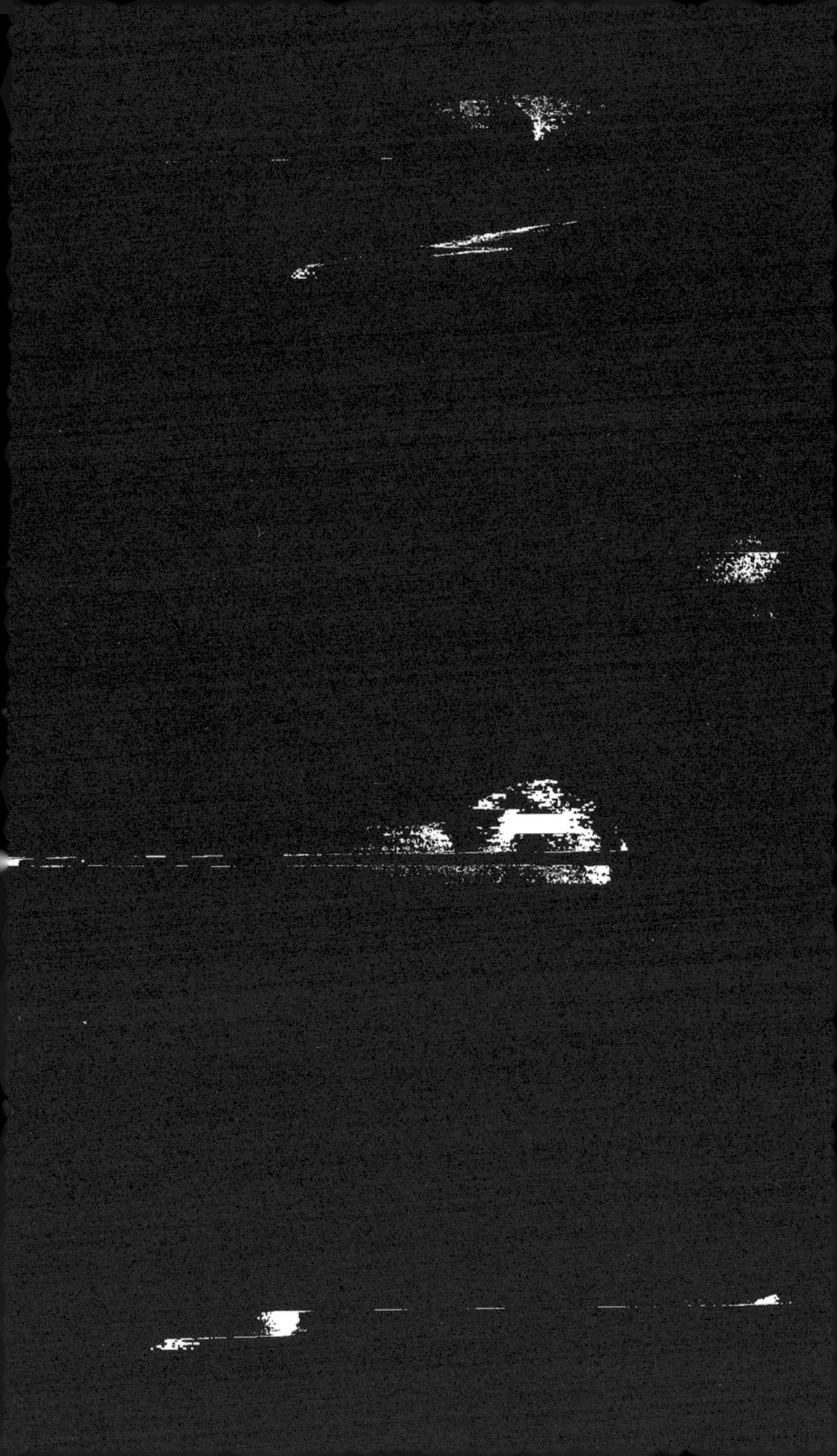

ING

AND

NOT

DOWN

As the selfie exploded as a form of representation in recent years, artworks began to appear alongside well-angled portraits. They became the backdrop to new imagery, passive participants in our visual engagement with the world around us. This trend was exploited by online magazine *Dis* in their #Artselfie project. Part art project, part viral meme, the artselfie revealed the audience's desire to capture themselves alongside, even inside, artworks. The subjects become temporary collectors who are able to have their experiences intertwined with a digital ownership of the work in some form—even if only within the screenscape. The results feel like a prosaic take on performance documentation. In this way, the art object becomes something communal, sharable and conceptual rather than physical.

The rise of the artselfie demonstrates how viewers seek a way to merge with art and lose the self. Reflection makes the viewer confront their own position, their own existence. It is a perfect metaphor for the age of narcissism. We become engrossed and addicted to our own image. Photographing the self in, or alongside, or in front of an artwork elevates the self(ie) to something immortal and transcendent. We become the objects rather than flawed, changing, living things.

If the point of art is to dissect our contemporary existence, it is no surprise the screen is something many artists are addressing. I would argue artists are addressing the screen in ways that demonstrate our passive and active involvement. The passive screen is one observed, a screen as object. In its most simple form, it is a screen we watch. Camille Henrot's *Grosse Fatigue* (2013) is a beautiful example of a film, which documents our relationship to the computer screen. The piece examines the way we look at and accumulate information, depicting multiple image and video boxes on a computer desktop. There is a strong sense of rhythm and editing in the work, which was developed during a residency fellowship at the Smithsonian.

"I was doing a lot of Internet research on the Smithsonian database. I often had a lot of windows open on my desktop," she explained to me in 2013. "When you look at a cluster of windows on a desktop and try to find reason, it results in a kind of primitive thinking—a sort of ultra-rationality. You see the images together and then your mind makes these connections, not because there is a connection, but because your brain needs to resolve the images." Here the screen becomes the subject of work itself. Shown as a projection, nonetheless our engagement is one of observer watching the film from the point of a relatively passive audience.

Telling the story of the universe from the starting point of a screen desktop is an amusing conceit, but a very apt one. Henrot juggles how the thought process is transformed through our screen reaction. She makes a narrative from the tangential experience of Internet searching. Henrot creates a story from the neural pathways of thought and discovery. The artist is the invisible-yet-present hand and head in the work. We are passive viewers in her arms being led through existence, while at the same time her own agency is questioned by the interface itself.

THE SCREEN AS OBJECT

The London-based artist Adham Faramawy has embedded the screen in his work in sometimes literal ways —sticking screens within complex sculptural objects or painting fields. Here, the screen is a passive participant thrust into the artist's world, in the same way it is thrust into our daily experience. Faramawy was originally influenced by the arrival of flat screen TVs and how they were replacing cathode ray monitors. He saw how they changed how we receive and perceive an image.

His use of the embedded screen emerged after he began working with animators to produce sculptural computer programmes, and later, particle animation; "I started to get familiar with the logics and the languages of the interfaces to the programs producing these moving images. They're inherited from analogue, physical traditions like film editing, clay modelling and masonry, but unlike the given conditions of these traditions, with computer modelling you can't make assumptions, you have to assign physical conditions and physics to an object."

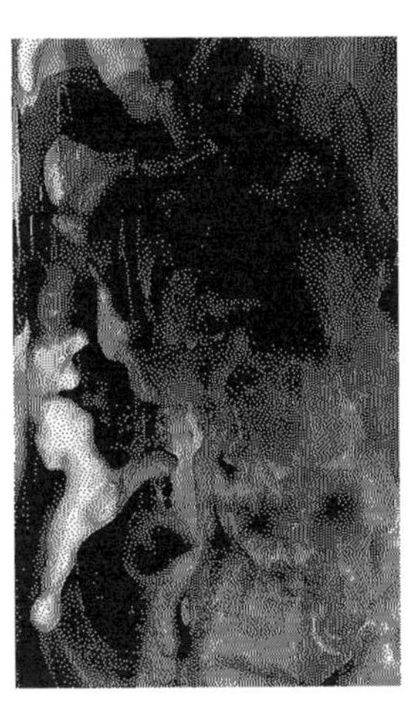

His screens are contained within highly textured cases and plinth structures. Often the screen is upturned in his work. He explains, “Shifting the angles at which a viewer receives an image was, for me, intended to point at the physicality of the image, thinking about the substrata carrying that image as a sculptural body, a form within a composition.”

The passive manifests in artists who deconstruct and take apart the screen, while highlighting its functions. The early work of Yuri Pattison, an artist who was part of the collective Lucky PDF, involved taking the screen apart, showing its inner workings and revealing the mechanisms of display. As a result, we can see a small number of manufacturers are making these parts —Samsung panels are being used by numerous brands for example. Pattison removed the façade of slick design and marketing. “The stripping of the screen's cosmetic body and branding also highlights the mechanisms that support the display of the image —these mechanisms are normally invisible, deliberately hidden by the manufacturer to present a seamless experience.” Pattison notes. “We view screens as a window onto something, so in the way we don’t think of the glass in the window we don’t think of the processes behind the representation on the screen. There are numerous layers we don’t perceive, or barely perceive, in the act of viewing something on a screen.”

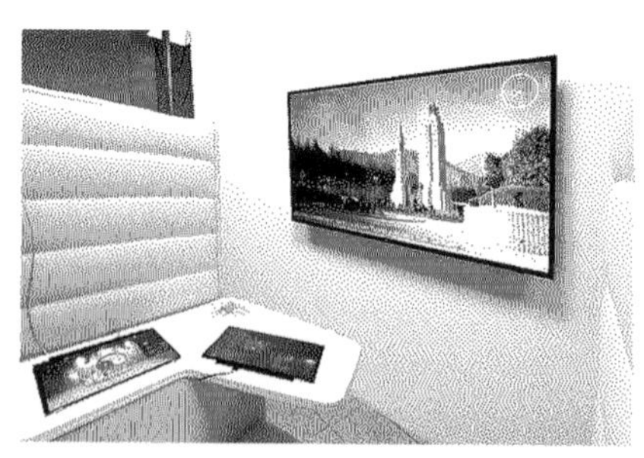

Pattison's practise in a wider sense explores the political and cultural impact and changes that technology has enacted on society. His installations and multimedia works explore how we work, the role surveillance and the physicality of the Internet. He presents the processes of the screen around us but we as viewers often helplessly watch.

Berlin-based artist Simon Denny has taken the screen as one of the fundamental tropes in his work. In the past, he has examined TV hacking, the thinning of monitors, how we receive information, the design, packaging and structure of the companies behind the consumption of technology and conferences that promote and position devices in society. He prints the screen on panels or perspex. Analogue materials replicate the structure and format of the digital. The screen is ripped apart, reimagined and revealed.

Denny has focused on technological industry events, aesthetics and packaging around technology beyond the actual content itself. "For me this is cultural information," Denny explains. "The people that make these businesses and the activity they create are prioritised in this moment. The tech context seems celebrated beyond its numbers. Not only the direct effects of what they do is important. The whole package is important—the images they produce, the design language they use and the way they

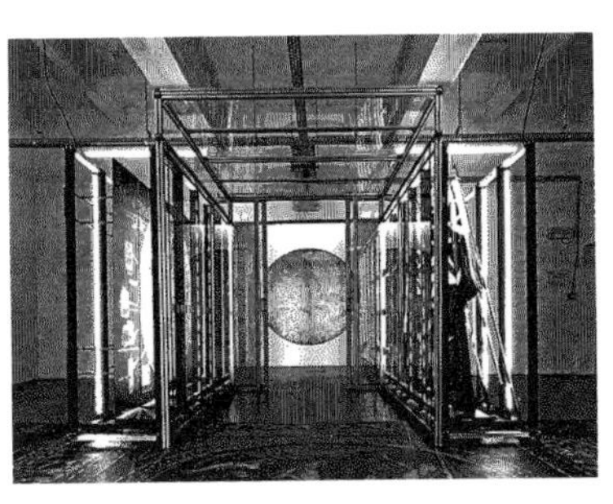

communicate values and systems." Taking apart the structures around the screen, even in their most basic physical sense, says far more about their relationship to reality.

THE ACTIVE SCREEN

Film director Brian de Palma made a documentary short at the early stage of his career, looking at the opening of *The Responsive Eye,* an exhibition held at MOMA in New York in 1965. It brought together artworks by Op and minimalist artists such as Bridget Riley, Josef Albers and Victor Vasarely. The curator William Seitz described the show as an "exhibition that would indicate an activity, not a kind of art." He argued in the exhibition's catalogue this was "non-objective perceptual art," art that "exists primarily for its impact on reception rather than for conceptual examination... Ideological focus has moved from the outside world, passed through the work as object, and entered the incompletely explored region area between the cornea and the brain."

Our interaction with the screen reflects decades of technological advancements that have played with human perception and physicality. The 'retinal' works of the 1960s provide a starting point for us to come to terms with GIFs or 3D animation. They were a blueprint for how we relate to the constant influx of movement, imagery, sound and informational content in modern screen life. They started the idea of the active screen.

Screen interactions can be lo-fi. Aram Bartholl's work questions the screen perspective: "Most of our reality today is taking place in that phone rectangle. The screen constantly moved closer to our eyes over the past decades (from cinema to phones). The screen will be attached to our eyes soon (glasses or lenses)." Playing on the exchange and selling of imagery through the screen, Bartholl's public installations of giant phone cut-outs are made for interaction and dispersion through social media. In these large, two dimensional uber-phones, people can pose as if within the phone screenspace for Instagram, Twitter or Facebook. His initial aim within an exhibition context was to get visitors to interact with each other. Now placing them in lakes or museums, that interaction becomes far more global.

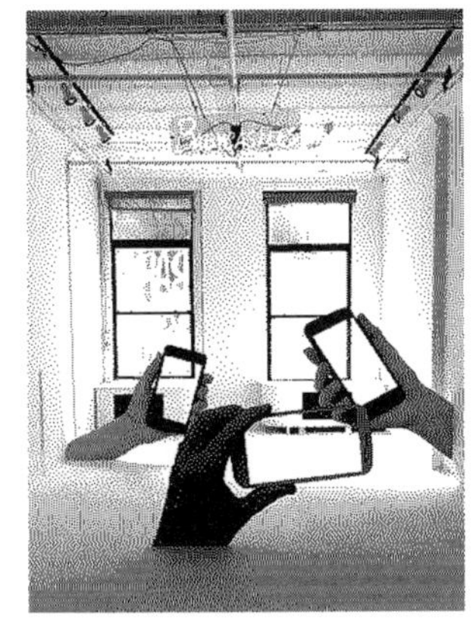

Selfie sticks, head-mounted cameras like GoPro or Google Glass play with the idea of the 'point of view' (POV) image. Bartholl created headpieces to mount phones during a workshop at the Atlantic Center of the Arts, experimenting with POV filming techniques. "In the end it appeared to me that the picture of someone wearing his/her phone on the forehead obviously filming is even more interesting than the actual clip shot with that head mounted phone," he explains. "The whole thing is a bit cyborg but in a silly, light way."

Another manifestation of the active or living screen can be seen in the work of Antoine Catala. In his video projection works and sculptural instal-

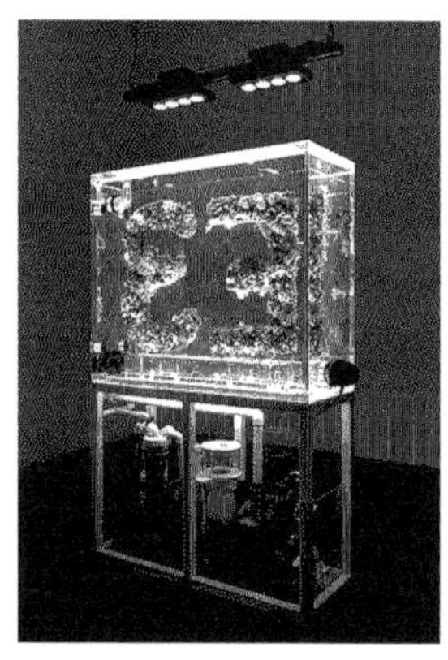

lations, the screen appears to literally come to life. He uses membranes that appear to be breathing, moving in a techno-organic way. He has streamed television into fluid blob shapes —'alive' in some form. He uses display technology and reflection to create screen-like space. Our engagement may still be as observers, but the screen itself comes to life in some way.

THE HUMAN TOUCH

The active screen can be activated by human touch or a click. The sound of a computer mouse has become so familiar we are barely aware of it. The tap of this hand-sized, ergonomic button-box or track pad as it is pressed and released echoes our mental engagement. We think therefore we touch. The invitation this presents to enter or activate something is a beautiful thing for an artist. There is almost something of a fairytale about this interaction. Like cake to Hansel and Gretel.

The most immediate way to incorporate the urge to interact is the website as artwork. Margot Bowman's piece *Heaven is for Quitters* (heavenisforquitters.com), which also functions as a very abstract music video for Faltydl, is a good example. As the viewer clicks around the screen, various animations of people and furry characters are depicted having sex. A scrolling text links these different couplings, stating, "You are sad,

You are so alone, You are very lonely". The viewer can download their unique version from the page to save. Here, the artwork lives online, where it has a sense of completeness and access, and lives in another form offline.

Brenna Murphy makes immersive installation pieces in real space, often with sound elements and performance, but her interactive pieces are largely based online. The intimacy of the screen relationship is key: "I make art that is meant to be viewed on the Internet by people privately browsing from their own device. I think this is an intimate and powerful way of transmitting and experiencing media." Here, viewers click on audio files so they overlap with rhythmic GIFs, video montage and scrolling images she makes from her own video footage. The results are very psychedelic.

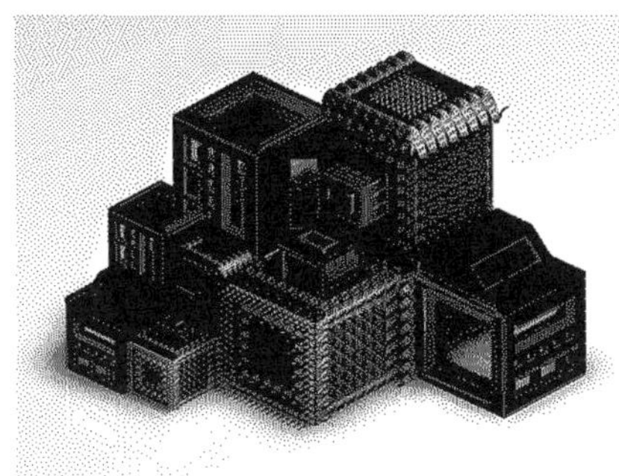

Clicking on images takes us through a maze of digital collage imagery. The aim of her web *Labyrinths* is to make us conscious of the role of the screen.

Her work is so successful because it relates to how we are used to using our screens for input and interaction. Other artists also create active screen works that replicate the interactive pathways and experience of exploring the Internet, such as the online questionnaires and page-to-page pathways of Cecile B Evans' online project for Serpentine Gallery AGNES.

A spambot that generates experiences beyond the virtual, and creates a sense of connection and emotion

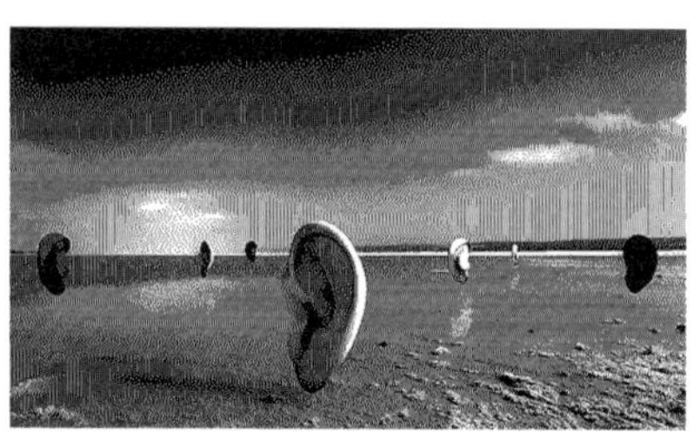

query. Here, the screen touches on those sensations of Lacanian transference. Her more recent works have drawn on ideas around AI and intelligent technology, manifesting in characters or motifs in which floating or disembodied objects have their own sense of autonomy.

The active screen relationship is very clear in artworks that draw on gaming. Games give the illusion of the active, but in fact, the audience is still largely controlled by the artist, the developer and the structure of gamespace. Game imagery is a metaphor for our relationship to technology and screens as a whole. These devices force us into a passive position.

Angela Washko makes games and video projects that examine and rework console-based role playing games such as *World of Warcraft*. Her work *The Game: The Game* is a dating simulator game where the player in the body of a female protagonist tries to avoid sleazy pick up artists in a crowded New York bar. Washko's work is very much about looking at how games reinforce and exaggerate cultural and gender stereotypes and violence. The screen interaction here is simple but that is part of what makes the content of the work so accessible and disturbing.

There are also structural and aesthetic aspects of screen game interactivity that emerge.

Ben Washington creates sculptural installations in galleries and then recreates these spaces, though often with strange failures and disintegrating pathways. The viewer—standing behind the controls of an arcade machine—will, for example, find themselves in a virtual version of the exact same physical gallery space in which they are standing. The result is an experience that contrasts seeing the real and the virtual version of something at the same time. They both become fused and influenced by each other. Washington explained to me, "the interest between screen space and real space arises at the point at which they converge and diverge. The focus in my work has been on these uncanny moments."

The interactive nature of the screen is of particular note to Washington from a more social perspective. He points out, "How much are we going to let the screen encroach into real space and into our social norms? Already it is evident that socially it is now almost totally acceptable to wander around with your face in a smartphone."

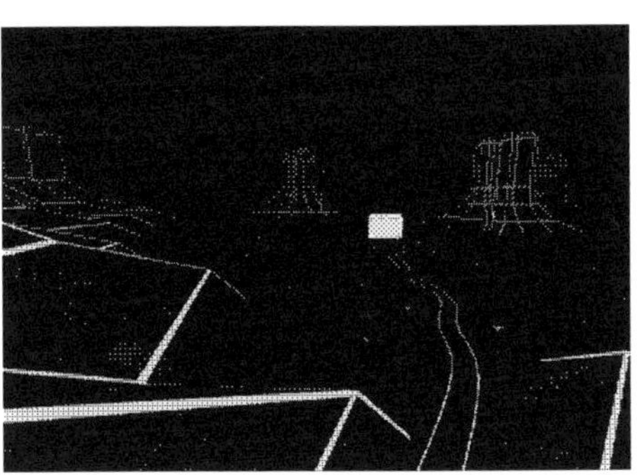

Washington was particularly excited by development kits being produced for *Oculus Rift* and the other contenders in the VR market—Sony's *Morpheus*, *Steam VR* and the *Sulon Cortex*. William Gibson's version of cyberspace made flesh.

Director and VR artist David Mullett describes the attraction of the VR screen: "VR has a frame in the sense that it is a screen tied to your face—but with a software coding sleight of hand and optics advancements alongside the accelerometers and gyroscopes built into smartphones, it appears as if there is no frame whatsoever. And our relationship to screens is so addictive and obsessive that we need to ramp up our stimulation to tug the emotions or get that dopamine hit we are so hungry for."

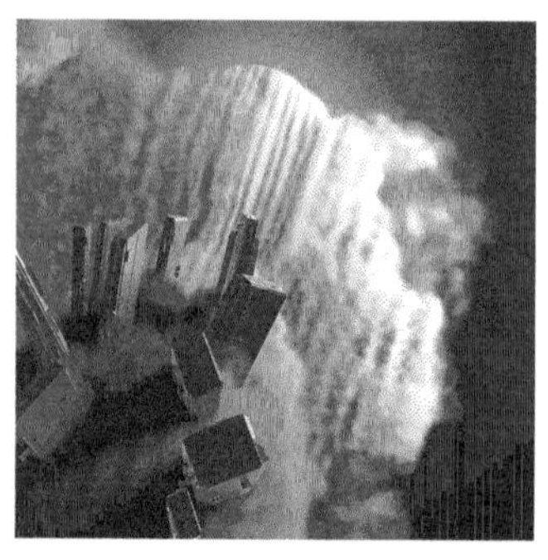

VR is being increasingly approached in more conceptual ways. Oscar Raby's *Assent* (2014) documented the artist's cathartic exploration of his father's traumatic memory of a mass execution in Chile in the seventies. Part interactive, part cinematic, it is a physical and poetic journey into trauma. A hybrid between first person gaming and the protagonist in a film narrative. *Perspective* (2015) by Morris May and Rose Troche reveals an extremity of first-person filmmaking where the audience is put in the shoes of a teenage girl being date raped at a house party, then in the shoes of the man committing the assault. Max Rheiner's *Birdly* (2013) is a flying-simulation installation where your entire body is used to fly like in a dream. As Mullet notes, "With VR immersion, your unconscious brain actually thinks that it is doing these things, indicating that the technology will rewire our brains in critical ways with extent of use and intensity of experience." He imagines flipping through immersive channels like TV surfing.

As the boundaries of the screen transform, the future is quickly transforming. Writer, curator and artist Sam Hart sees the post screen future for art as something more to do with the structure of the Internet itself. In fact, a new decentralised Internet—artwork coming out of the blockchain.

Getting to grips with the blockchain for a layman is notoriously obtuse. Hart attempted to describe it to me: "The blockchain is nothing more than a publicly visible, distributed database whose entries are immutable once instantiated. The 'blocks', or records, comprising the database are uniquely addressed and have a cryptographic key which entails ownership." Hart suggests this space could become a novel medium for digital art by encoding line and colour values, sequences and relationships. The platform for decentralised applications *Ethereum* (ethereum.org), for example, embeds an entire programming language for design. As Hart explains, "I think it represents a significant progression in digital artistry: a uniquely relational medium that circulates through body and network by way of the screen." The results are unknowable at this time, but these new languages point to new screen-based structures to create work within and upon. The structure of programming has a huge influence on the results we experience. Rethink our entire approach to that and you have a different future in the making.

So where does this leave us and our little black screens? Despite the anxiety around them, they are the site of a lot of creativity and hope. It is impossible to be comprehensive in the many ways artists are using the screen in their work—what is so interesting is how varied the approaches are. Interactive, passive, three-dimensional, flattened, virtual, literal—the screen has a lot more conceptual depth than a void. In fact, the void-like nature of the screen can be seen as what makes it so exciting. It is waiting to be filled with imagery, information and ideas.

ACCESS ALL AREAS

Alongside this balancing act between active and passive participation, the screen itself has become a space for viewing artwork. One of the most obvious triumphs of the Internet is the online dissemination of art via websites as galleries or institutions. There have been numerous online sites dedicated to showing online work, such as *Opening Times* (otdac.org), a British non-profit organisation that commissions works, creates online residencies and takes over third-party websites such as the Goethe Institute or Philips auction house's home pages with temporary online artworks. They have commissioned work like Ruth Proctor's *Always* (always.otdac.org), a standalone website that displays a clock, continuously counting from the launch of the *Opening Times* website. Every time the viewer visits you can press a button and download the time of your interaction.

Cosmos Carl (cosmoscarl.co.uk) is another online space that uses existing platforms. Each project is simply a new weblink presented on its home page.

This consists of the name of each different artist and a fresh URL. These temporary shows lead through to projects on sites such as eBay, Pinterest, YouTube, Vimeo, Google Maps, Soundcloud, Google Earth, Facebook or Kickstarter. These works live outside of *Cosmos Carl* as things people can accidentally discover outside of a web art context. This sliding into the Internet's infrastructures is both critical and accessible, detached and integrated.

Artist Faith Holland (faithholland.com) has made interventions into the porn hub *Redtube*, with a series of videos that are tagged with pornographic clickbait like 'amateur' and 'solo girl' and touch on ideas of sex or fetishes but are much weirder. One video for example depicts the artist shaving her legs. The results are detached and almost uncomfortable—which perhaps is a very appropriate comment on the videos uploaded to the porn site in a wider sense. Her largest online piece, *VVVVVV*, was an in-depth exploration of the relationship between the erotic and the screen. Her site, which drew traffic from sex sites, examines the abstract and the fragmented in moving imagery particularly porn. The results are a fascinating balance between feminism, humour and activism in a space that has become innately eroticised. The screen is a place to look at sex, and in turn, becomes sexualised.

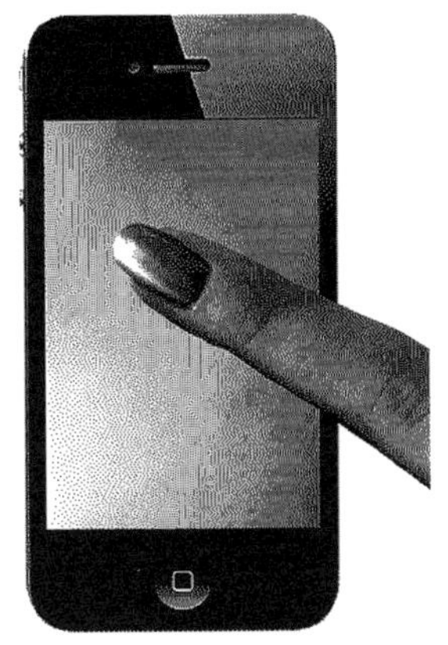

Kari Altmann has used Tumblr in works that explore ideas around evolving tags, images and videos. For example, in sites such as gardenclub.tumblr.com and softmobility.tumblr.com, she explores ideas around feminism, posthumanism, survivalism and alternative currency. Her chosen images and ideas are linked by social media tags such as #jailbreakgesture, #softmobility or #vitalcontent. Yet Altmann has had serious issues with Tumblr. In Kari's words, "At some point Tumblr got bought out and went super corporate. At that point, a lot of my accounts got shut down without warning, either for having a name like pier1, which Pier One Imports decided they had a right to, or they were shut down for URL camping, if they had only one post or no posts. It was considered 'hoarding'—part of the problematic way that these platforms eventually try to whittle your identity options down into a very small consumer unit, so they can monetise and wrap information around you via a single algorithm."

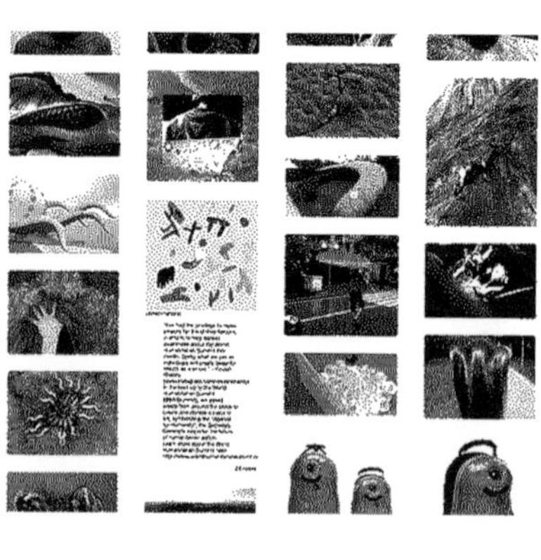

The increasing corporatisation of social media is leaving no space for conceptual approaches, privacy filters and different kinds of content. The writer Dennis Cooper notably had his website shut down by Google. His blog, *the DCs*, which contained over a decade's worth of work and research as well as GIF novels in the style of the collage-like *Zacs Haunted House* (now archived on kiddiepunk.com/zacshauntedhouse) was deleted entirely without any notice—as was his Gmail account. Cooper is a writer whose work is notoriously controversial, often inhabiting the intersection between horror and homoeroticism. His blog inhabited the same space, for example showing profiles of Russian rent boys. He hadn't backed up his blog and for three months was given no explanation to why his work had been entirely removed. He was exceptionally lucky that due to very high profile interviews and online campaigns, he was given his archive back and is working on reposting it to a dedicated site slowly over time. However, this is something that is not available to less well-connected artists.

These examples highlight the innate problems around the dissemination of art online: corporate ownership, corporate censorship and the commodification of social media and the individual. Instagram has been lauded as a space for artists to show work and reach an exceptionally wide audience outside of the limits of the art world. Yet in its heart, it is a form of marketing where someone's body and creativity are positioned into a structure predetermined by branded desires. Instagram, now under the Facebook umbrella, owns our pictures.

Advertising is being increasingly inserted into apps and sites. There are ads in-between posts on Twitter, Facebook and Instagram. There are ads popping up inside Google searches, in email feeds. In the same way that street art once occupied ignored spaces within urban architecture before they were aggressively taken over and commodified by ad sales companies, so the wild west utopian possibilities that accompanied the early days of the Internet are clearly over.

There are obvious pros presented by the Internet—a space to exhibit, to experiment and to distribute art; a space that is cheaper, faster and looked at by a huge portion of the population every day. But it is also the source of fears, stress and exploitation. Perhaps this is also part of the legacy of modernism and the entire concept of cultural progress. It is impossible to make work about, or using screens, technology, social media or the Internet without being strongly aware and critical of its relationship to global capitalism. To put it simply, shopping isn't going to change the world.

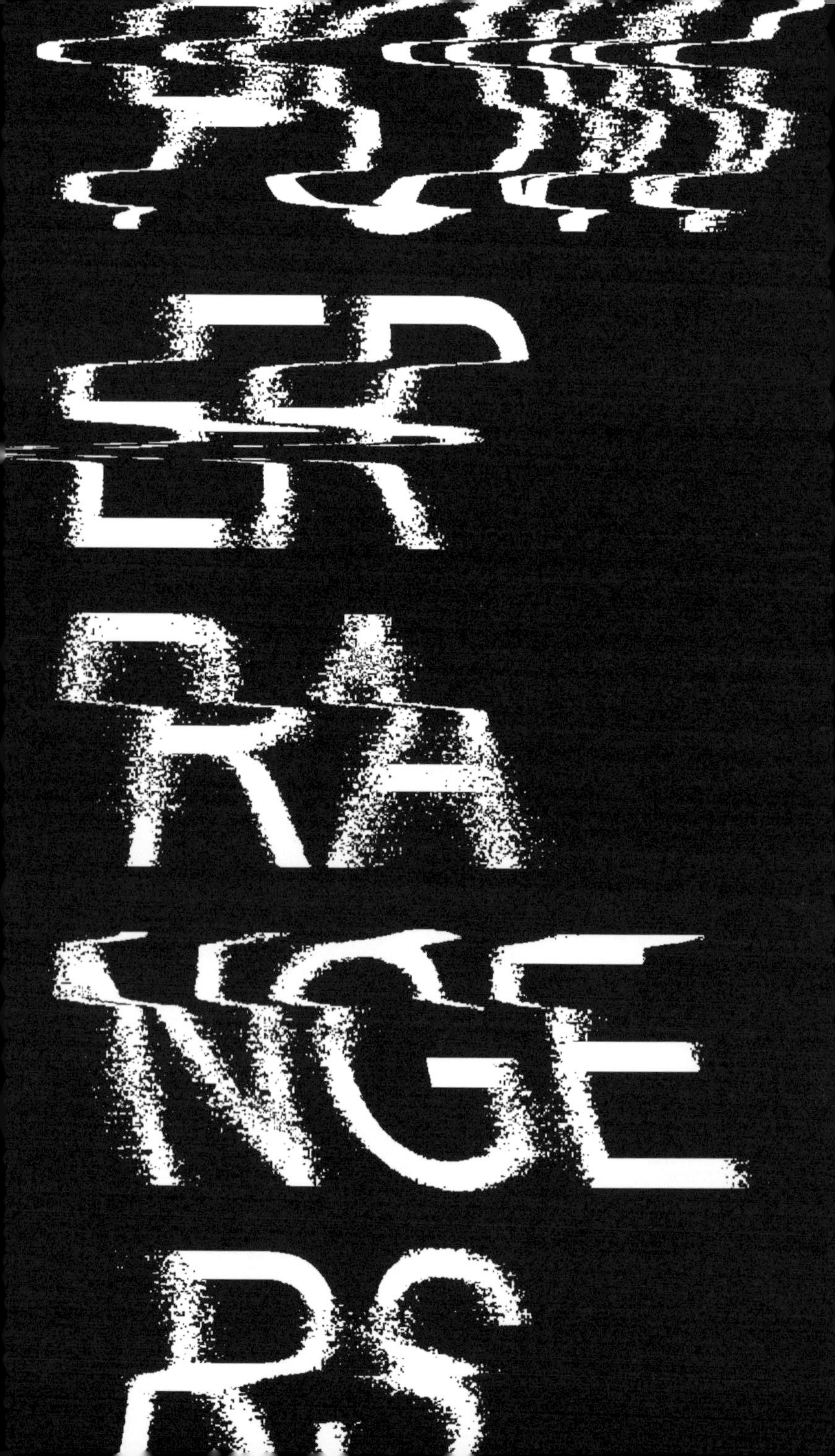

What does power look like? The media is a forum where it manifests. The Catholic Church controlled much of European literacy through the Bible for a good few centuries. In the sixteenth century, the rise of print technology led to the seditious culture of pamphlets. At this point, media information became politicised. Martin Luther, the leader of the Reformation, was the first pamphlet icon. In 1589, Henri III issued an imperial edict in Germany prohibiting pamphlets, citing their violent and coarse language. (Violence came first—satire took another century.) Twentieth-century newspaper moguls like William Randolph Hearst and Rupert Murdoch were well aware that whomever owned the press, and later telecommunications, had enormous power and influence on society. Own the media and you control the world.

Today, screen space is the focus of power. The carefree utopia of a cybernetic future promised by the Space Race in the 1960s did not manifest. The 'mediascape' we inhabit today displays the cryptic working of power and ideology. As Timothy W Luke wrote in *Screens of Power: Ideology Domination and Resistance in Informational Society*, "The communication of information became critical tools for producing power and privilege for those who own, control, or manage them." When Luke was writing way back in 1989, power lay firmly in the hands of Cold War superpowers, alongside transnational corporations. Today you can throw China, the Military Industrial Complex, cyber criminals, Internet moguls and extremist political agitators into the mix.

MONEY TALKS

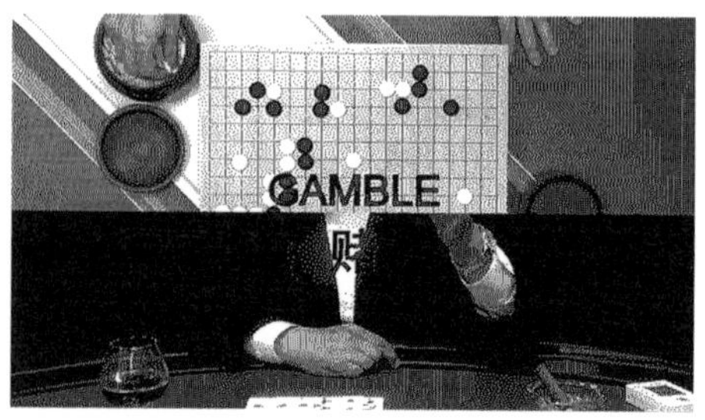

For a moment, put aside the decline of urban life, failing communities and the destruction of the environment and damage to our health. Let's focus on how the informationalisation of the screen connects humanity with commodity. How has the logic of the market—the speed and scroll of the NASDAQ and Globex—changed and insinuated itself into society? How have we become a replica of the economic system?

In 1923, Georg Lukacs criticised the commodification of society in his essay *Reification and the Consciousness of the Proletariat* (1923). He questioned how commodity exchange was capable of influencing the outer and inner life of society. He argued that how we relate to each other had taken on the character of a 'thing'. By extension, we have become a hyper-fast stream of information. We are the scroll of numbers on the stock exchange, the digital text at the bottom of 24-hour news channels, and ever-moving imagery on social media feeds. Society is no longer about comprehension, meaning or narrative, but about plugging in and becoming part of the flow.

Jean Baudrillard was very aware of how the commodification of consciousness was affecting society and symbolism. For him, the fact that money was no longer founded in the concrete meant signs no longer referred to any objective reality. This lack of meaning also was reflected in the media landscape. "We live in a world where there is more and more information, and less and less meaning," he wrote in *Simulations* in 1981. "Only the medium can make an event—whatever the contents, whether they are conformist or subversive." This changing landscape feels even more apt after the mass adoption of social media. Autonomy is almost void. Capital produces only consumers. Media exists only as a conduit between one reality and another.

"CERN's *Large Hadron Collider* in Geneva has become the perfect symbol of a postmodern return of illuminism, the illuminism of the cult of light speed for a history operating in a different time zone from all common reality," wrote in Paul Virilio in his book *The Great Accelerator* (2012). Virilio points out how the concept of seasons, even the idea of the week, has been replaced by the cyber-systemic. His view of the future is undoubtedly bleak: "The 'speed box' (gearbox) of technical progress will go into automatic mode and the stock market crash brought on by speculation will end, sooner or later, in the crash of all job production. The futurism of the instant requires it and will force it tomorrow on the generations to come."

It is impossible to think of the increased market meltdown of society without looking at the people who own the media, and how they are benefiting from the changing landscape. How does controlling the symbolic meanings of things we consume on screen affect us? Now we are in 'their' hands, what are 'they' doing?

The early Internet brimmed with utopian motivations. People developed new technologies without any financial expectation. It was an egalitarian space of shareware, open source giving motivated by communication, not overt financial interest. We grew used to a world of free 'content'—the new word for culture. That all changed when the US military stepped in and implemented a policy in which all firms working under Defence Department contracts were forced to test their employees' blood and urine for illegal drug use (only one company refused). The counterculture of computer era was over. Without that small dose of resistance, the Internet was quickly reduced to a direct marketing platform.

Advertising has grown to underpin our daily media diet. We want free apps, access and information. Business is happy to cover the costs, if it means consumption grows. New, often fabricated, needs for new products mean new consumers, so capitalism can tick along nicely. Sitting on the London Underground recently, I looked at the four advertisements above the seats of the people opposite me. They seemed a perfect manifestation of twenty first century post-tech needs. One was for easy broadband that could be delivered the same day: "relish broadband rebooted". Next to it was an ad for on-demand TV, *Discover Sky Entertainment*, presented on an image of a curved, top-end LCD screen. The third advertisement was for an Eve mattress; "everybody should be able to bound out of bed in the morning, fully energised, ready to face the day's challenges." A bed, rather than a space of respite is transformed into a place to become recharged as a productive, tech ready individual. (The last ad reflected the fallout from the new market demands of entertainment and speed. It stated: "It's time to give a xxxx about mental illness in young people—text swear to 70660." Its connection to the advertisements next to it felt notably ironic.

The power of the screen also has serious implications in terms of law enforcement, bureaucracy and governmental power. It is no accident George Orwell presented a hyper-dictatorship where people were spied on and ruled by the media. The eighteenth-century social theorist Jeremy Bentham was central to the creation and building of the prison system in Britain. His architectural concept of the Panopticon, involved a single guard at the centre of a space designed so he could see all the cells. Prisoners were unable to view him in return, and could not tell when they were being watched. The assumption was that the prisoners would behave as if being observed at all times. The state as systems operator is a digitised version of the same thing—a continuous gaze exerted through surveillance, the police and military, as well as institutional bureaucracy.

Owning the media means owning visibility. The state is able to hide its operations while on public display. This is an international approach that applies to countries including Turkey, Russia, China and USA. Journalists in war zones are controlled, corralled and given mediated information. Laws are implemented to criminalise whistleblowers and any complicit members of the media. The printed press died at the advent of the online free circulation of news. US print advertising revenues fell by 55% between 2006 and 2011. Sponsored journalism has increased. Those in political power are not complaining: compliant media that has less power to hold governments to account means it is easier to get work done.

Go ahead. Attend a march. Protest. Sign a petition. Like a tweet. This, however, does not necessarily mean you are free in the modern police state. Your face is now onscreen, so police can keep you under surveillance. The rise of political protest in 2016 and 2017 was arguably intentionally encouraged by those in power to foster the idea of protest ennui. Reveal who dissents early. The rest of the populace will become bored by their actions and be more easily controlled.

Even if we do not protest, we also contribute to our own sense of subjugation—by constantly turning ourselves into images. This is a world of selfies and self-presentation, where the conception of success and integration in society is something connected to our online presence and the marketing of the individual. Like Debord on hyper-speed, we feed the image machine.

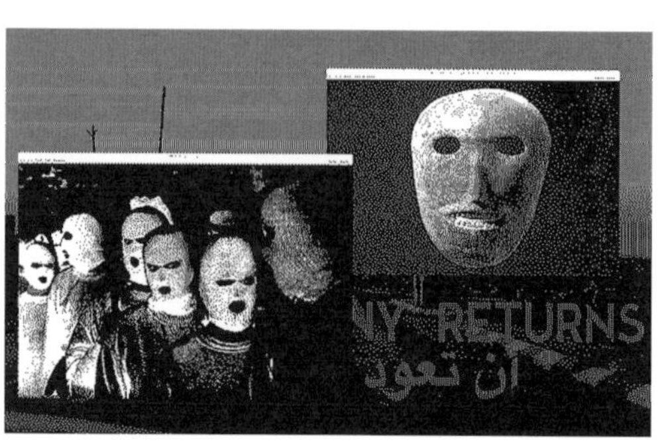

Situationism demonstrates how corporate capitalism leads to an image-based society, rather than an authentic one. In 1957, Debord in *The Situationist International* called for a "Platform for a Provisional Opposition", for revolutionary action. He was writing at a time when life was replicating images seen in advertising and on TV and led a strong movement to create new forms of behaviour and resistance. "To do this, we must from the beginning make practical use of the everyday processes and cultural forms that now exist, while refusing to acknowledge any inherent value they may claim to have," he wrote. "We should not simply refuse modern culture; we must seize it in order to negate it."

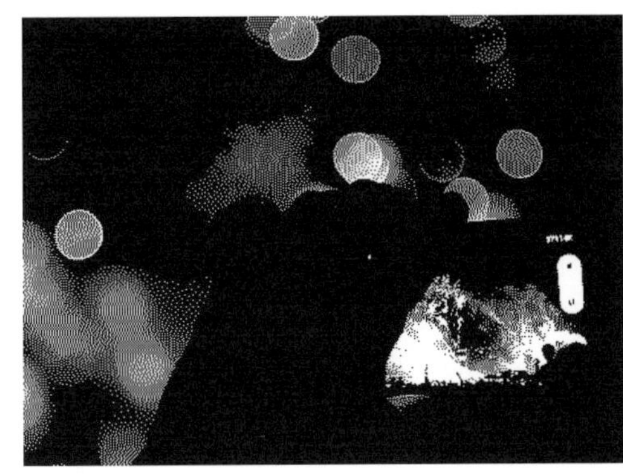

Some of the forms of suggested resistance from 'the spectacle' proposed by Situationism, such as the subversion of everyday imagery through art, interventionist action and alternative pathways through urban space, have became assimilated into the capitalist machine over the past 50 years. A straight ad for a cleaning product Cillit Bang was later twisted into a manipulated techno soundtrack. This satirical consumerist ad at first seemed like a DIY twist on capitalism—until it later emerged it was sponsored by the company itself. Arguably even the Situationist idea of the psychogeographic *dérive* has fed into and been absorbed by GPS surveillance analytics.

None of the information or imagery we put online is owned by us. It is ALL owned by the tech companies we collude with, that benefit and become increasingly powerful by our engagement. In February 2017, Mark Zuckerberg released a 5700-word manifesto on his Facebook page, which was greeted with increasingly worried responses. "Facebook stands for bringing us closer together and building a global community. When we began, this idea was not controversial. Yet now, across the world there are people left behind by globalization, and movements for withdrawing from global connection." Join Facebook's uber state above the nation state, or be forgotten.

Recently, again on public transport, I overheard someone who worked at Facebook selling the concept of data manipulation to a possible buyer on their phone. He talked about the replication of fringe audiences using data sourced from the social media platform could lead to more 'ROI' (return on investment). "Reach is irrelevant if you're not reaching the right people," he said. It was all about data analysis and how to use it. Need more information? Not to worry. "Do a couple of little competitions to give away things to get more data we can use."

Our desire to be noticed makes us into things that are increasingly owned by other people. To quote Frankfurt School philosopher Herbert Marcuse in *One-Dimensional Man* (1964), "Under the rule of a repressive whole, liberty can be made into a powerful instrument of domination. The range of choice open to the individual is not the decisive factor in determining the degree of human freedom, but what can be chosen and what is chosen by the individual."

WHERE DID IT ALL GO WRONG?

It feels naïve to see the Internet as an opportunity for democratic change, open participation and genuine engagement. Instead just as capitalists took over the Internet in order to make us shopping slaves, radicals have take over much of social media as a space to spread nationalism, fundamentalism, and the self-interested focus on the individual.

It began with the innocuous acceptance of the troll. Everyone thought trolls were harmless. Maybe because of their name—halfway between a garden gnome and a creature in *Lord of the Rings*. Comment threads and social media feeds were their lairs—spaces to vent anger, racism, sexism and terrorism, where any extreme view and violent fantasy could run rampant. No one was policing trolls or their comments. Like plucking grey hairs, if one account was closed down, and three more would grow in its place. The anonymity of the Internet revealed humanity's hidden frustration and foulness.

Rather than view the troll as a real thinking individual, we dehumanised him. (The troll's invisible gender is often portrayed as male). We could imagine the troll as a spotty teenager who couldn't get laid or an angry office worker taking their anger, boredom and lack of autonomy out on the screen. Yet in the wake of Brexit, the election of Trump, the rise of terrorism and neo-reactionary politics, trolls don't look harmless anymore. Social media may not be the cause of extremist thinking, but it has fed it. Negativity has flourished, first on blogs and then was disseminated via news feeds on Facebook and Twitter.

Trump is President of the Trolls. His political speeches became an extension of his Twitter feed—unedited, unrepressed. Short, fast, retweetable, immediate thoughts shared with the public in seconds. Out of his mind and onto the screen. Would Trump have become president if his fans didn't feel he represented the everyman? He was just like us, wasn't he? He even tweeted at four in the morning when he couldn't sleep, just like the rest of us.

I first noticed the relationship between social media and extreme political views in August 2014. My Facebook feed was filled with a wave of hatred and anti-Semitism in the wake of the Israeli invasion into Palestine. It began with some comparisons to the Holocaust. Liberal artists, fashion stylists, photographers and musicians who were my acquaintances and friends started posting strange blog posts with increasingly violent content. I saw images of Jews being lynched. People began quoting 1930s Fascist speeches. I was so upset by the content of my feed, I couldn't sleep. I decided to get off Facebook and deleted 1500 'friends'.

And yet I stayed on Twitter. I grew to love Instagram. I slowly began to dabble with Facebook again. I was choosy about whom I followed, whose feed I wanted to look at. I increasingly created a bubble of my own interests—a mirror of my view of the world. After Brexit,

I realised I was not the only person to create a buffer of like-minded virtual souls around me. What became clear is people with opposing views were also doing the same thing. We were all living in an echo chamber of our own politics. There was none of the even-handed political detachment that journalism and the law was said to uphold. Newspapers increasingly began to echo the extreme anger of the troll. Headlines (largely from Rupert Murdoch's empire) were written in troll-speak. The world became binary—us versus them, good versus bad, right versus wrong. There was no nuance. We lived in world where there was only a yes or no without any discussion of the in-between. You're wrong and here's a death threat to go with it.

A wave of petitions began to emerge online—a social media version of good fairies. I signed numerous online petitions—against war, to protect the NHS, stop Monsanto, save the bees. I would receive passionate emails from 38 degrees and its like. They felt like positive ways to have a little say and reminded me of the Amnesty International letters I would copy and sign and send off as a teenager to save someone lingering in some foreign jail. I imagined children who wanted to change the world presenting these heartfelt petitions on the steps of Downing Street. Yet nothing seemed to quite come from these notes sent into the ether. No serious political change. When over four million people signed a petition for a second Brexit referendum, people were calmly sent a transcription of a small meeting between 20 people, ignoring the request. If four million digital signatures have no effect, that online click form of resistance isn't working.

Meanwhile, social media companies have said nothing. In fact, it is in their interest to keep quiet. They want our shock, our outrage. They want us to post lists from *BuzzFeed* and blog responses to media stories. The screen has become a space that encourages ideological outrage and anger. These all increase advertising revenue. Youths in Macedonia began to create fake, pro-Trump websites in order to entice Facebook thread clicks that earned them pocket money. As Adam Curtis said in an interview with the *Evening Standard* in 2016, “The fact is that angry people click more and clicks are gold dust, clicks are the measure of success for all corporations and media platforms. So the more angry you get, the more you actually keep everything stable. Your anger fuels those systems.”

Conservative businessman, early Facebook investor and Trump supporter Peter Thiel has endorsed a theory created by the French Christian philosopher René Girard, in his book *Things Hidden Since the Foundation of the World* (1978). Girard laid out mimetic theory, where human behaviour imitates desires, leading to conflict. When that conflict builds up, people look for a scapegoat. “According to Girard, imitation is inescapable. As a rule, we do what we do just because other people are doing it, too. That’s why we end up competing for the same things,” Thiel told *Business Insider* magazine in 2014.

It is here that things get strange. Girard was also interested in the idea of the apocalypse and the Book of Revelations in relationship to the world after 9/11. Geoff Shullenberger argued in *The Society Pages* in

2016, "Thiel invested in and promoted Facebook not simply because Girard's theories led him to foresee the future profitability of the company, but because he saw social media as a mechanism for the containment and channeling of mimetic violence in the face of an ineffectual state." Online platforms are drawn to express envy, violence and anger, as the existence of the troll and both ISIS and Fascism's use of social media proves. Own, harness, profit from and manipulate this anger and you run society. This also means directing the populace at scapegoats—away from those in power in the Silicon Valley pseudo-monarchy.

The algorithmic filtering of information is having an increasingly dominant influence on our lives. Algorithms predict our choices. They are used to auto-fill online forms, direct you to information, assess your risk profile, observe workers' productivity and abilities, and predict policies. This is an unregulated and highly lucrative area of contemporary data gathering—and arguably impossible to limit or police.

Emerson T Brooking and PW Singer, in the cover feature 'War Goes Viral' published in *The Atlantic* magazine in 2016, examined how social media empowered the ISIS international recruitment of at least 30,000 foreign fighters from 100 countries to go to Syria and Iraq. Their use of Instagram-ready, staged photos and choreographed videos, such as the beheading of American journalist James Foley, depicted the movement in a particularly filmic way. The intimacy and authenticity embedded in the language and immediacy of social media was vital. They created hashtags. Social media was part of the success of the new vein of terrorism. "Social media platforms reinforce 'us versus them' narratives, expose vulnerable people to virulent ideologies, and inflame even long-dormant hatreds. They create massive groundswells of popular opinion that are nearly impossible to predict or control."

Russia Today has become the most popular television news network on YouTube, maintained by bloggers and fake accounts working in 'troll factories'. The entire purpose here, as Adam Curits notes in *Hypernormalisation* (2016), is to make all truth fragile and conflicting so that the public is easier to manipulate and control. Similar approaches were made by the Turkish government, Venezuelan President and undoubtedly in the campaigns of Brexiteers and Donald Trump.

WHICH WAY OUT, PLEASE?

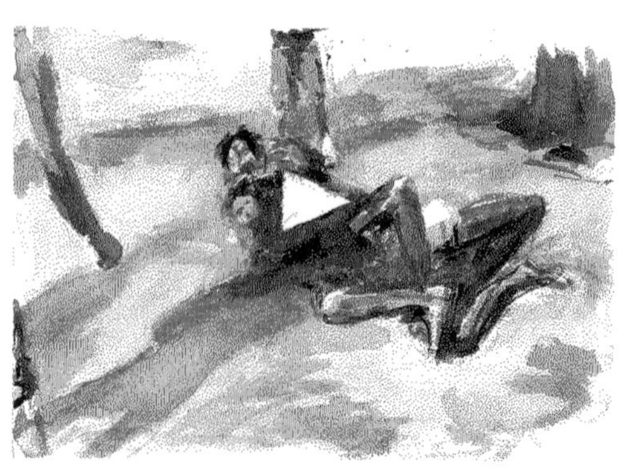

Artist and activist Clayton Patterson was a pioneer in the blurred area between the layman and the screen. He documented the changes of New York's Lower East Side for over 20 years, collected over 2,000 videotapes and one million photographs. His emphasis was on the documentation of his cultural environment, from drag clubs or the graffiti art scene. He bought his first video camera in 1986, when access to the technology was very new. In August 1988, he filmed the eviction of the city's homeless from the public park, Tompkins Square. His footage of the ensuing riots filled the mainstream media and shamed the police. Patterson went to jail for 10 days in 1988 for refusing to give up the original copy of the tape. Amateur phone footage is the norm today. Patterson set a precedent.

There is a grit to DIY screen imagery—bad angles, unclear lighting. You can feel a hand holding the screen. The screen can create a sense of personal resistance—cue heartfelt films from people dying in Aleppo that became momentary viral videos. Yet these cries for help quickly fade into the past. Old news gets cold very quickly.

The Black Lives Matter movement was ignited by the screen—in particular how the documentation captured on mobile phones highlighted systemic violence, injustice and murder. Louis-Georges Schwartz in his article 'In Plain View' in *Artforum* (2016), suggested the role of video calls for a fundamental re-evaluation of the moving image as evidence as it often reinforces structural racism. The March 1991 video footage of the brutal beating of Rodney King by Los Angeles police, broadcast on the evening news KTLA, may have sparked the LA Riots but it did not change systemic racist behaviour. It did, however, put a fire under the opponents of violence who questioned how government and law enforcement agencies could ignore what was plain for all to see on the screen.

Seeing and being seen is at the heart of visual activist and author Nicholas Mirzoeff's e-book *The*

Appearance of Black Lives Matter (available for free from namepublications.org). He explores "the doubled experience of revealed police violence and subsequent protests in the same or similar spaces," what he defines as the 'space of appearance.'

We watch police violence on screens and the protests against this violence on the same screens. Mirzoeff proposes a new way of looking, a multisensory seeing. He considers how the hashtag #blacklivesmatter, created in 2012 in response to the murder of Trayvon Martin by George Zimmerman, has led to the possibility of meeting the police gaze. This is looking as looking back. "This persistent looking, meaning a refusal to look away from what is kept out of sight, off stage, and out of view… calls for us to see what there is to see, to be vulnerable, but not to be traumatized. Looking here is both witnessing and the embodied engagement with space."

The networking of screens through searchable hashtags on social media, such as Facebook, Instagram, Snapchat, Twitter and Vine, has created a form of resistance to the persistent seeing of the state through body cameras, CCTV and surveillance. Yet is seeing enough? According to cnn.com, between 2005 and 2017, 80 police officers were arrested on murder or manslaughter charges for on-duty shootings. Only 35% were convicted, while the rest were pending or not convicted at all. Black men are three times more likely to die from police force.

How does resistance emerge in this screen savvy context? Digital activism, crowdfunding and even social media networks reflect utopian aspirations of freedom and independence of communication. Yet, we live in an illusionary powerful landscape, controlled by increasingly hidden mechanisms. As Astra Taylor, one of the co-editors of the *Occupy! Gazette*, notes in *The People's Platform: Taking back power and culture in the Digital Age* (2014), "online, some speak louder than others." We can all broadcast our views but are far from cultural democracy. The problems with the old media system—"consolidation, centralization, commercialism" —have carried over. She calls for a refocus of attention back to social structures and how power operates.

There has been a flurry of blog posts on the Internet encouraging methods of hiding from our screen society. Join Signal for encrypted conversations. Try Ello for social media that is not observed. Dip into the Black Web. Set up something on the blockchain. All these moves are arguably important, but also feel futile. Is it truly possible to escape what Taylor describes as "the creep of algorithms and automation that has fed into every corner of our lives; The trend toward filtering and personalization; The lack of diversity; The privacy violations."

A growing number of companies offer services that analyse social media profiles to determine whether individuals are a lending risk—a move that may enable creditors to consider information they are banned from requesting on certain loan applications (for instance race and religion, what we read and who we associate with), and facilitating unfair treatment and exclusion.

In recent years, there has been a wave of literature deconstructing our relationship to technology —often criticising it, even from within. Jaron Lanier, an American computer scientist and pioneer of virtual reality, in his book *You Are Not A Gadget* (2010), criticised the limitations of the structure of programming and how it restricts human expression and communication. Devices, he notes, are "inert tools and are only useful because people have the magical ability to communicate meaning through them...The most important thing to ask about any technology is how it changes people."

The most influential text to sum up our experience with technology and what it means to exist now is Jonathan Crary's *24/7: Late Capitalism and the Ends of Sleep* (2013). The book is deeply critical of the political and commercial interests that oversee our relationship to technology. If you're checking your emails or feeds in the middle of the night on the tablet next to your pillow, this book will make you feel very uncomfortable. Much of Crary's focus is on the speed of consumption —the current accelerated formats of image and information absorption. Nothing is ever really off—just resting, waiting to be activated at a single gesture, touch or glance. Here, the screen becomes a device that is limiting, not increasing, our activity. As Crary writes, "Devices are introduced (and no doubt labelled as revolutionary), they will simply be facilitating the per-

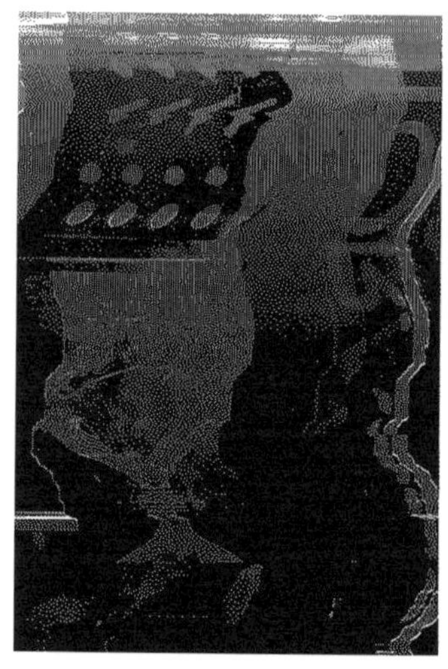

petuation of the same banal exercise of non-stop consumption, social isolation, and political powerlessness."

Crary points out how the myths of open source egalitarianism and the empowerment of technology have been cultivated. "The idea of technological change as quasi-autonomous, driven by some process of auto-poesis or self-organisation, allows many aspects of contemporary social reality to be accepted as necessary, unalterable circumstances, akin to facts of nature. In the false placement of today's most visible products and devices within an explanatory lineage that includes the wheel, the pointed arch, movable type and so forth, there is a concealment of the most important techniques invented in the last 150 years: the various systems for the management and control of human beings." To paraphrase, we voluntarily kettle ourselves in cyberspace.

There are rumours of Facebook's messenger app recording people's conversations and ruffled feathers over Samsung's amended terms and conditions warning users their Smart TVs that records conversations within earshot. The screen is watching us as much as we are watching the screen. Stories of things mentioned in social conversations appearing in social media feeds is now the norm. Television today is often a two-screen experience—with phones and tablet interaction encouraged to revive traditional passive media. Interactive adverts already exist on services like Hulu. Sony has just patented methods, systems and computer programmes for converting television commercials into interactive network video games. In one method, a broadcast or streamed commercial is accompanied by an interactive segment. A media player would present users with an enhanced and interactive mini-game commercial that could be played with other viewers. It could be inserted within the television program, overlaid on frames or last the duration of a commercial spot.

A blog post by Salim Virani, a writer and founder of the peer-to-peer education programme *Source Institute*, has been viewed over a million times. Entitled 'Get your loved ones off Facebook', it was promoted on Twitter by political provocateurs Anonymous. Virani argues that removing oneself from Facebook "isn't just necessary to protect yourself, it's necessary to protect your friends and family too." Drawing on a thorough examination of the changes in the platform's terms of service, he desperately explains, "It's not too late to take back control." He notes that none of the data on Facebook is safe or anonymous; that there have been serious privacy policy breaches, with data being given to 'third parties' through apps, a serious level of spying including reading of private messages, the contents of the links you send privately and using facial recognition to track your location and the people you know. Most frighteningly, Facebook has introduced features that turn your phone's microphone on, and is enacting audio surveillance largely through their messenger app. They can change settings without letting you know, track your location and sell any information to whomever it wants.

What are the prospective problems? Influence on an individual's credit rating, their ability to get insurance or a mortgage, their chances of getting a job.

If you've ever referred to something illegal, if you've ever supported a political cause "this can be used against you in the future, especially by another country's government. You may find yourself arrested for being at the wrong place at the wrong time, or just pulled aside at an airport one day, now facing jail time because you revealed you did something that government considers illegal five years ago."

I removed myself from Facebook once again, yet became aware of the company's presence over many other things on my phone. Facebook now owns Instagram and Whatsapp—two social apps with currently less worrying public profiles. However, the information they both provide to their parent company is worrying. Google is another company with a huge breadth of control—they had to rename themselves Alphabet as they had so many other companies under their wing, such as Android, Blogger, YouTube and the many different companies with Google prefixed to their names. Advertising with these two companies is vacuuming up budgets from all other outlets, as well as any rival digital ad companies.

So where does that leave us and what can we do? Leap off social media like lemmings over a cliff? Facebook is apparently getting worried people have stopped posting and thus they have less data to draw on. In *Fuck Off, Google*, a chapter in The Invisible Committee's last book *To Our Friends* (2014) they also present an alternative: "Understanding how the devices around us work, brings an immediate increase in power, giving us a purchase on what will then no longer appear as an environment, but as a world arranged in a certain way and one that we can shape. This is the hacker's perspective on the world." We have to shape, and take control of, the virtual structures of the Internet. We need to pull ourselves away from private companies with strong financial stakes. We need to create a brave new virtual world.

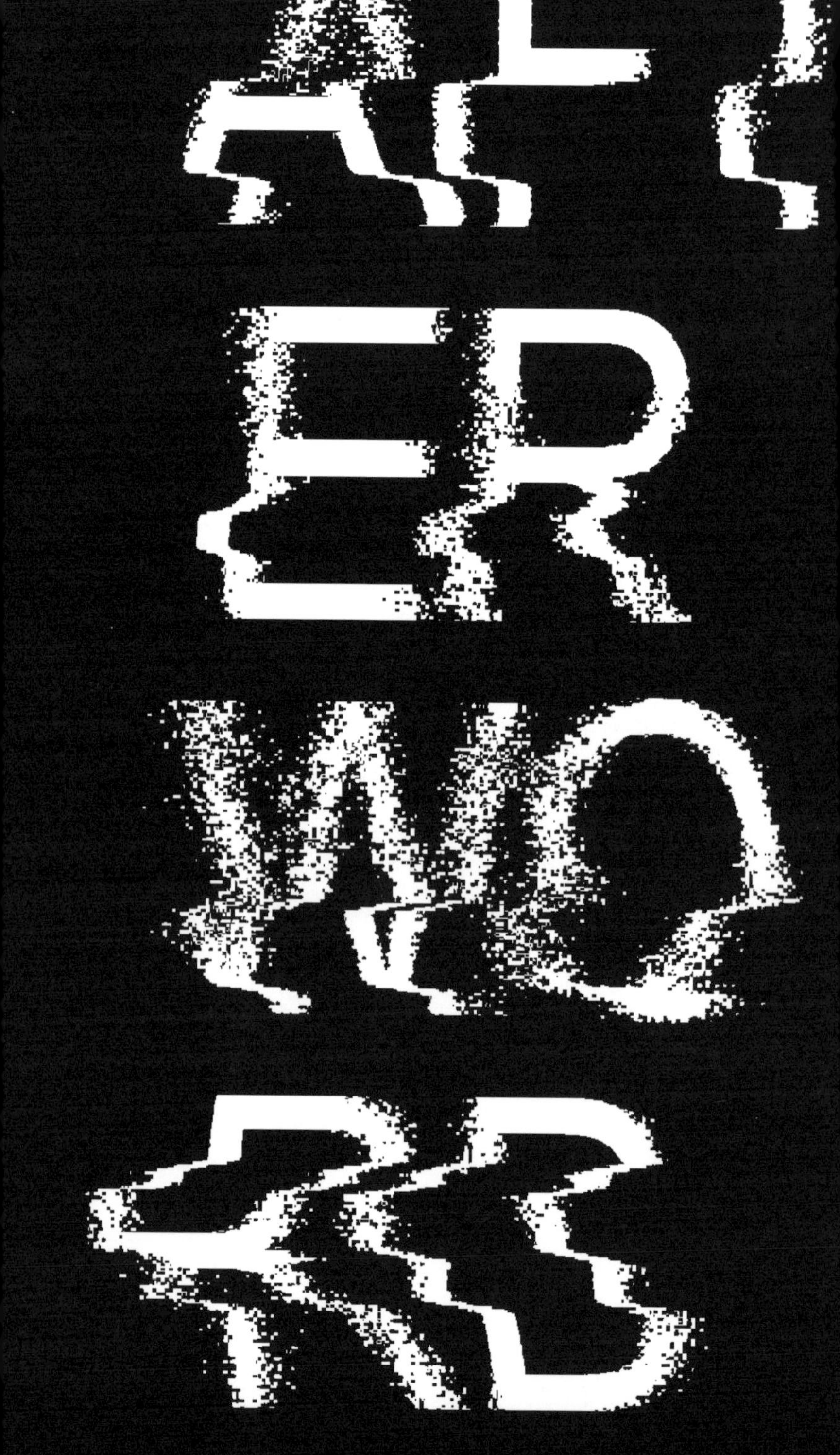

SLOW FUTURISM

As Western capitalism appears to unravel, grasping at totalitarianism and environmental destruction in an attempt to continue, the screen has increasingly become an object of information and distraction. Finding new models of imaginative possibility are hard. However not everything connected to the screen is disturbing.

Narrative is transforming away from the usual structure of plot that arguably emerged from ancient Greek theatre. Instead of mourning the end of the simplicity of the 90-minute movie, the broader approach to new narratives is, perhaps, exciting. I still remember being eight-years-old in bed reading my first *Choose Your Own Adventure* book by Steve Jackson, viscerally overwhelmed that a story could be something which I had influence upon. The sprawling, epic narratives of box-sets or tight, short, phone-accessible texts both provide new possibilities for expression and communication. Short doesn't necessarily mean less powerful, as haiku prove.

There are many political and cultural possibilities that can emerge from a post-screen world. The concept of Afrofuturism was coined in the 1990s, around the intersection of aesthetics, philosophy and history informed by science fiction, fantasy and an esoteric take on reimaging the African diaspora. Cultural examples of Afrofuturism include the novels of Octavia Butler, music of Juan Atkins, Parliament, Sun Ra and

Drexciya and some of the art of Laylah Ali, Neil Beloufa, Jacolby Slatterwite and Martine Syms. Part of the intention of the movement is to draw on ideas of the future as a way to reimagine and address the contemporary. The concept is innately positive and has had fascinating results from manifestos to artworks. In recent years, there has been a move to reposition Afrofuturism within a more technological space, drawing on the possibilities of digital connection, post-humanism and technological advances as a way to manifest actual change. The political dimension of these cultural imaginings provides a very interesting and hopeful model for new ways of relating to, and developing, our connection to the screen.

Another ray of hope is the reimaging of the technological to be more in tune with nature. New ways to exist with the organic and natural world is perhaps the ideal antithesis to the pull of the screens. There is a temporal drive built into screens. This constant ticking forward is innately part of ideas around progress, agency and capitalism. Is is build into the idea of the future. Without the screen, we may notice other forms of temporal movement from the seasonal to the lunar. There has been a rise of retreats where the main draw is a lack of wifi or poor connection. It may not be over the top to say phone screens are the new cigarettes, having the same level of addiction and physical damage that nicotine inflicted in the last century. Old school phones without apps or cameras are gaining new followers. The brave new world may in fact be slower and, hopefully, more authentic.

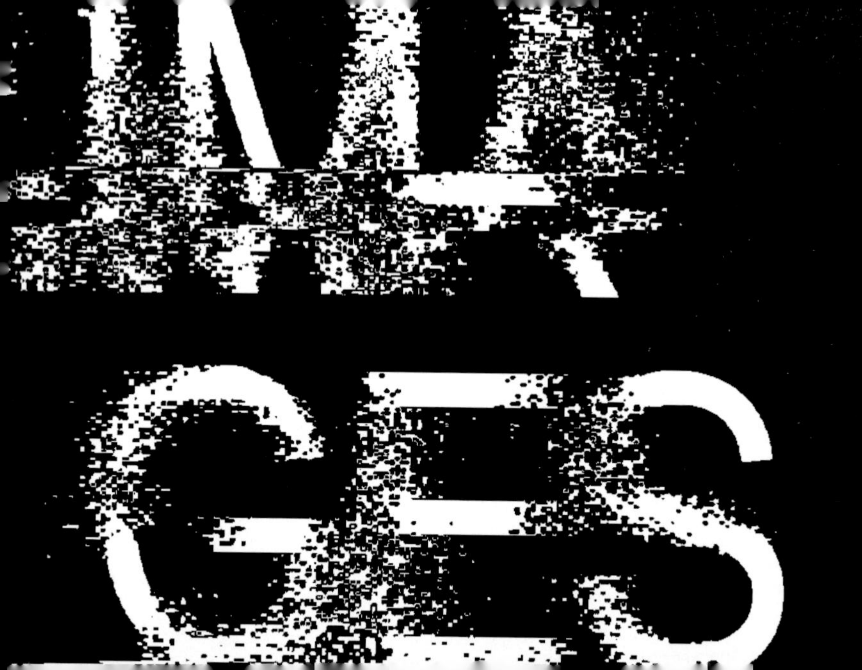

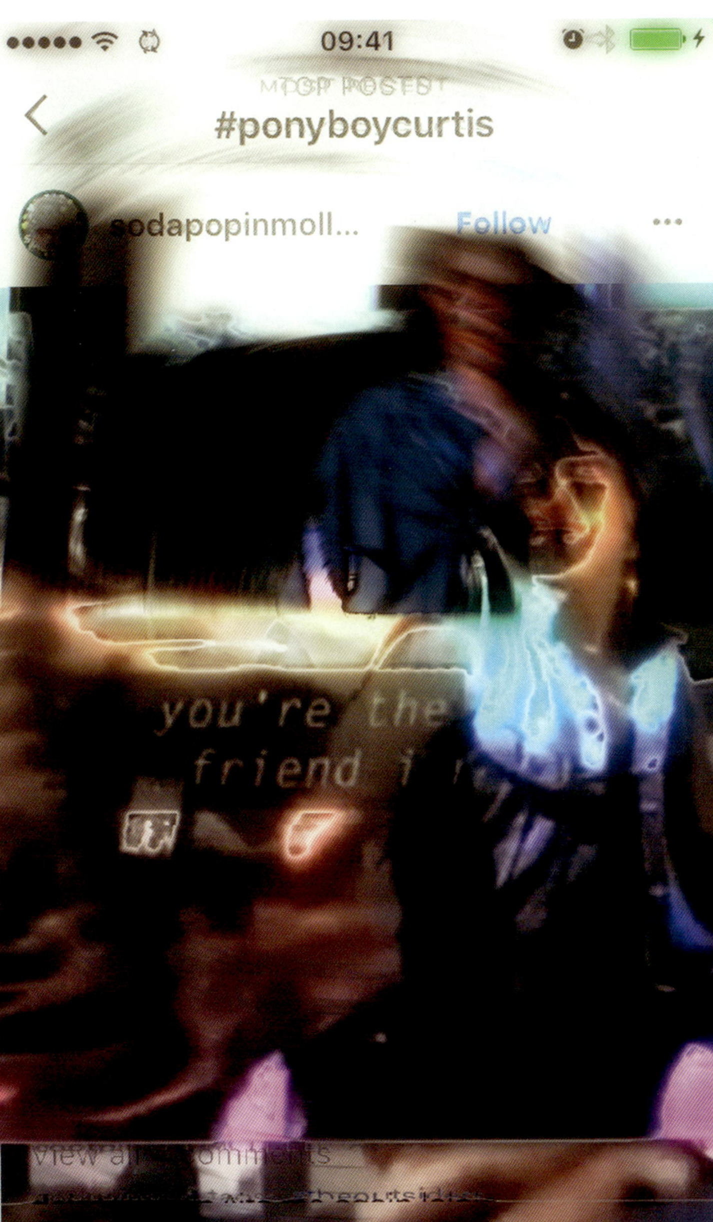
09:41
#ponyboycurtis
sodapopinmoll...
Follow
you're the
friend

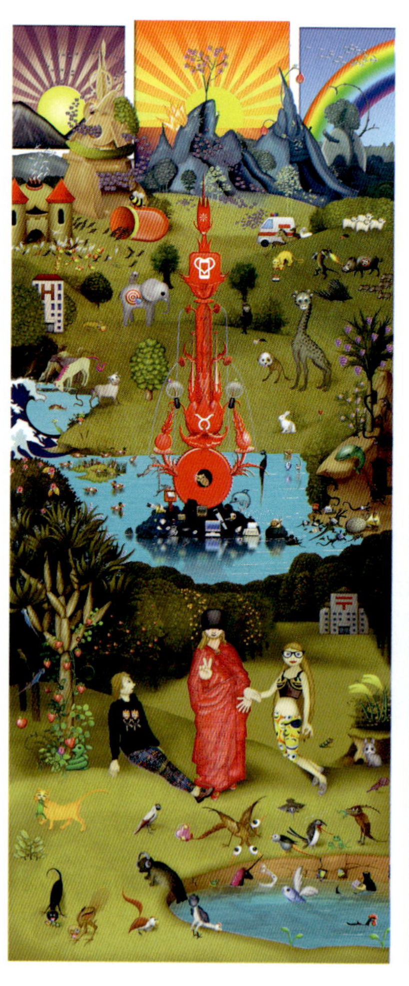

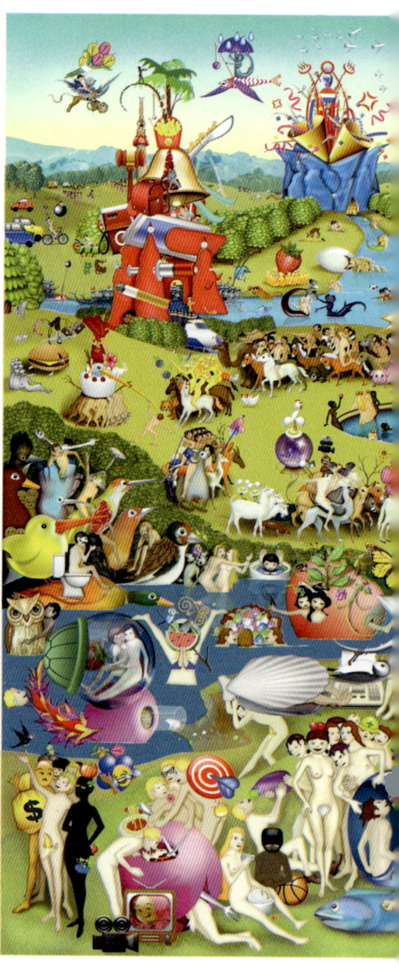

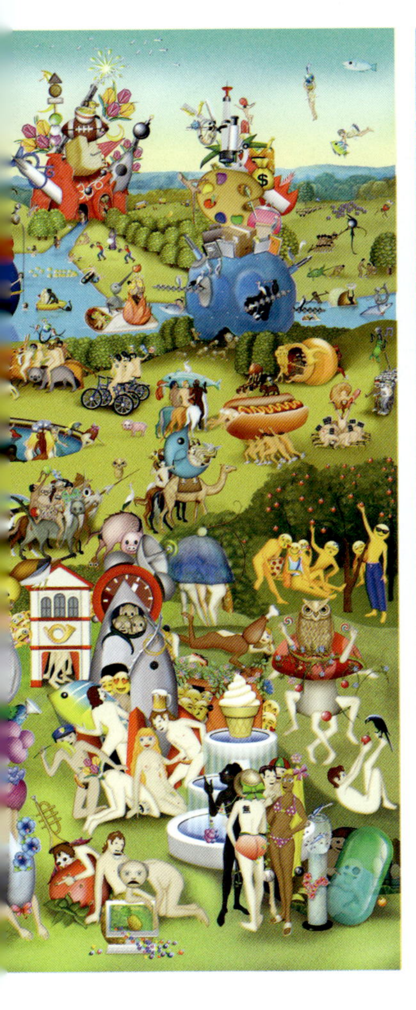

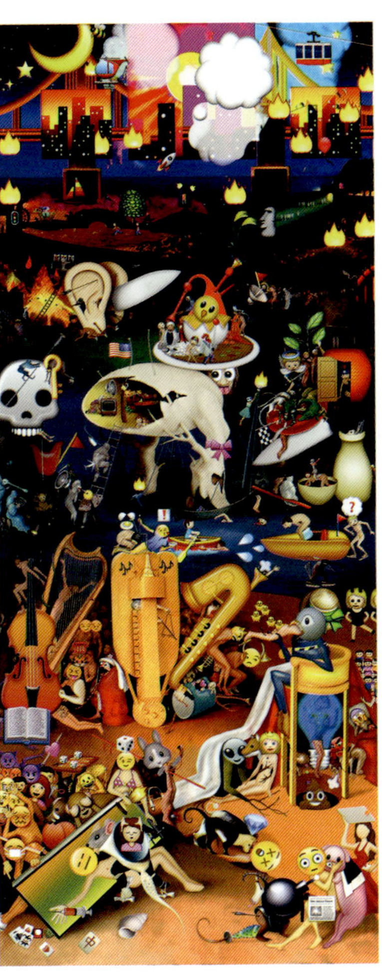

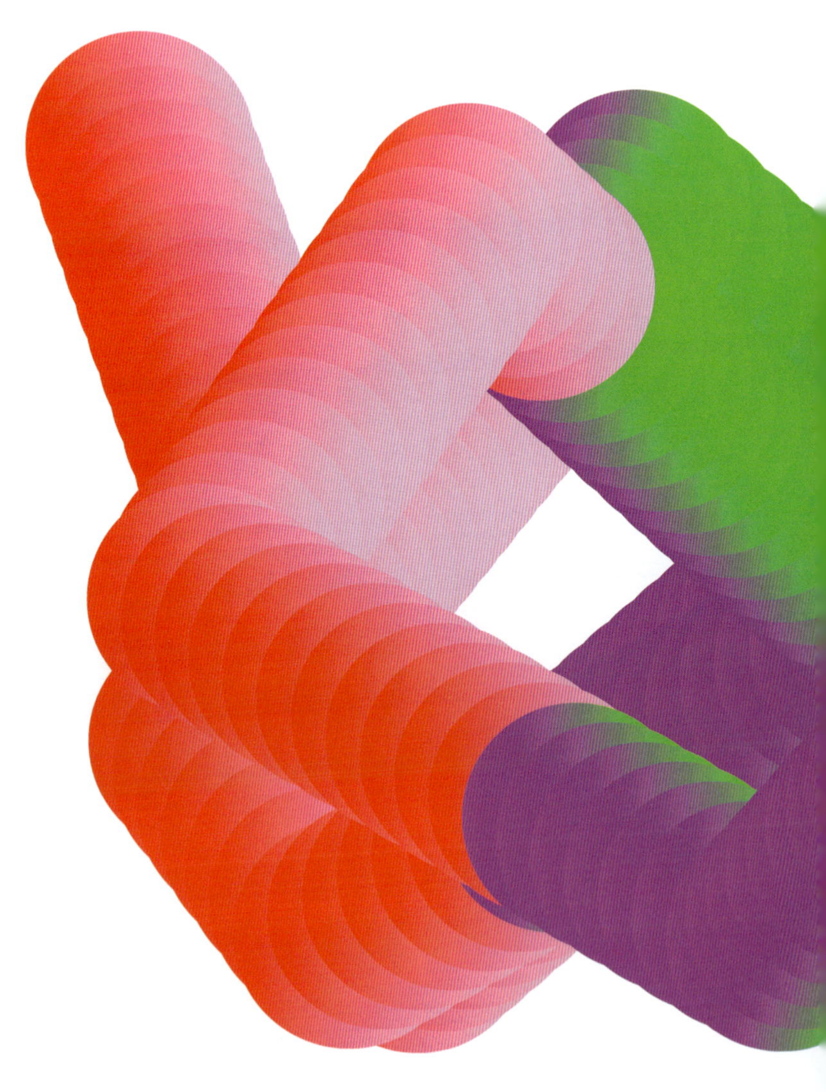

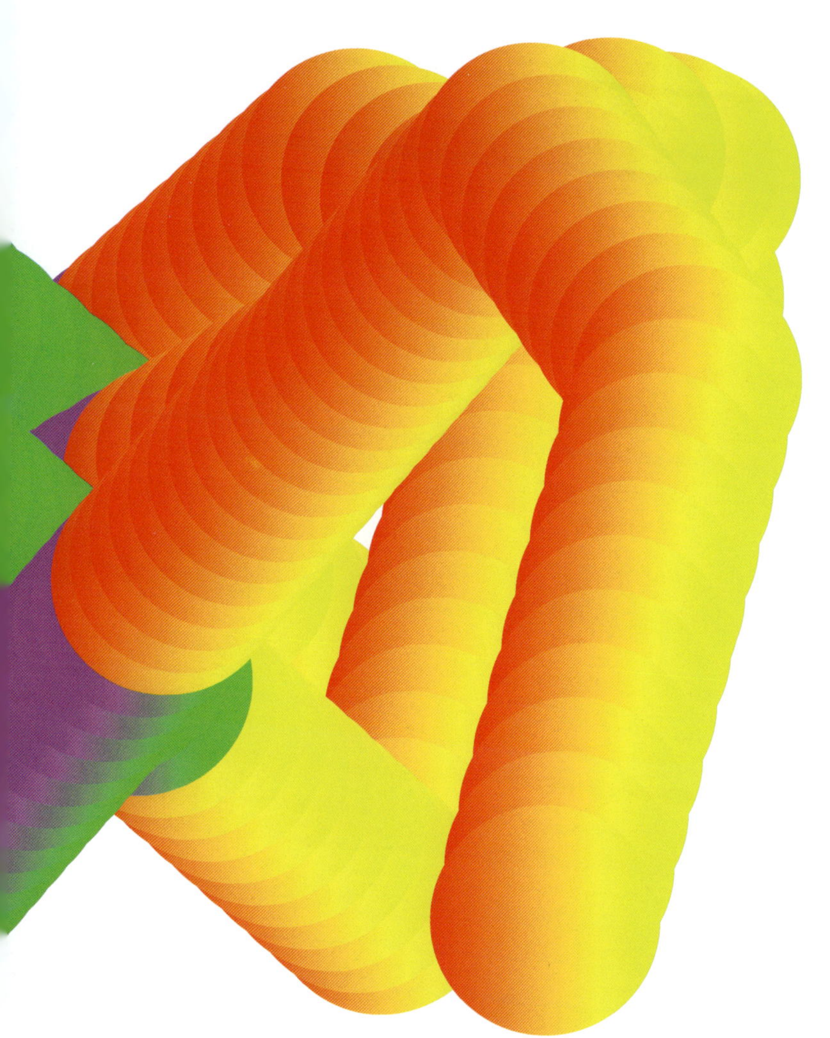

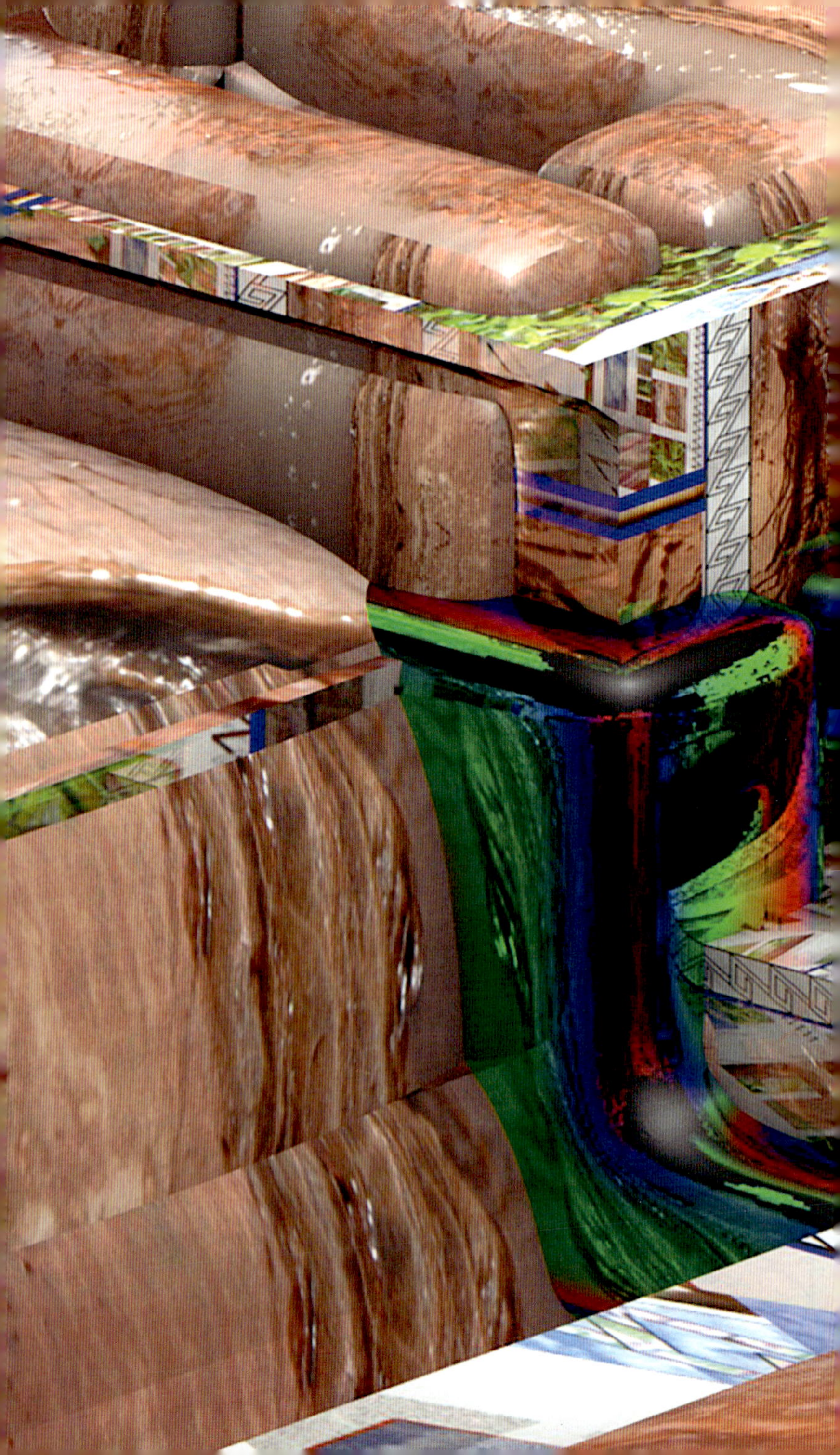

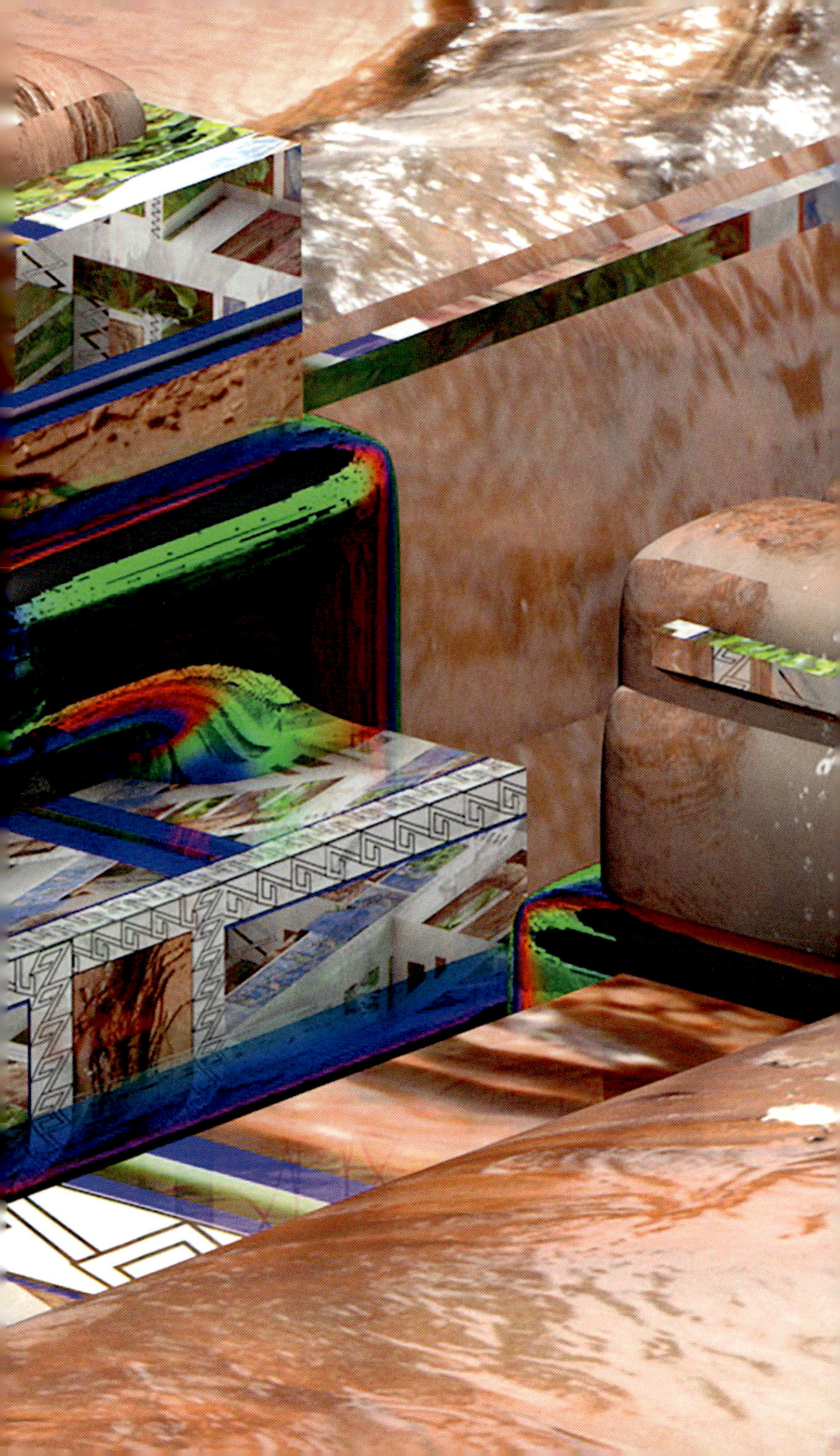

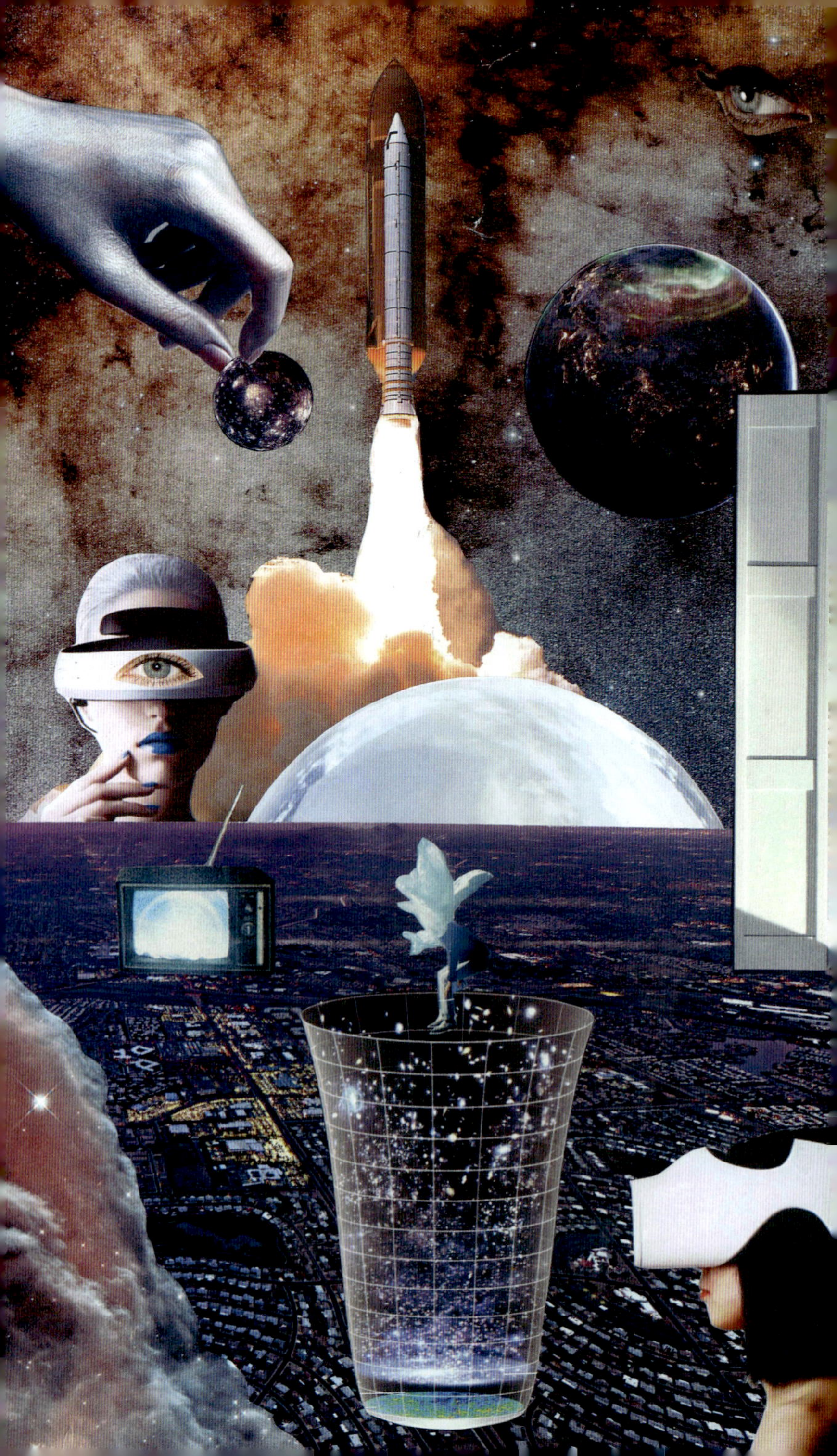

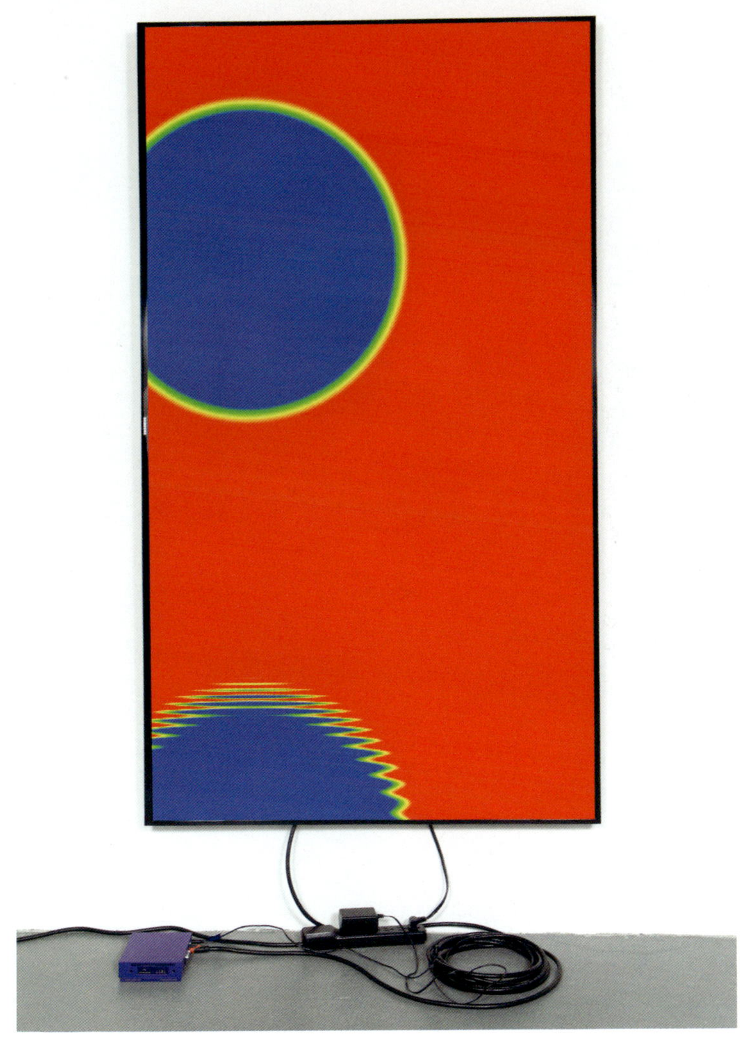

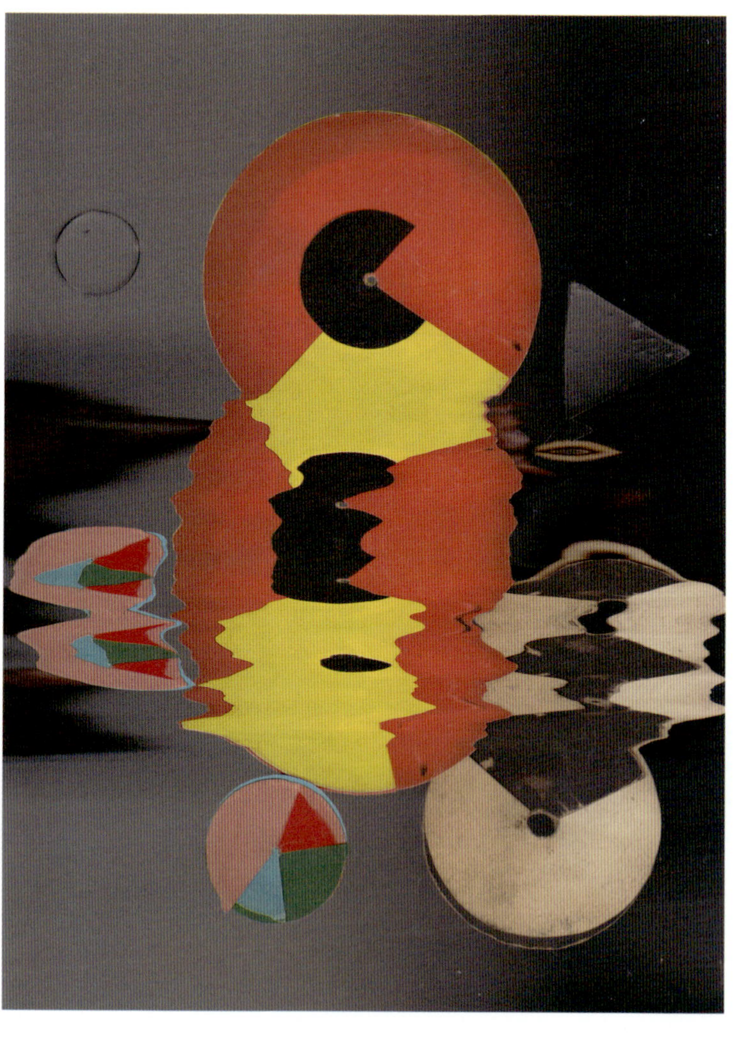

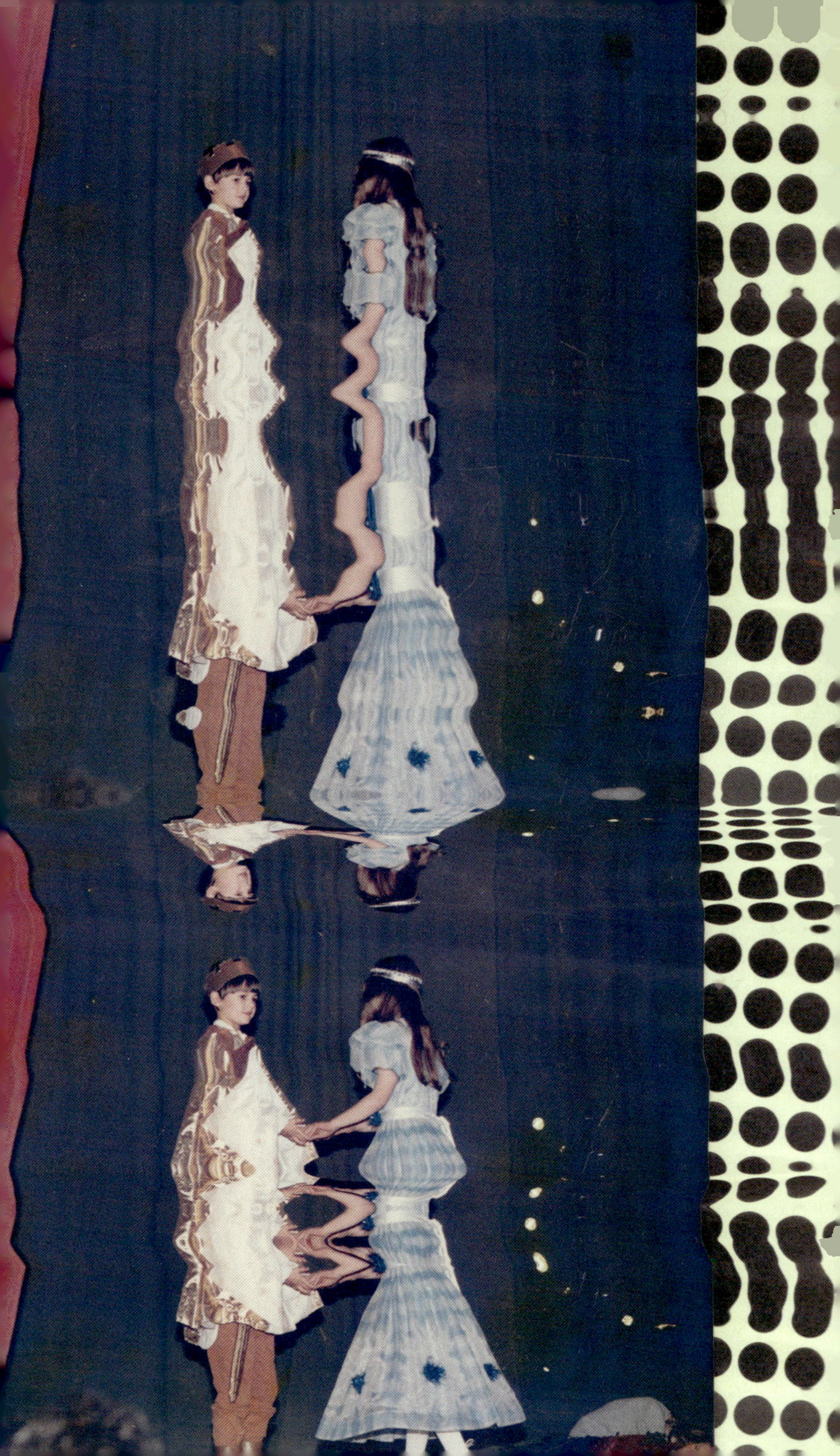

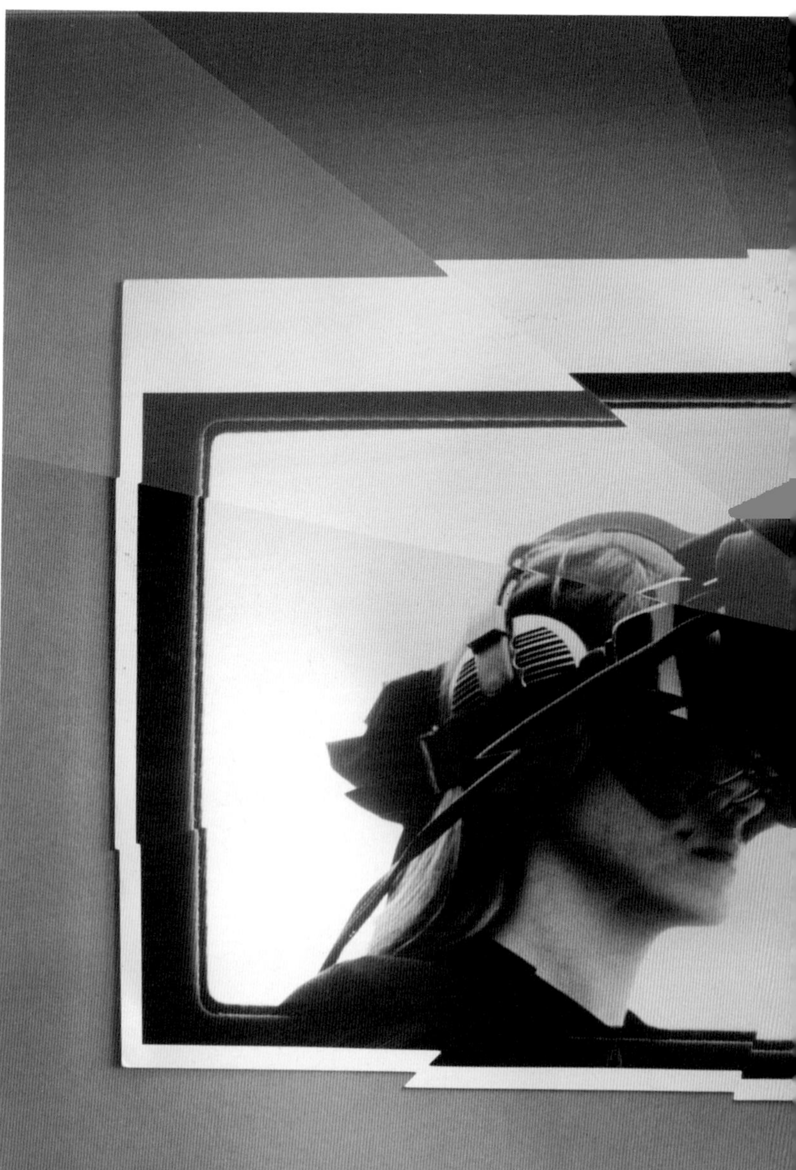

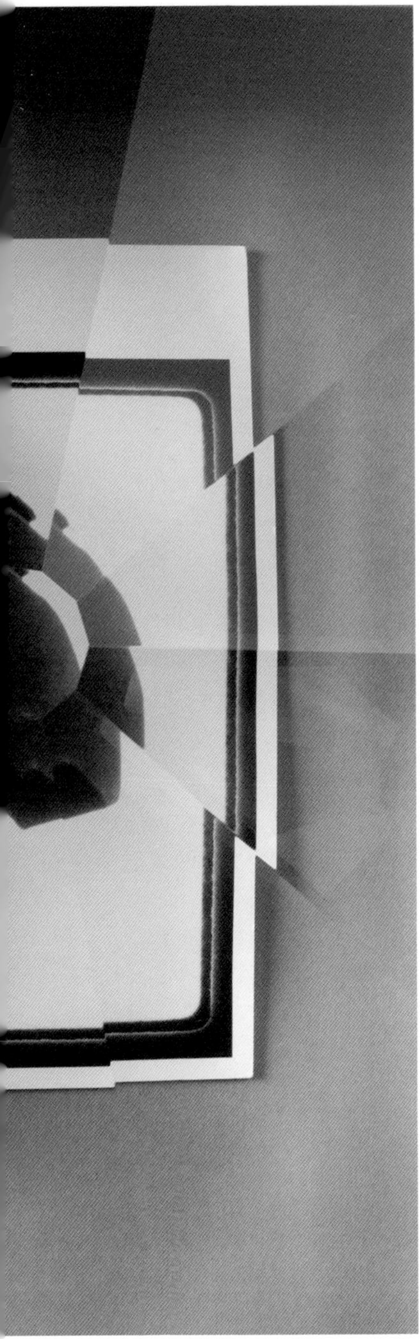

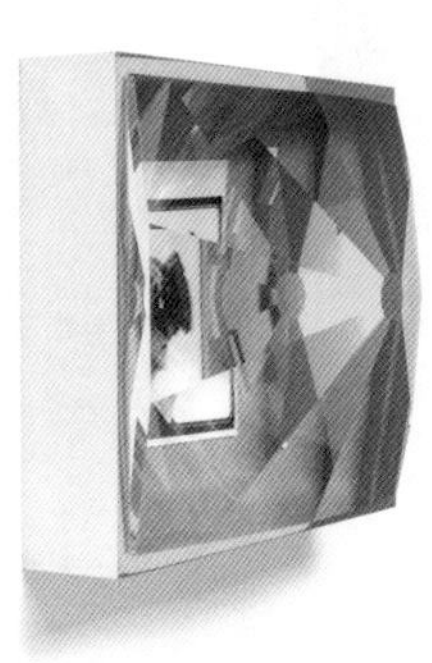

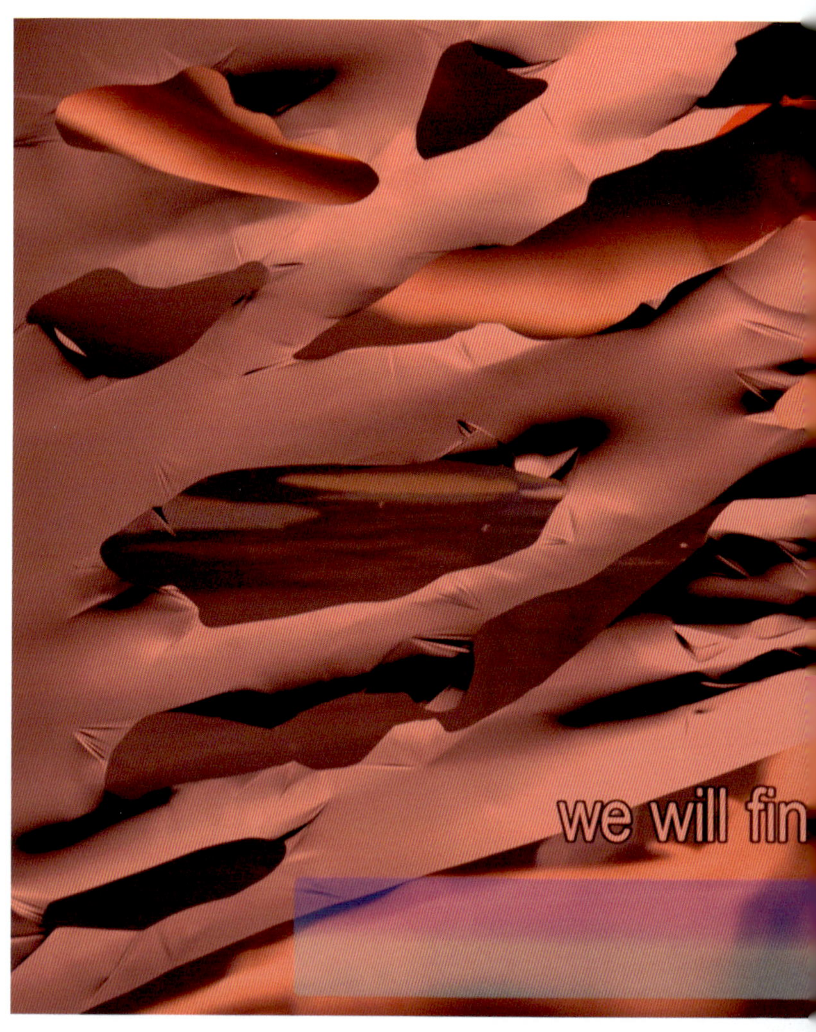
we will fin

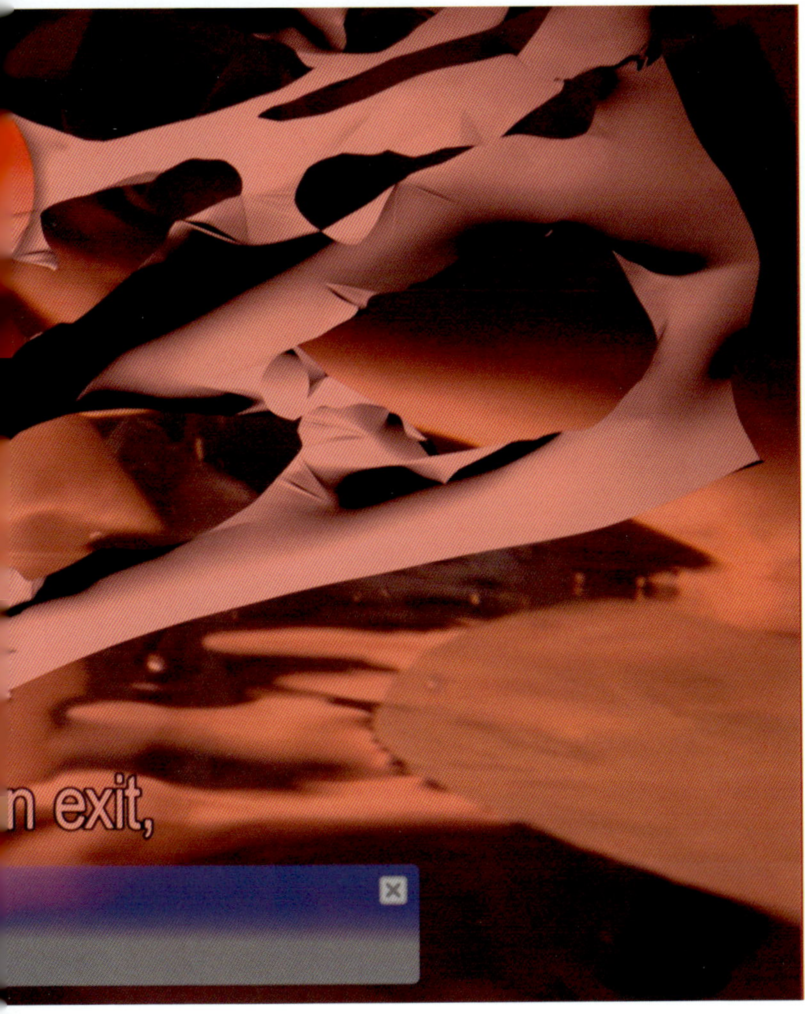
n exit,

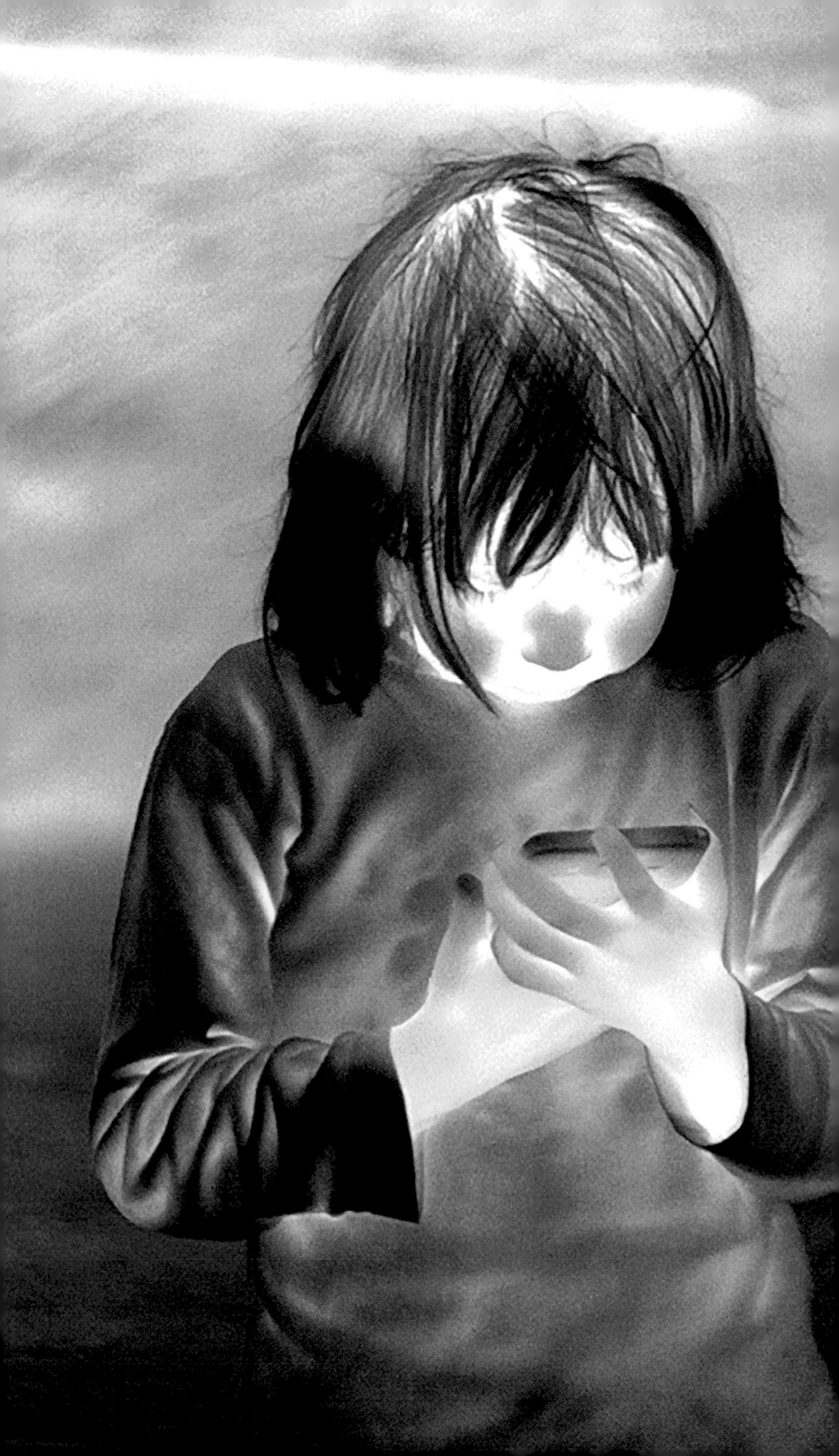

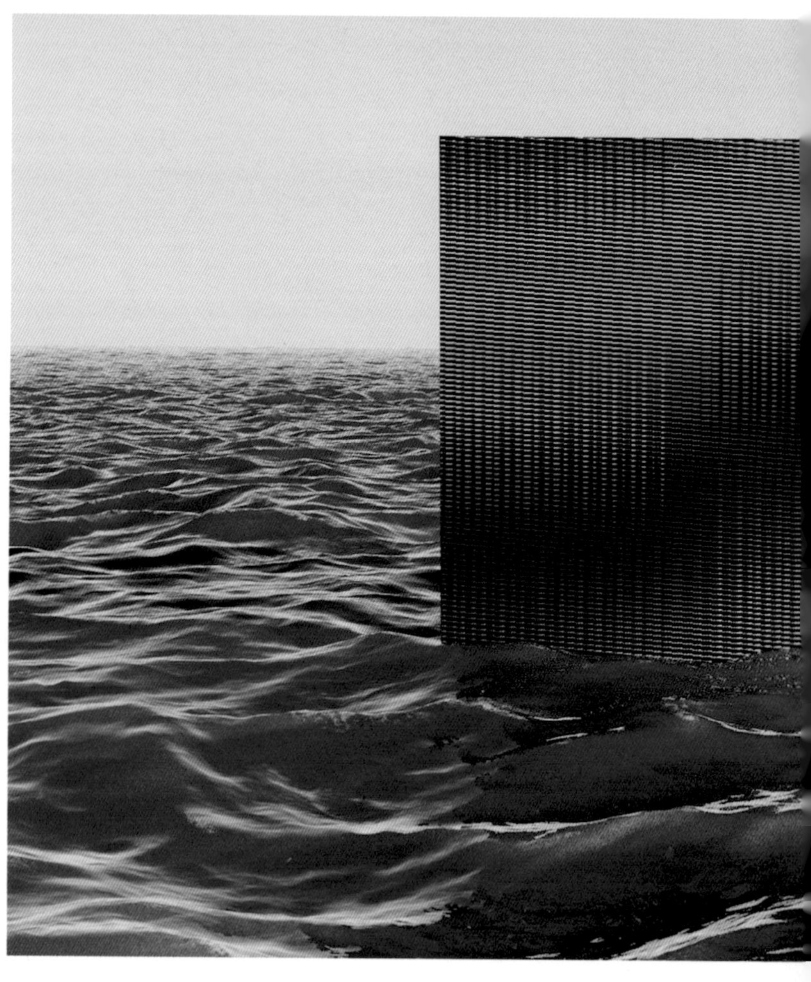

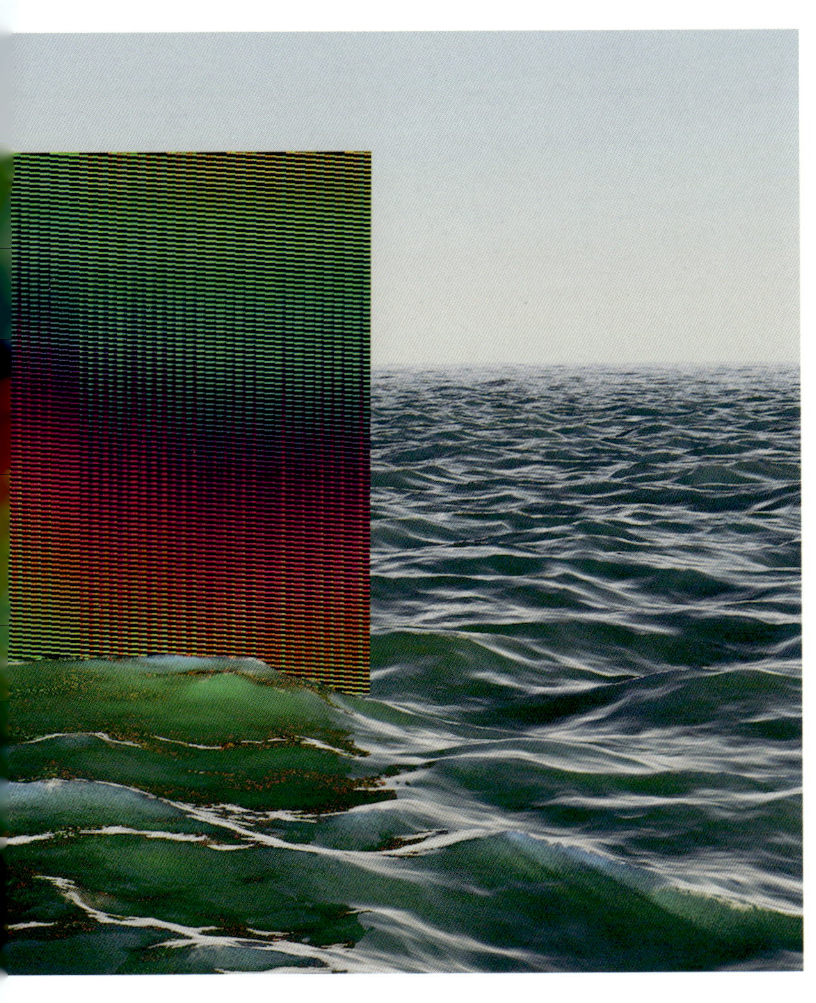

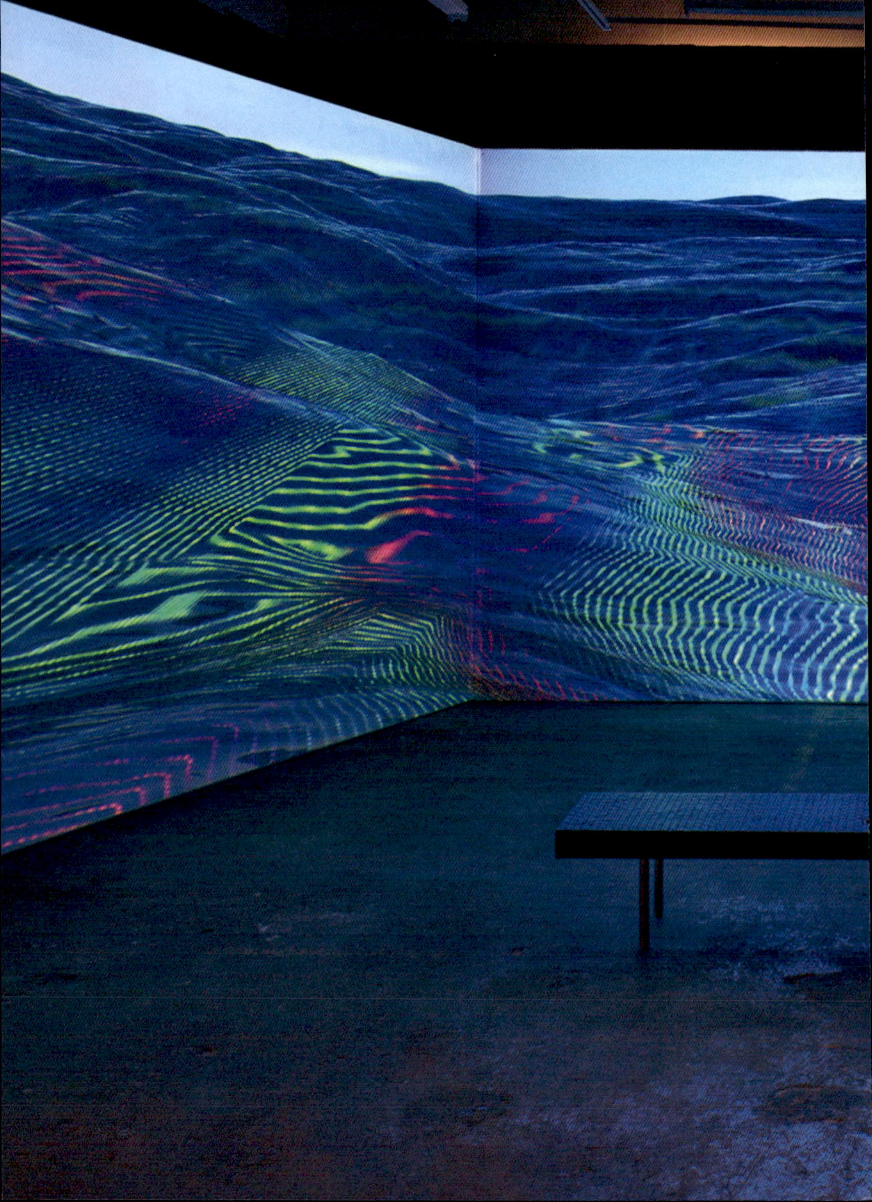

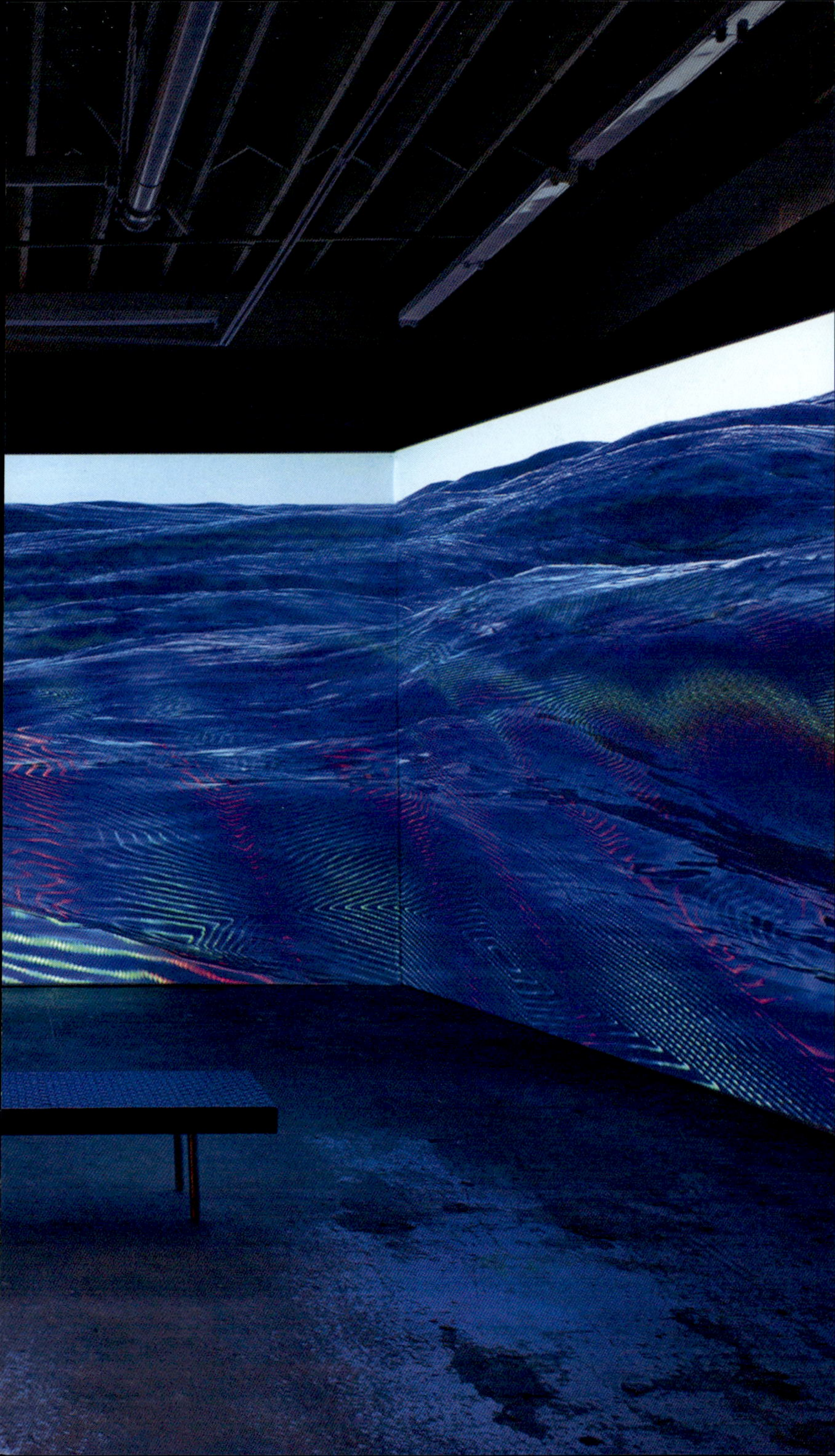

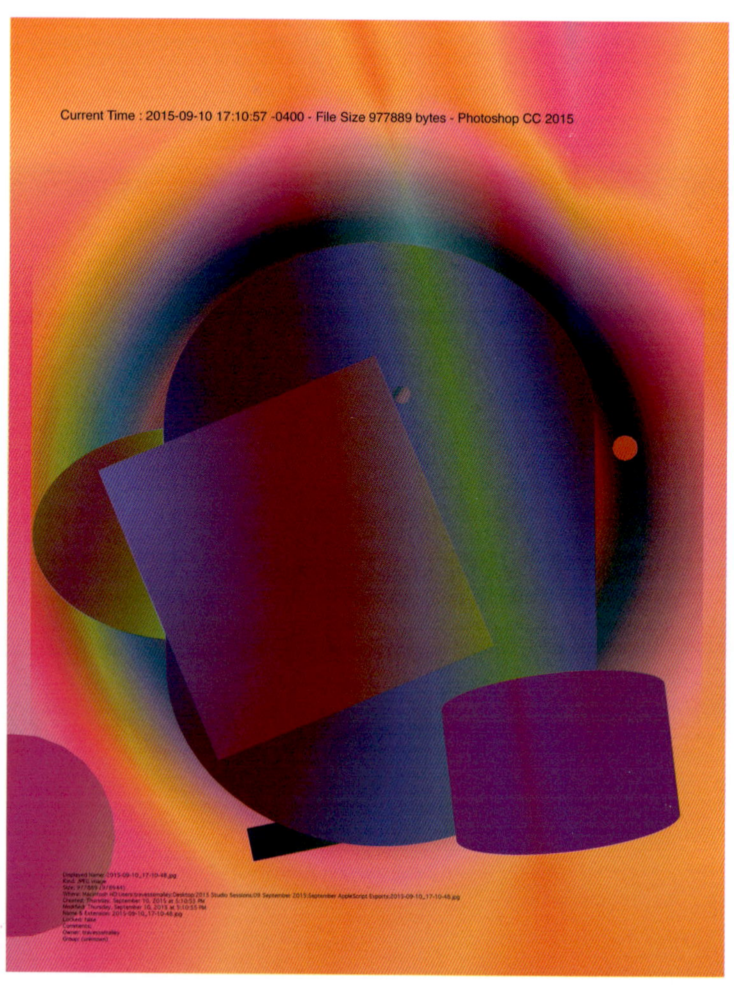
Current Time : 2015-09-10 17:10:57 -0400 - File Size 977889 bytes - Photoshop CC 2015
Displayed Name: 2015-09-10_17-10-48.jpg
Kind: JPEG image
Created: Thursday, September 10, 2015 at 5:10:53 PM
Modified: Thursday, September 10, 2015 at 5:10:55 PM
Name & Extension: 2015-09-10_17-10-48.jpg
Locked: false
Comments:
Group: (unknown)

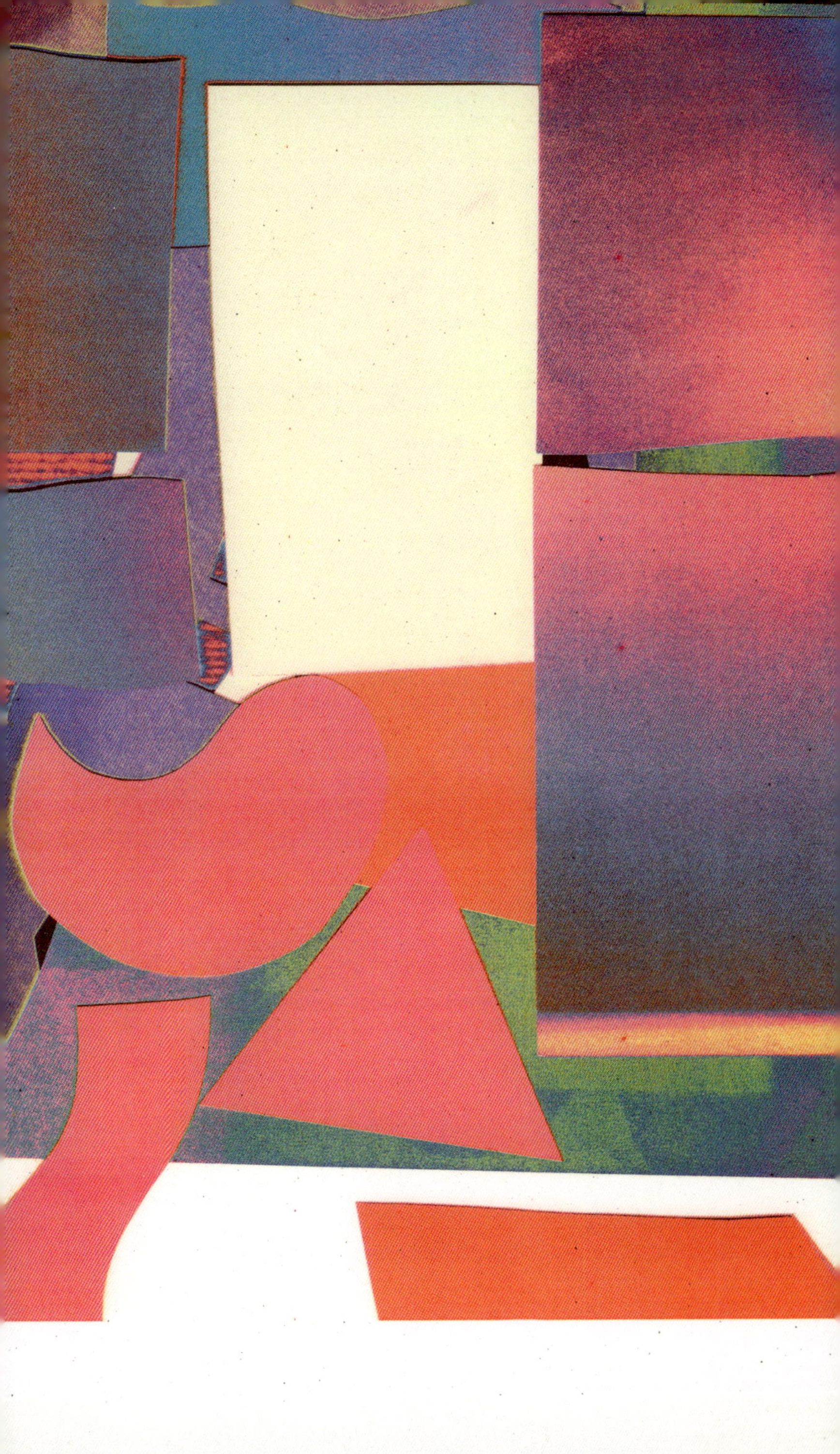

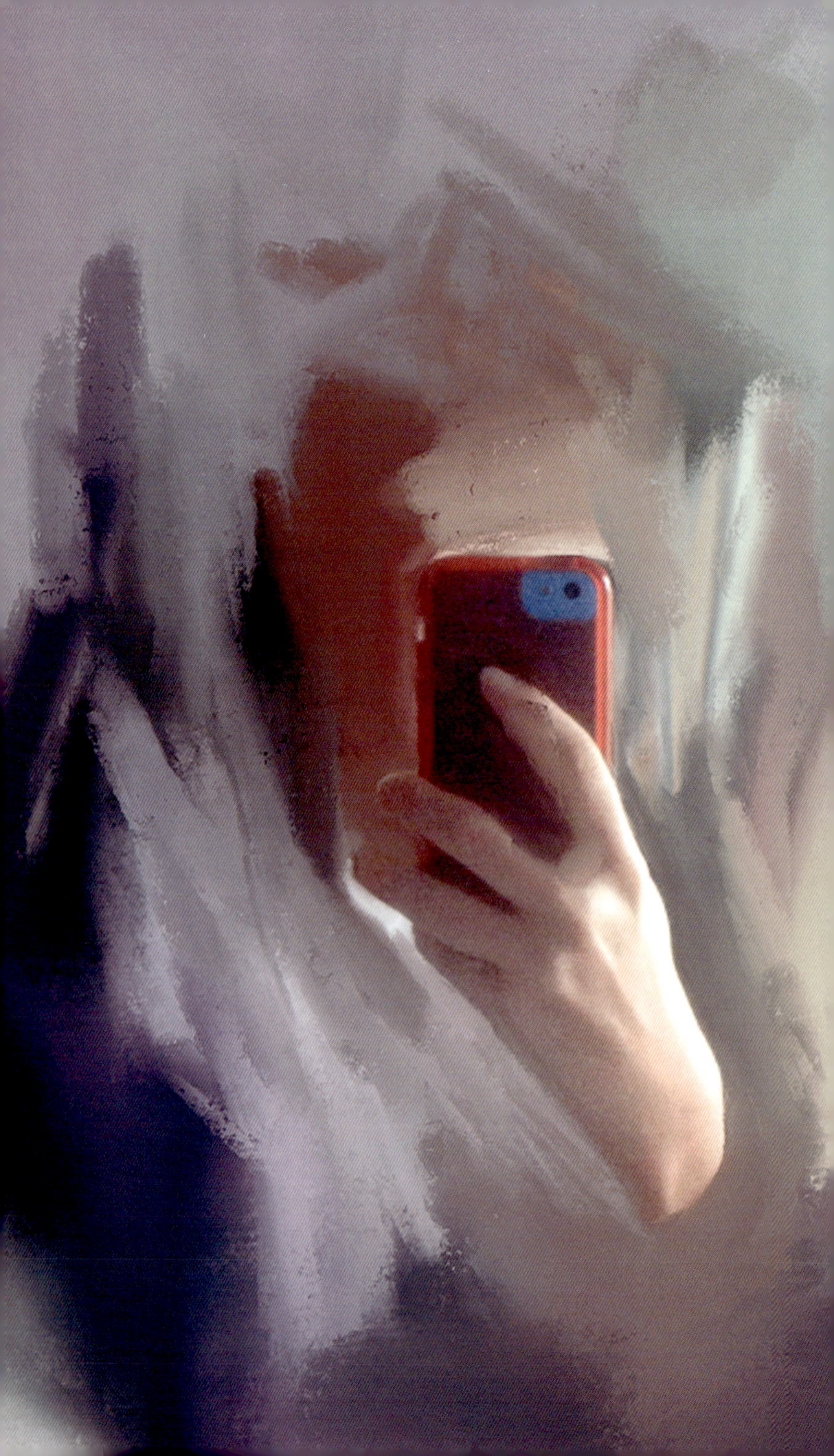

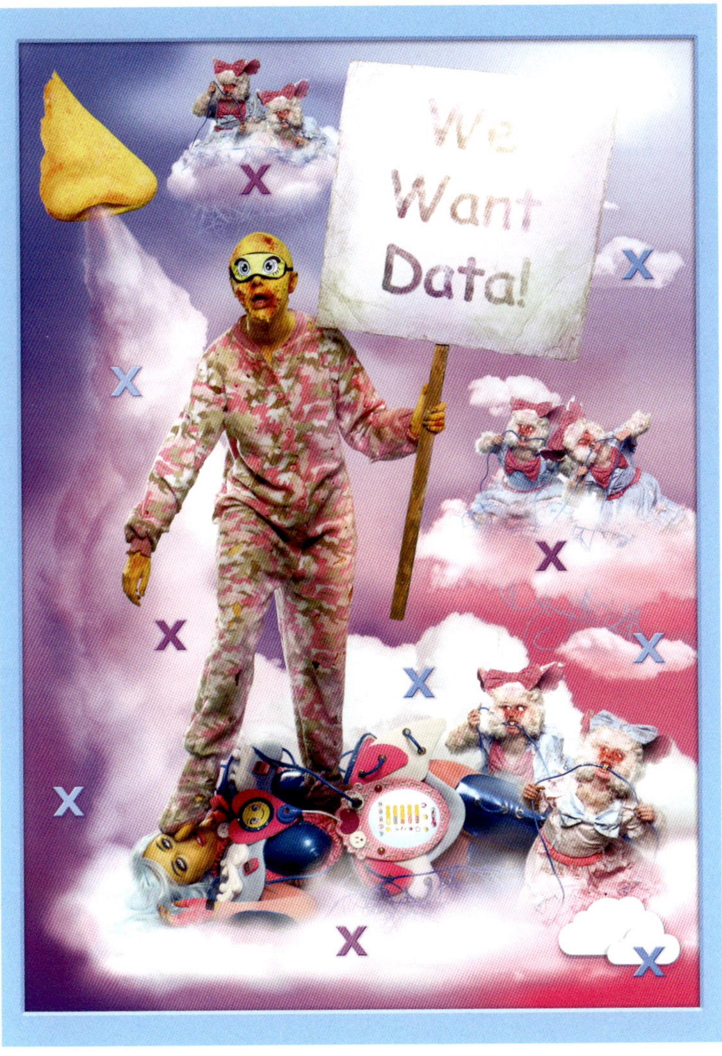
We
Want
Data!

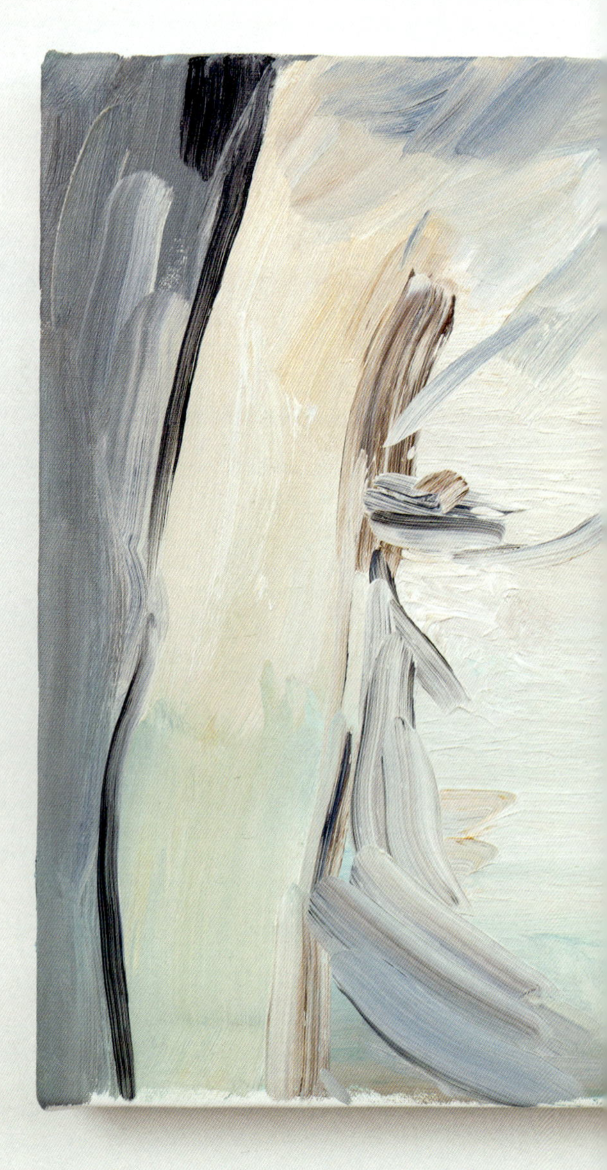

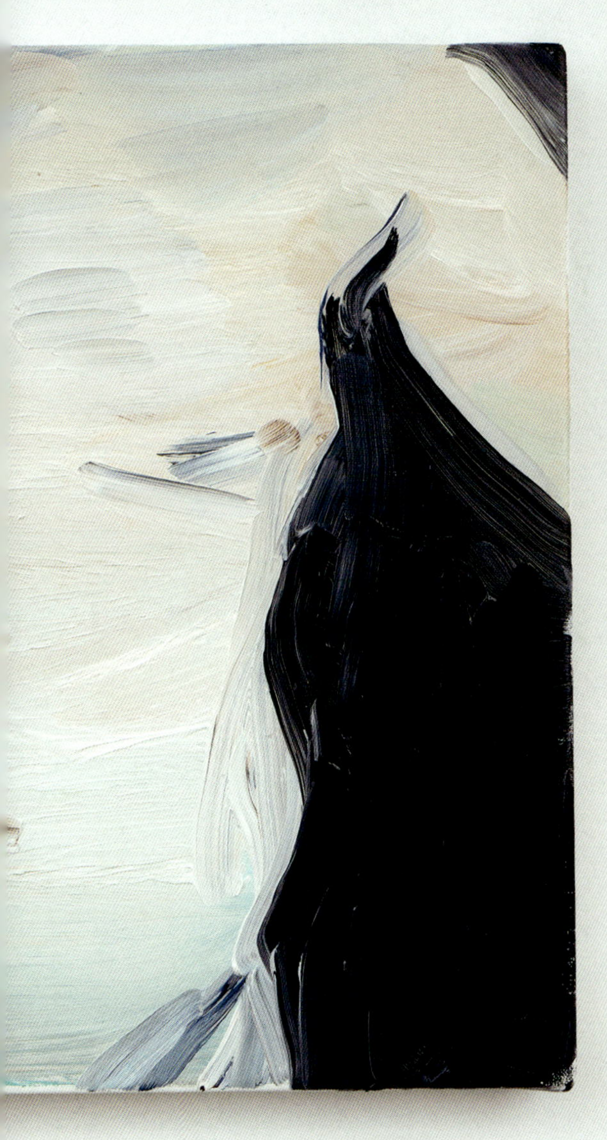

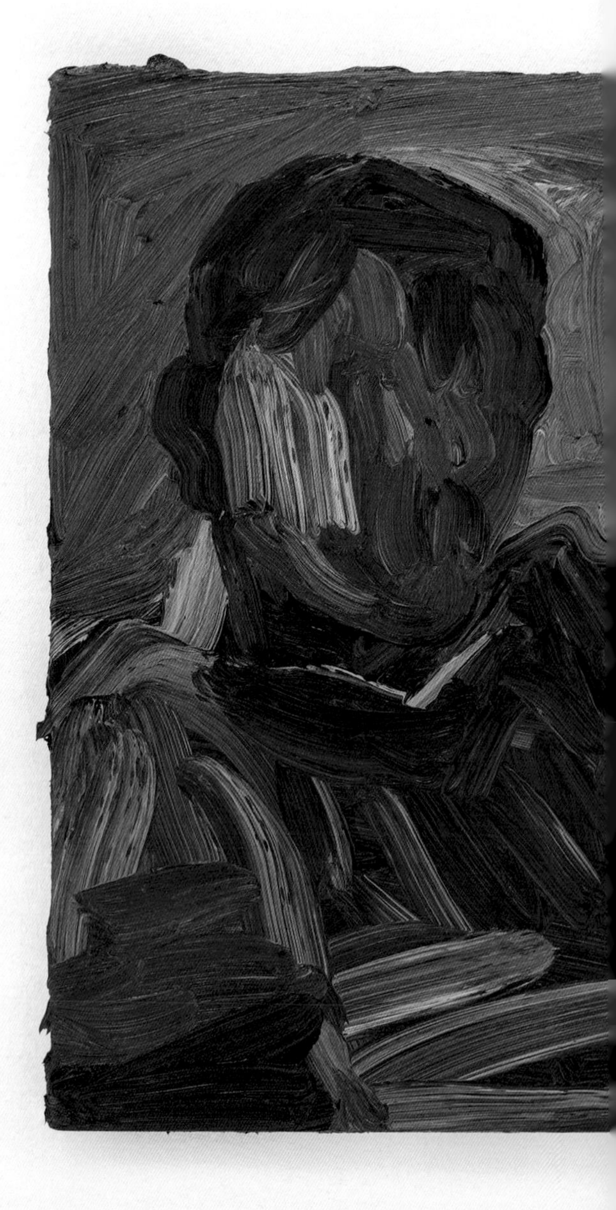

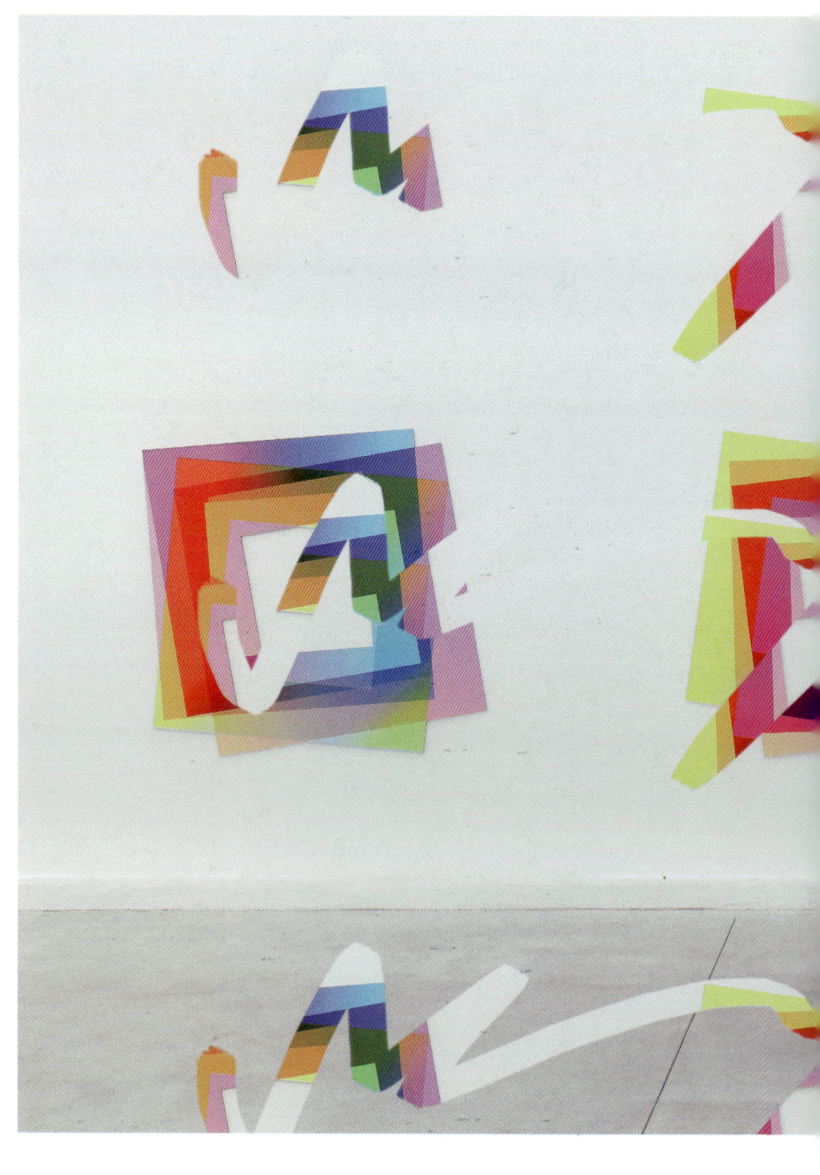

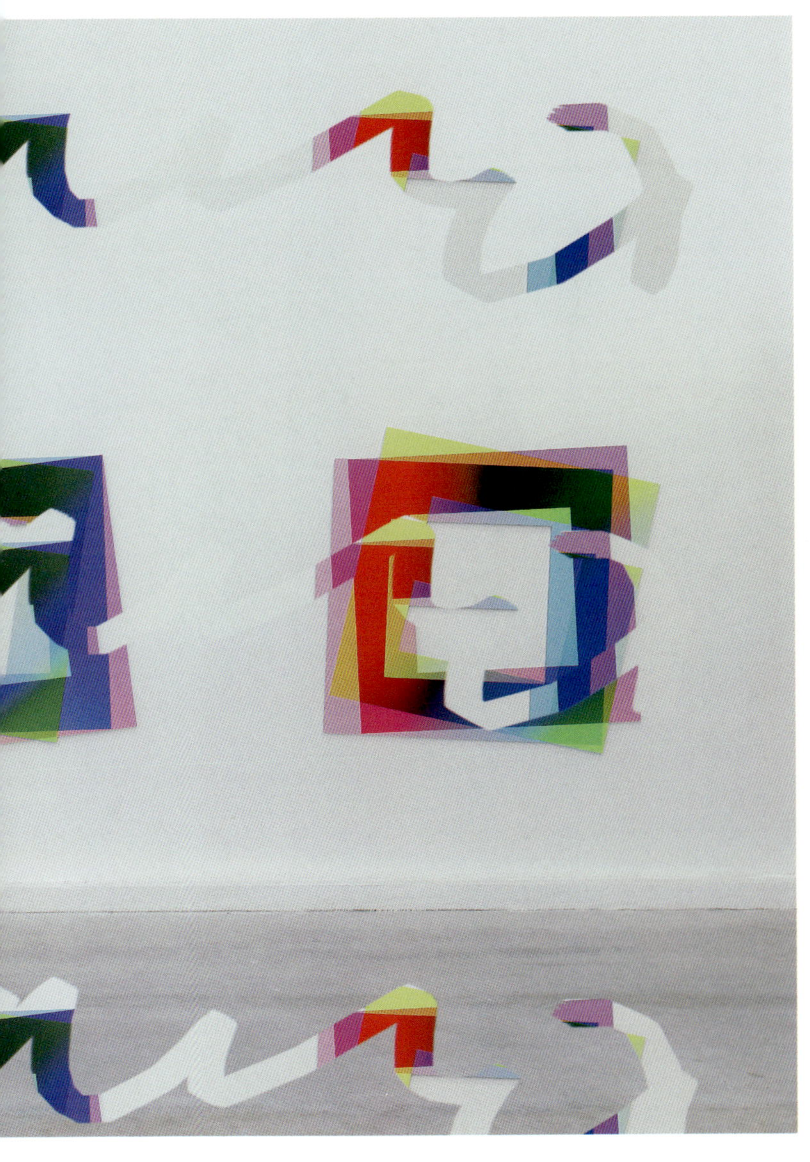

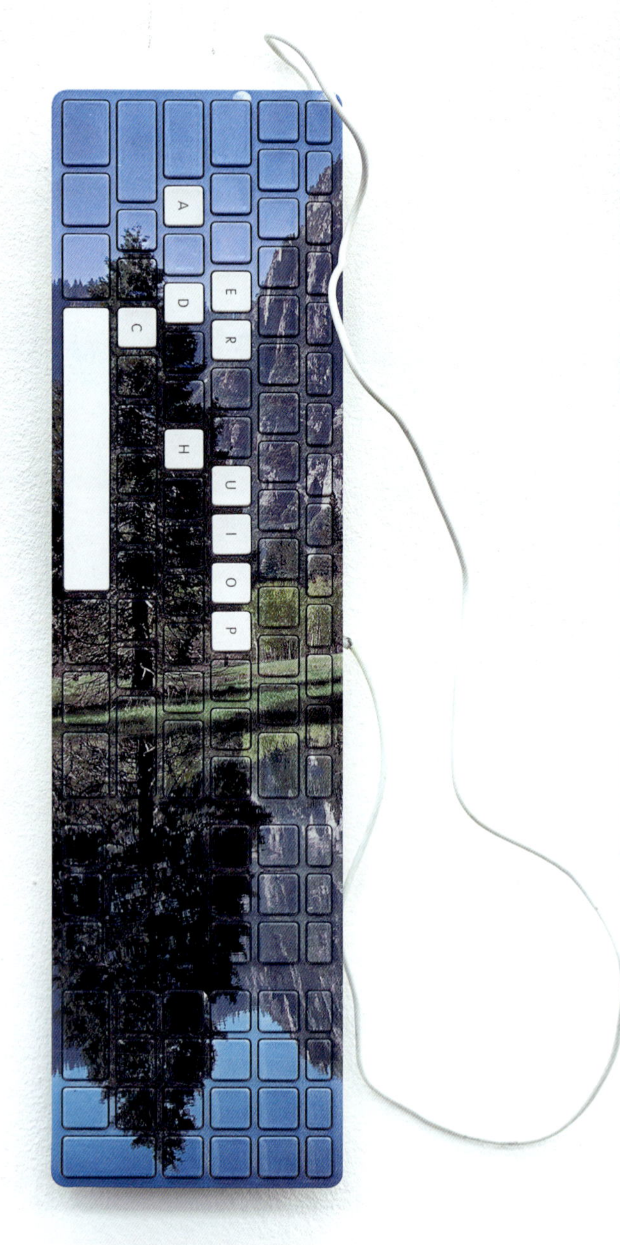

I MISS MY PRE-INTERNET BRAIN

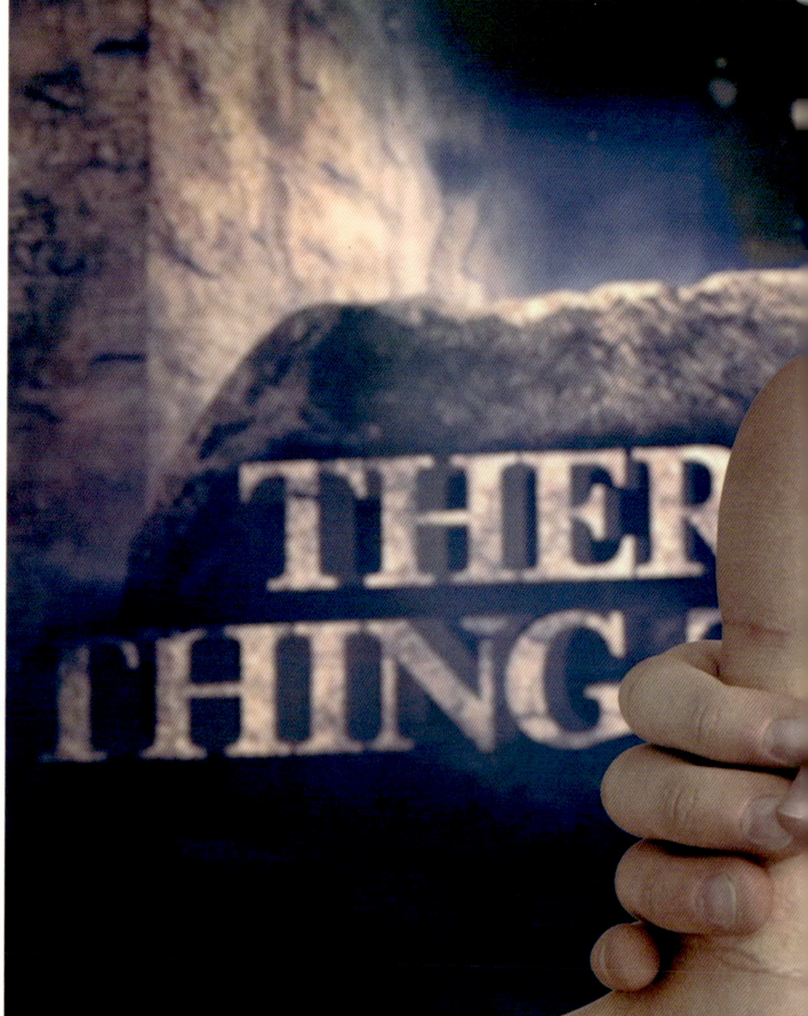
THER
THING

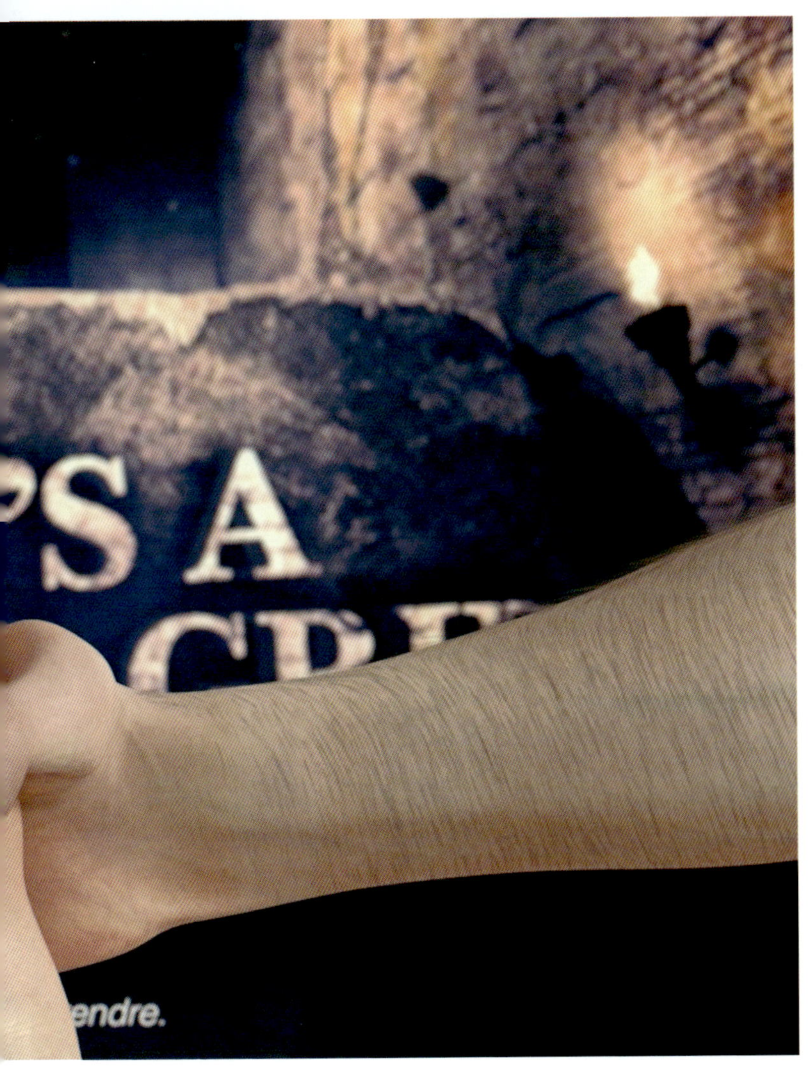
S A
endre.

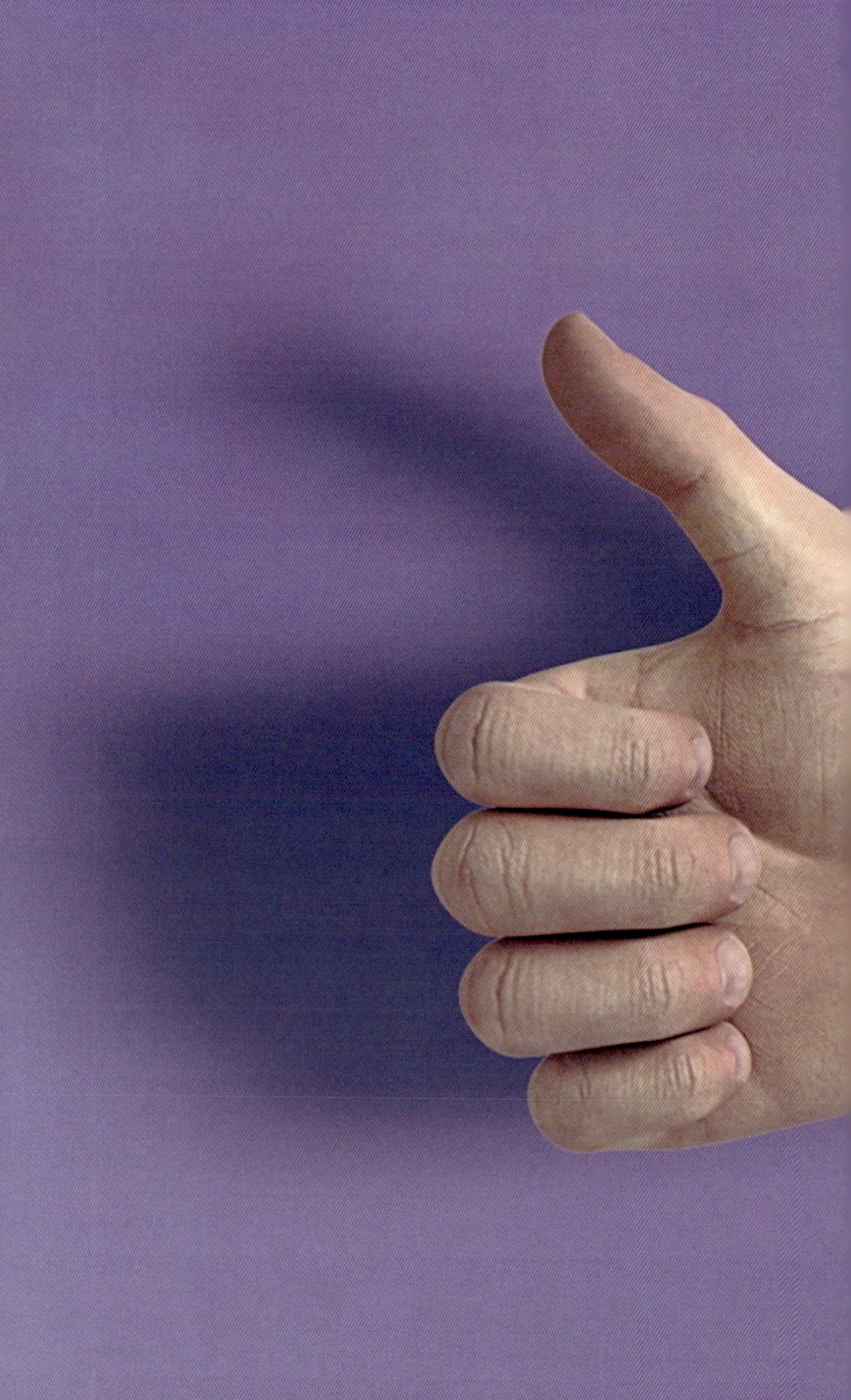

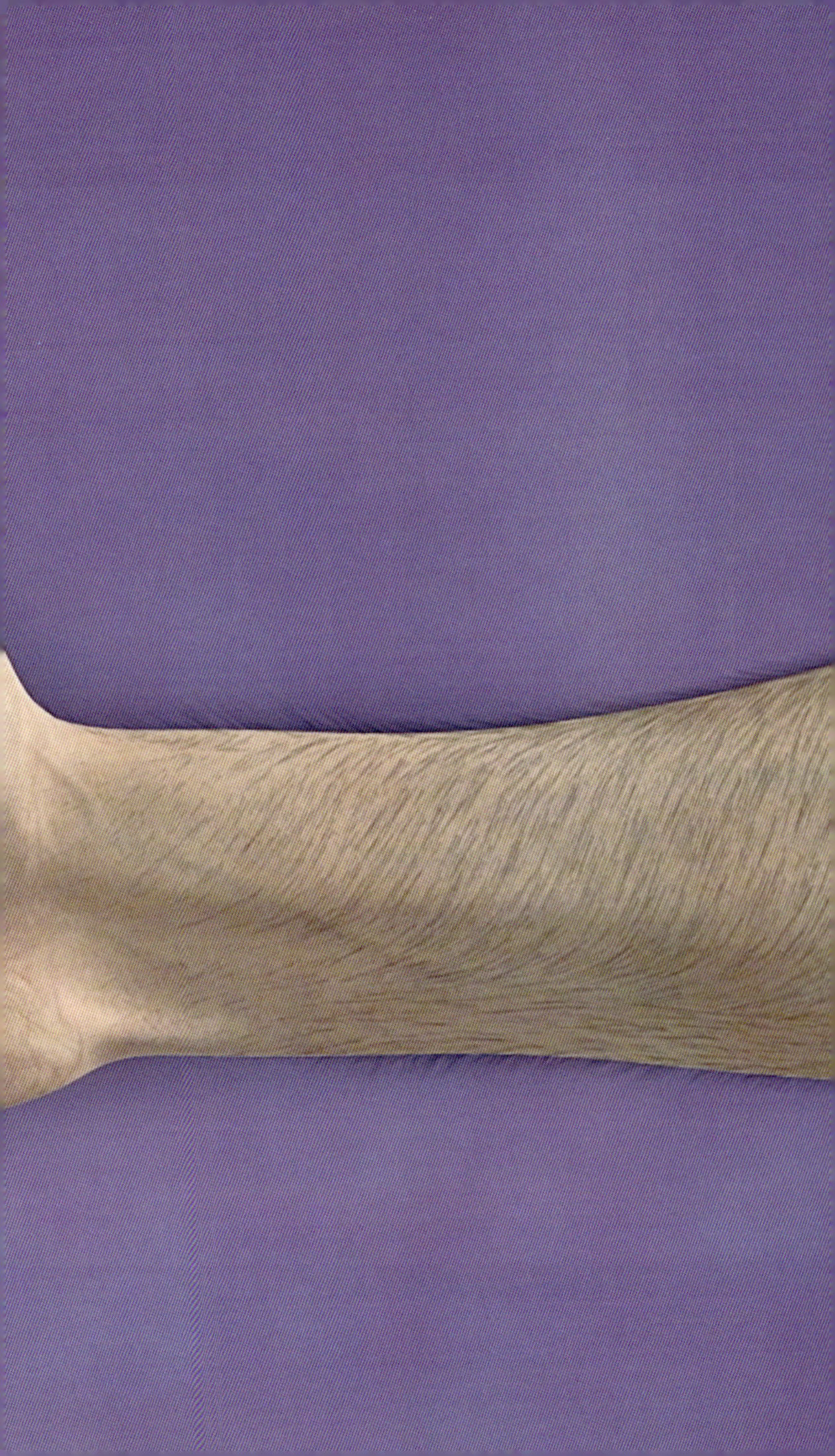

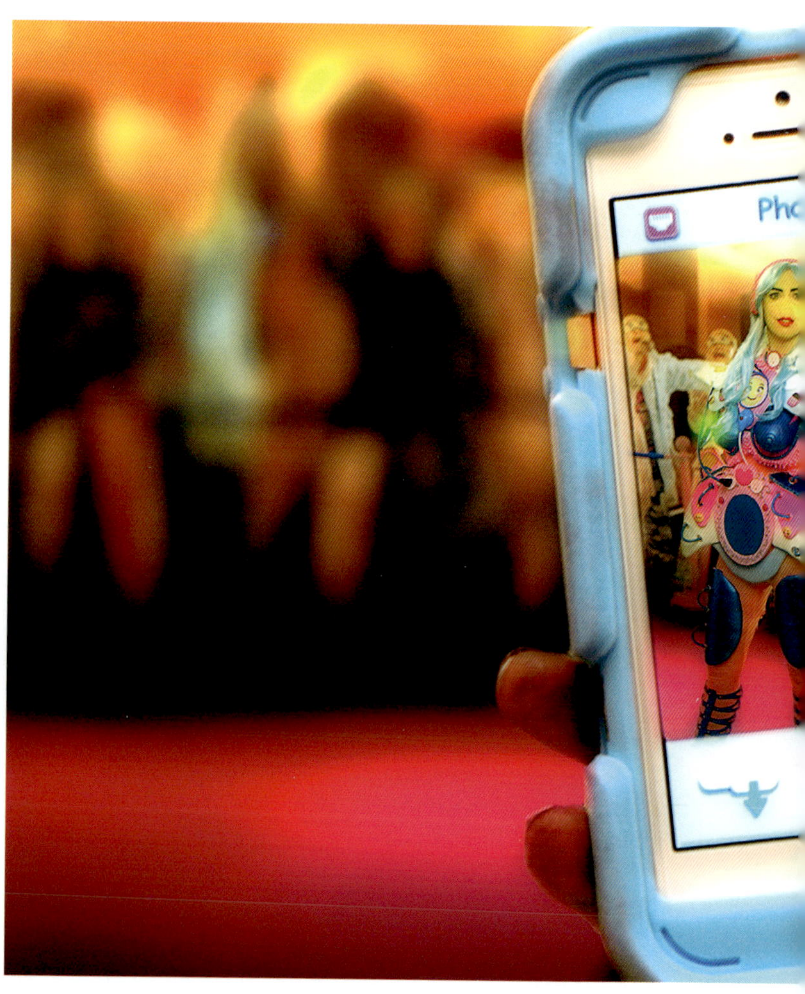

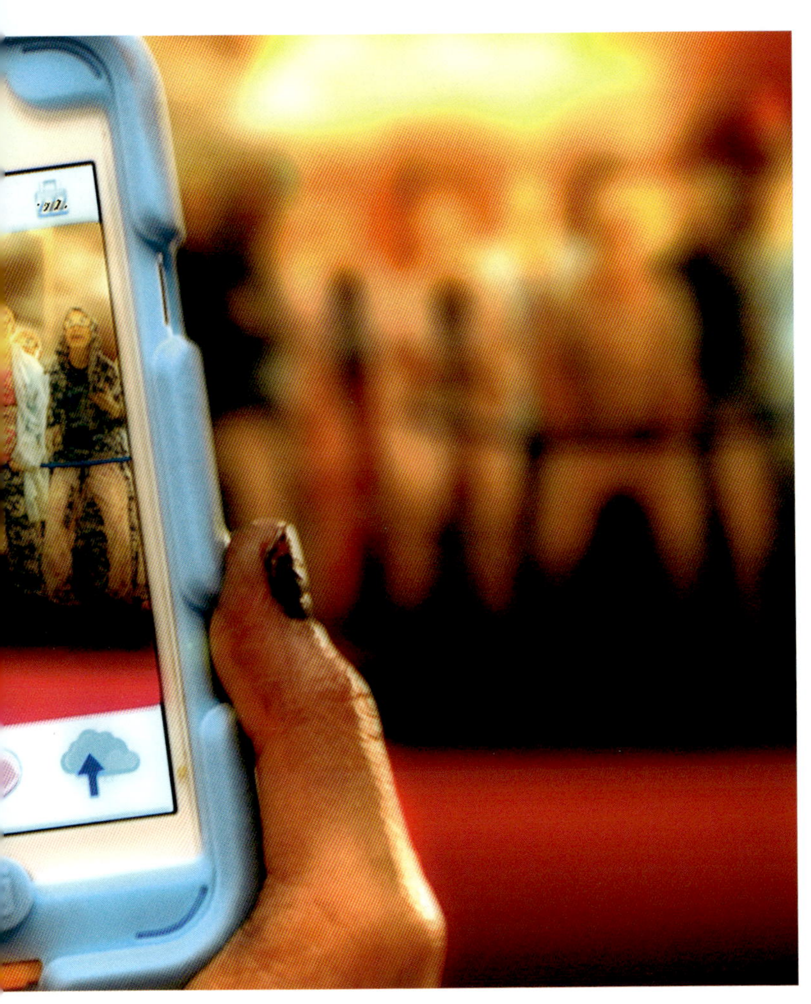

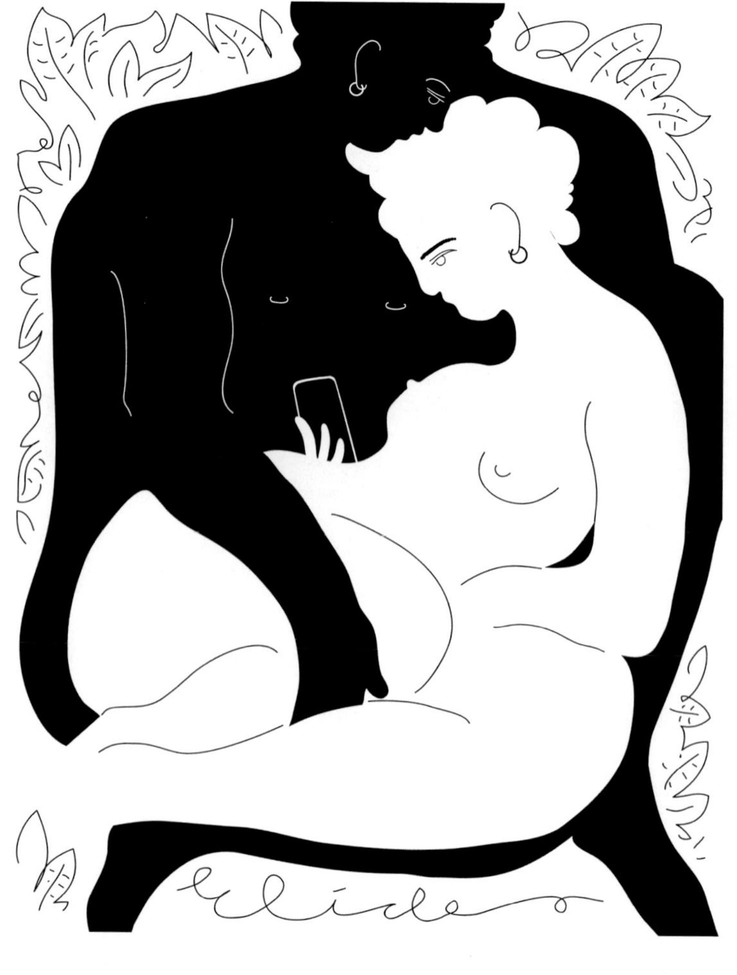

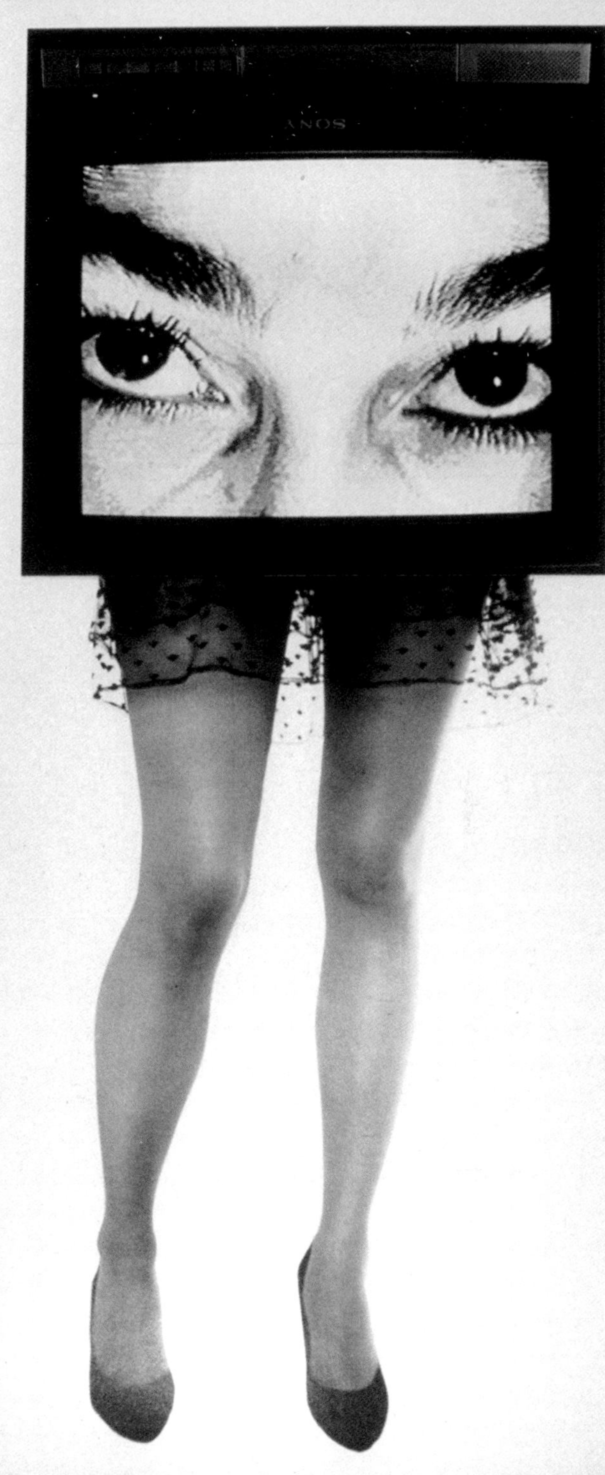

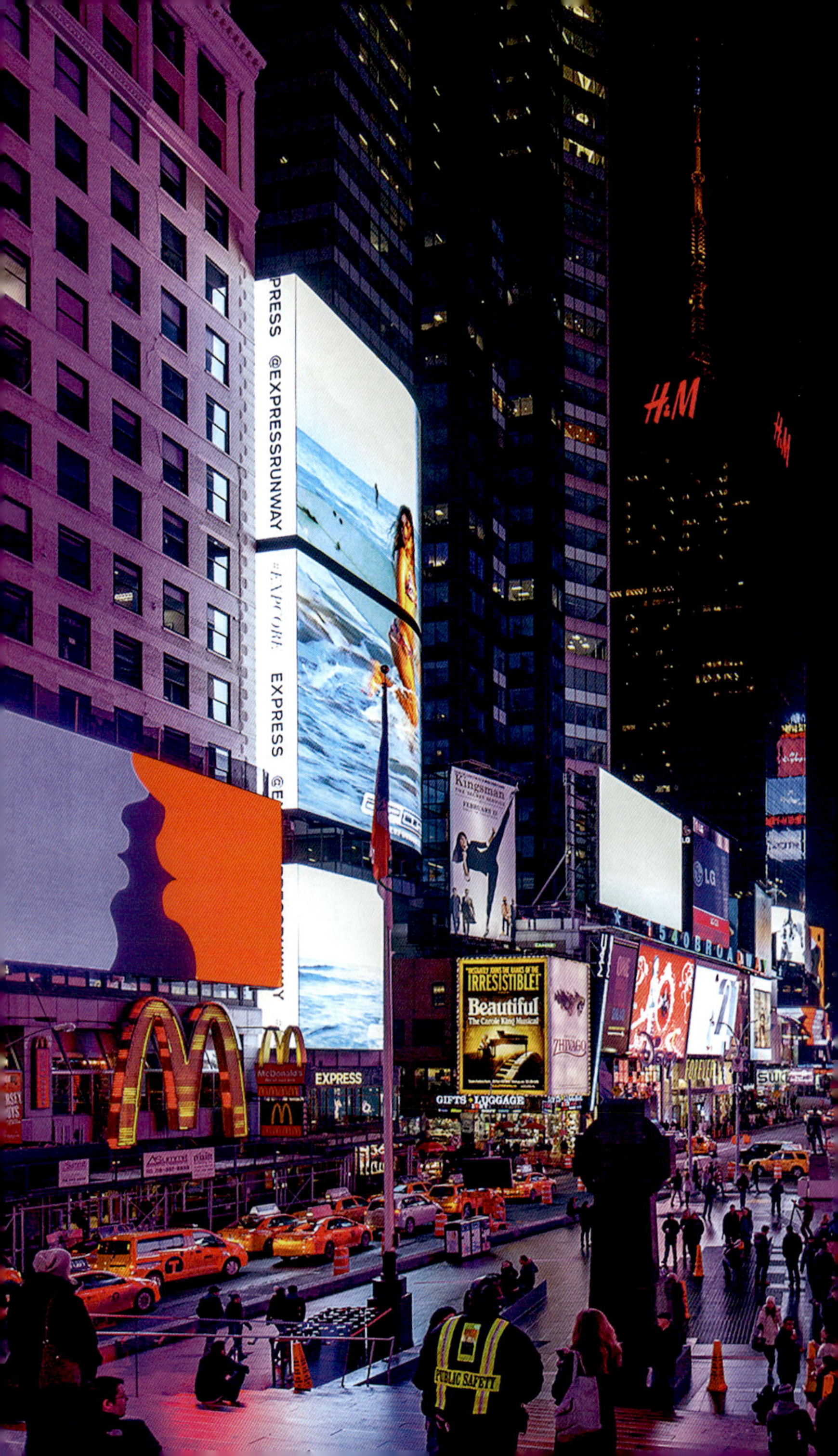

PRESS @EXPRESSRUNWAY
EXPRESS
H&M
Kingsman
IRRESISTIBLE!
Beautiful
The Carole King Musical
ZHIVAGO
LG
1540 BROADWAY
McDonald's
EXPRESS
GIFTS LUGGAGE
PUBLIC SAFETY

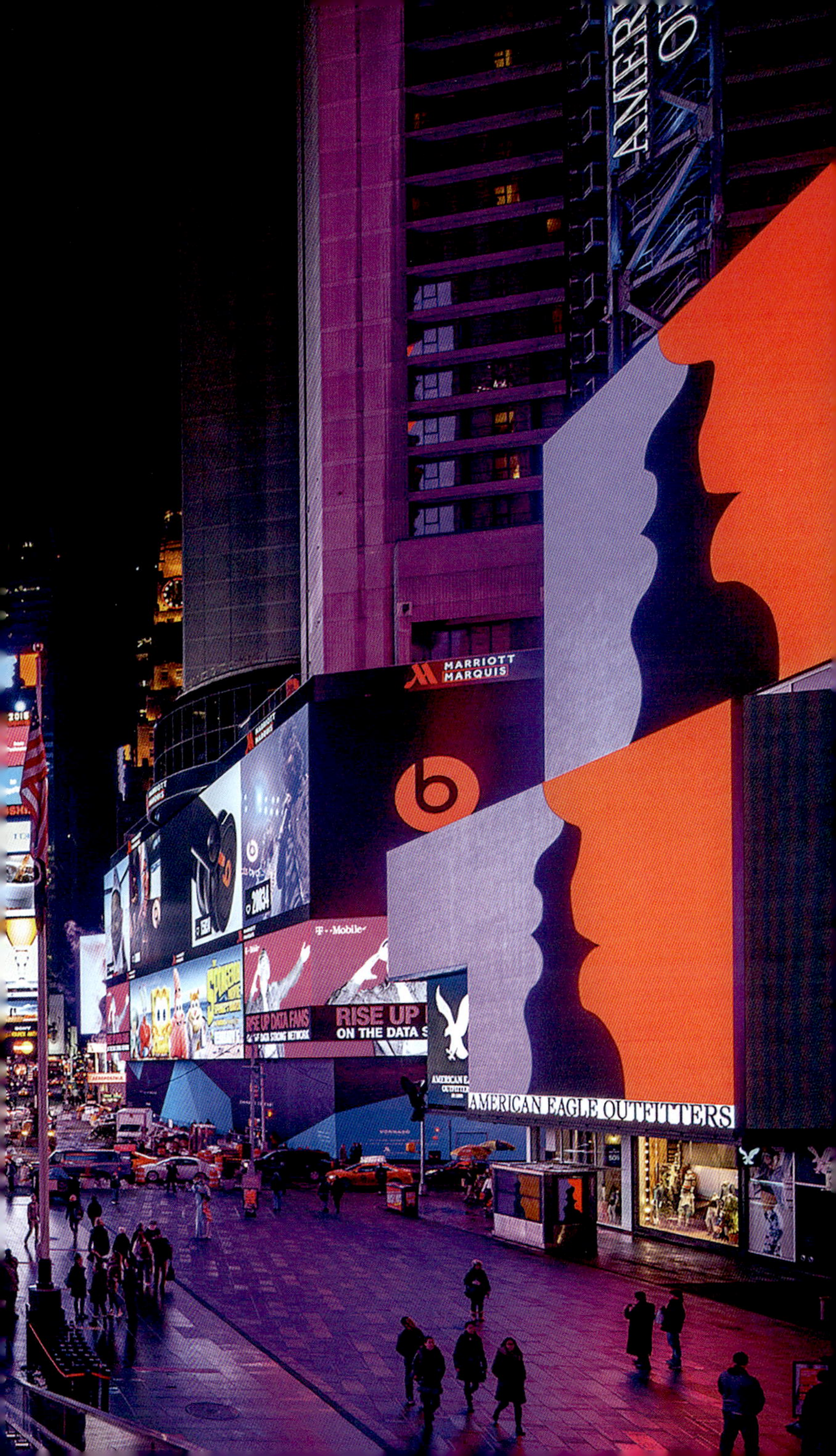
MARRIOTT
MARQUIS
T-Mobile
RISE UP
ON THE DATA S
AMERICAN EAGLE OUTFITTERS

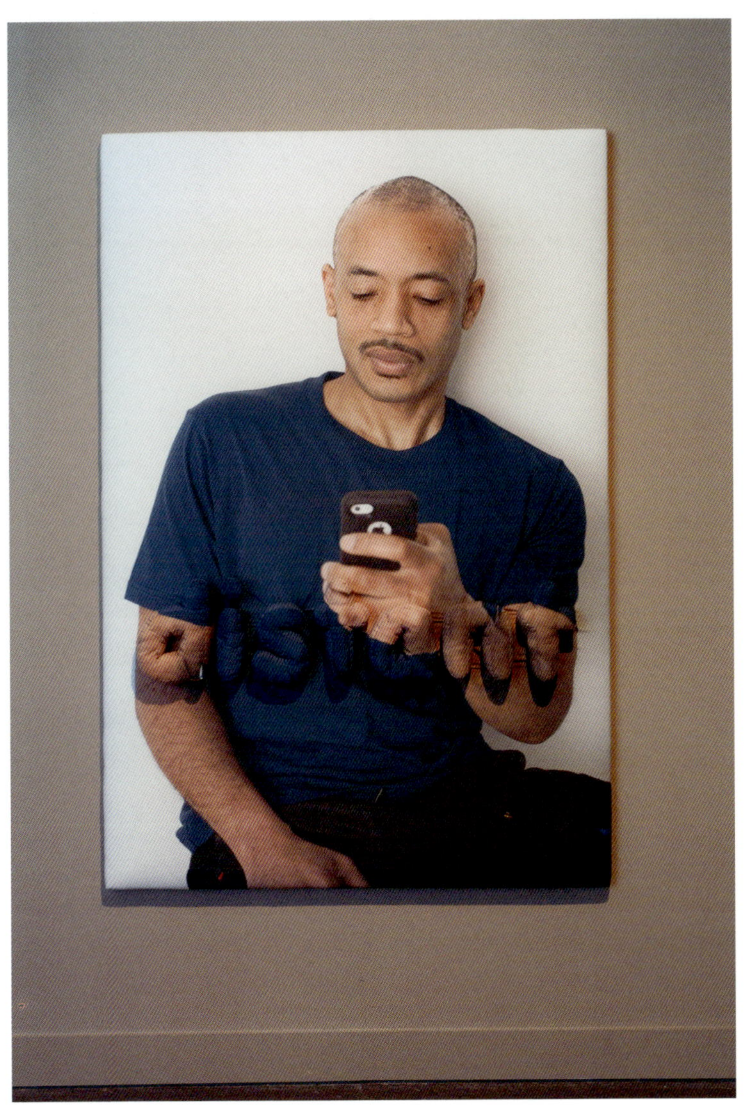

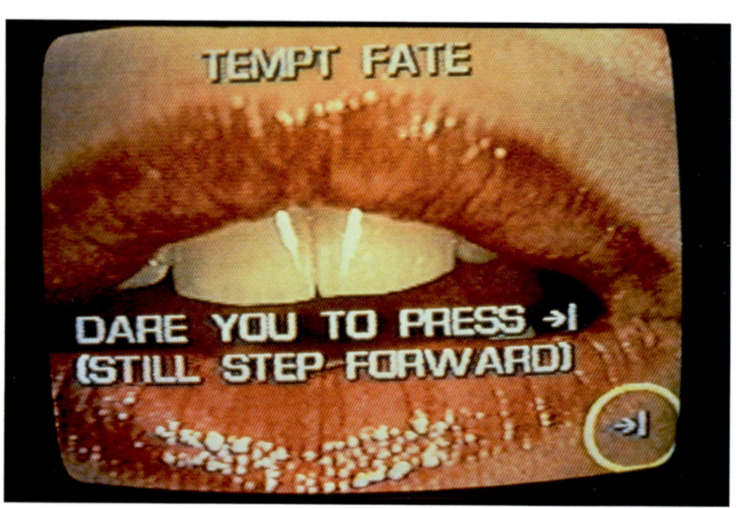
TEMPT FATE
DARE YOU TO PRESS →|
(STILL STEP FORWARD)
→|

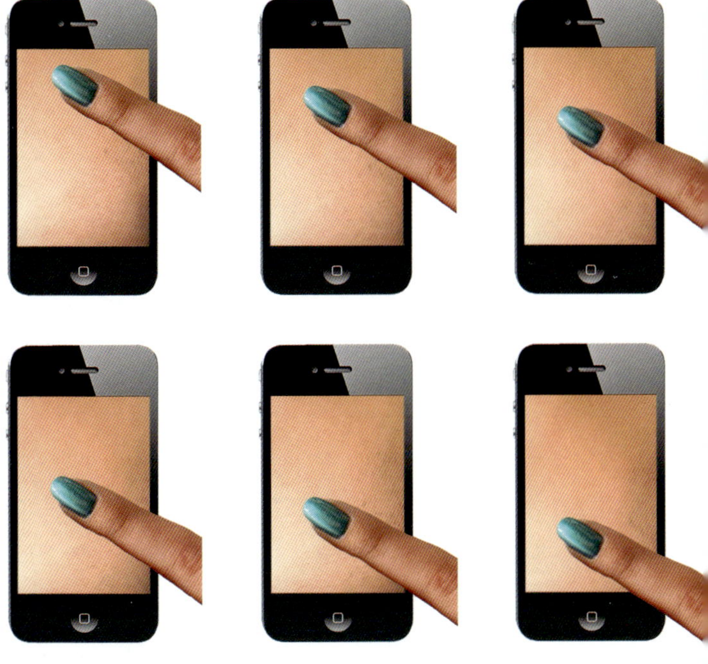

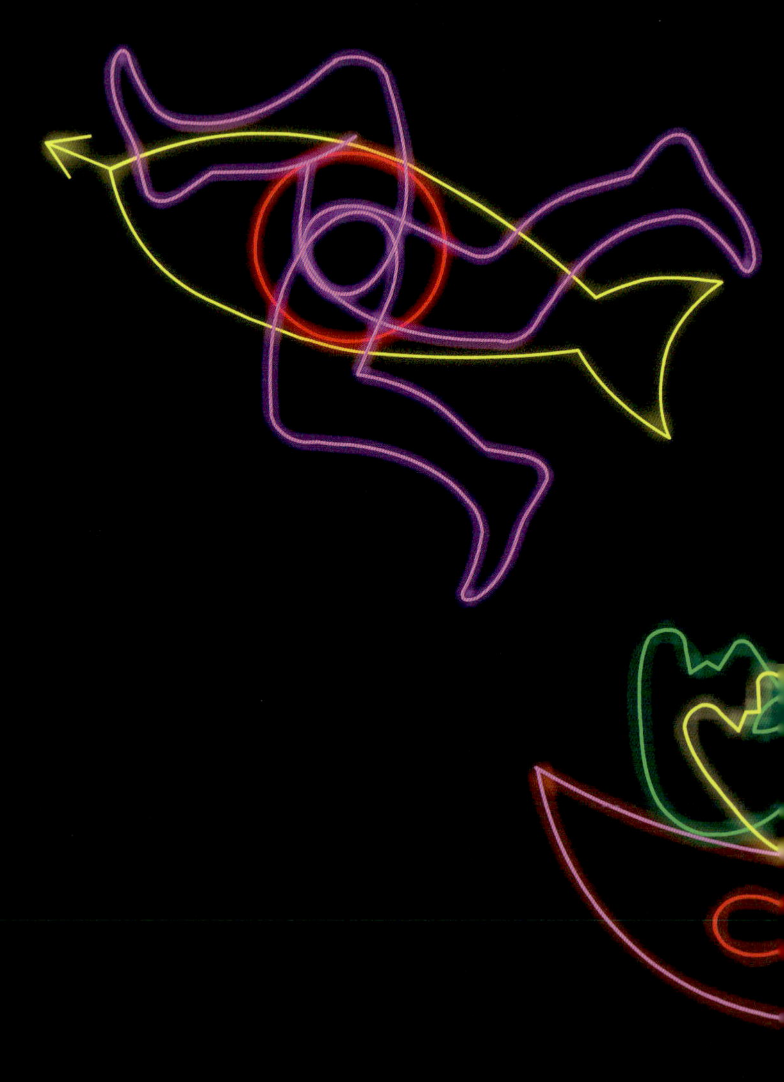

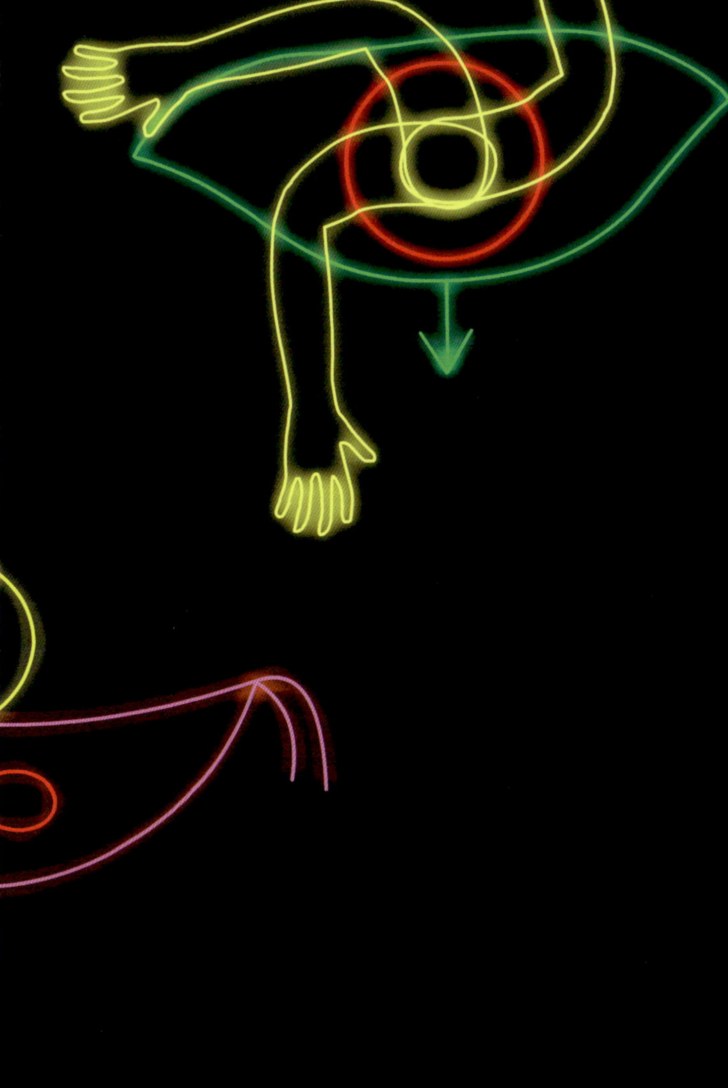

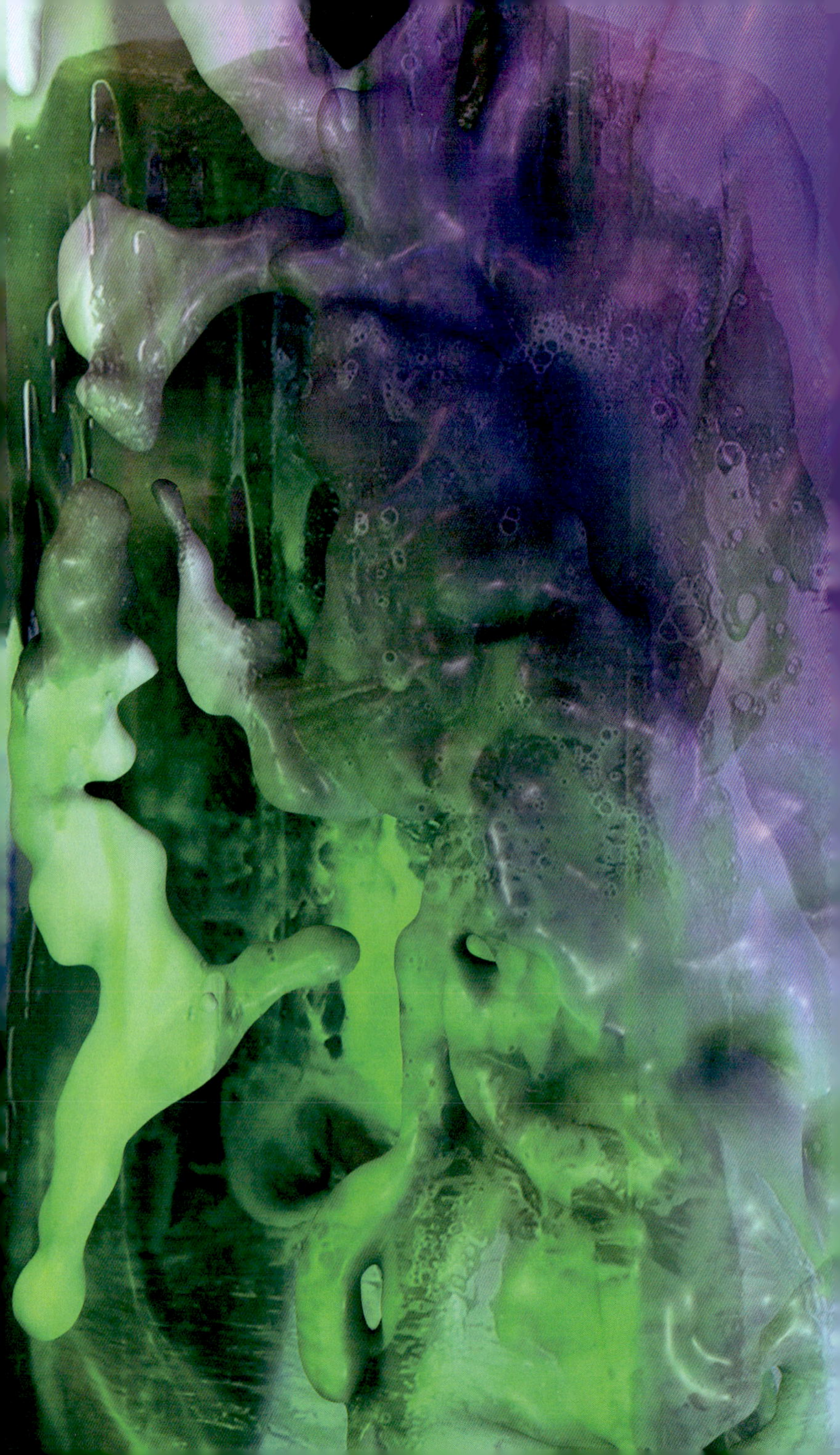

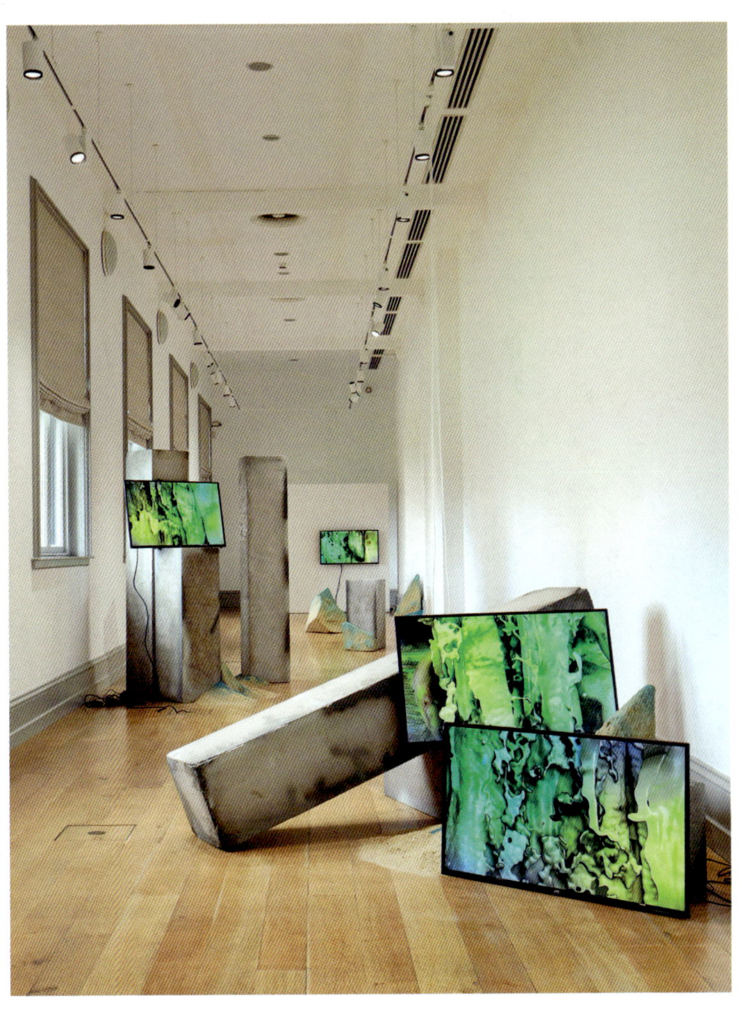

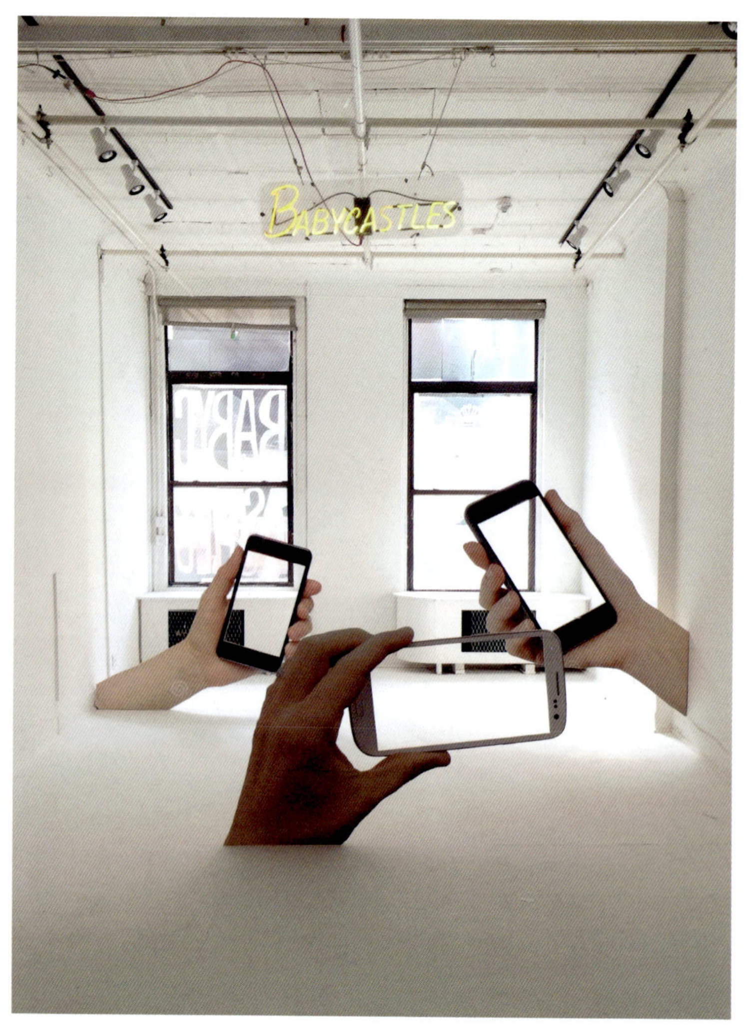
BABYCASTLES

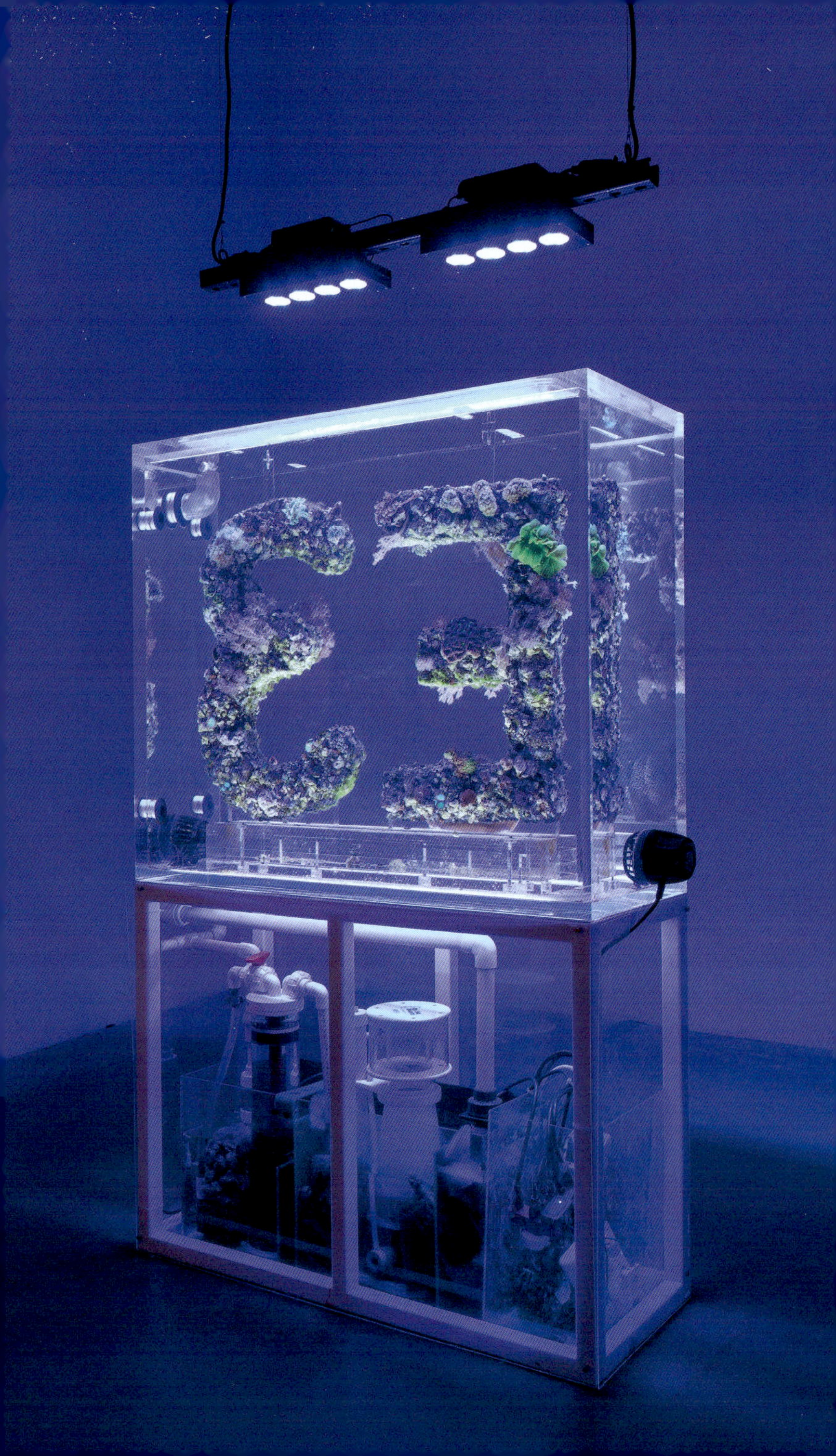

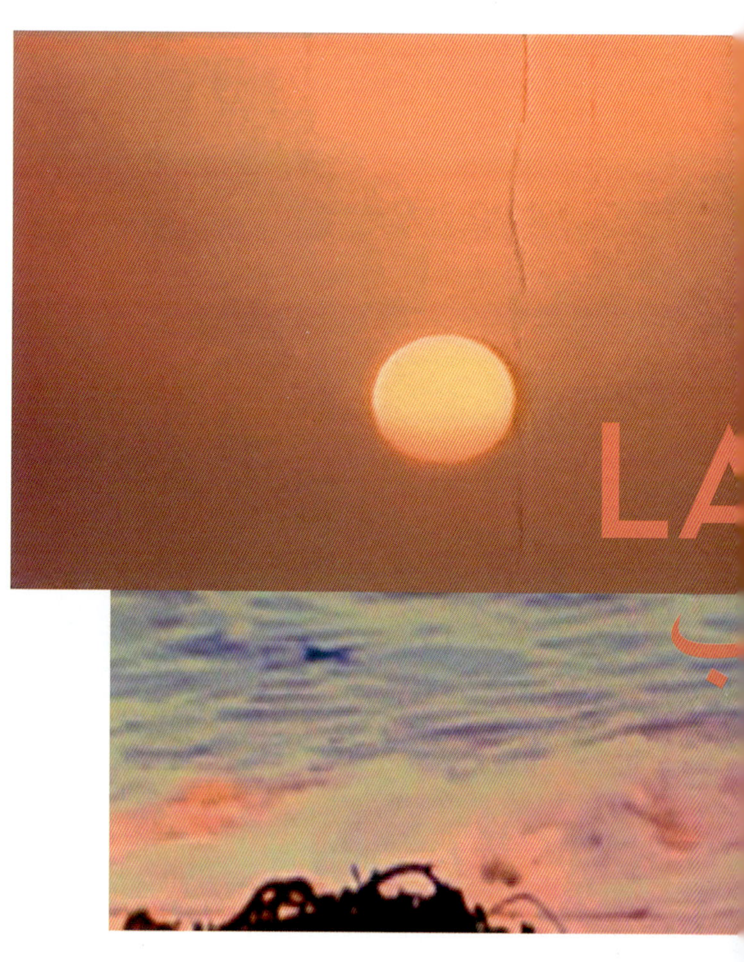
LA

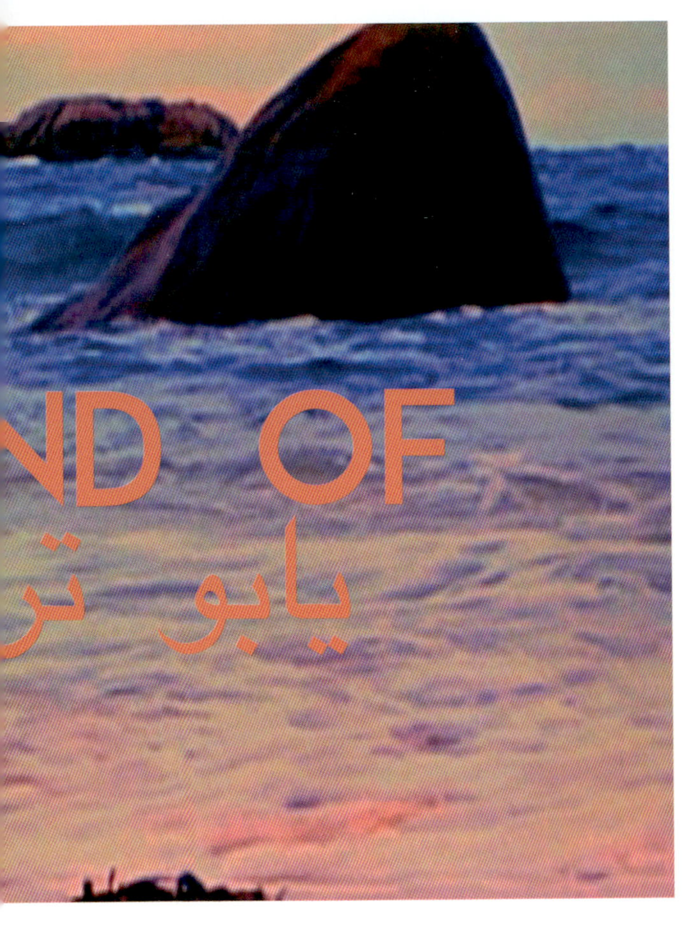
ND OF
يابو تر

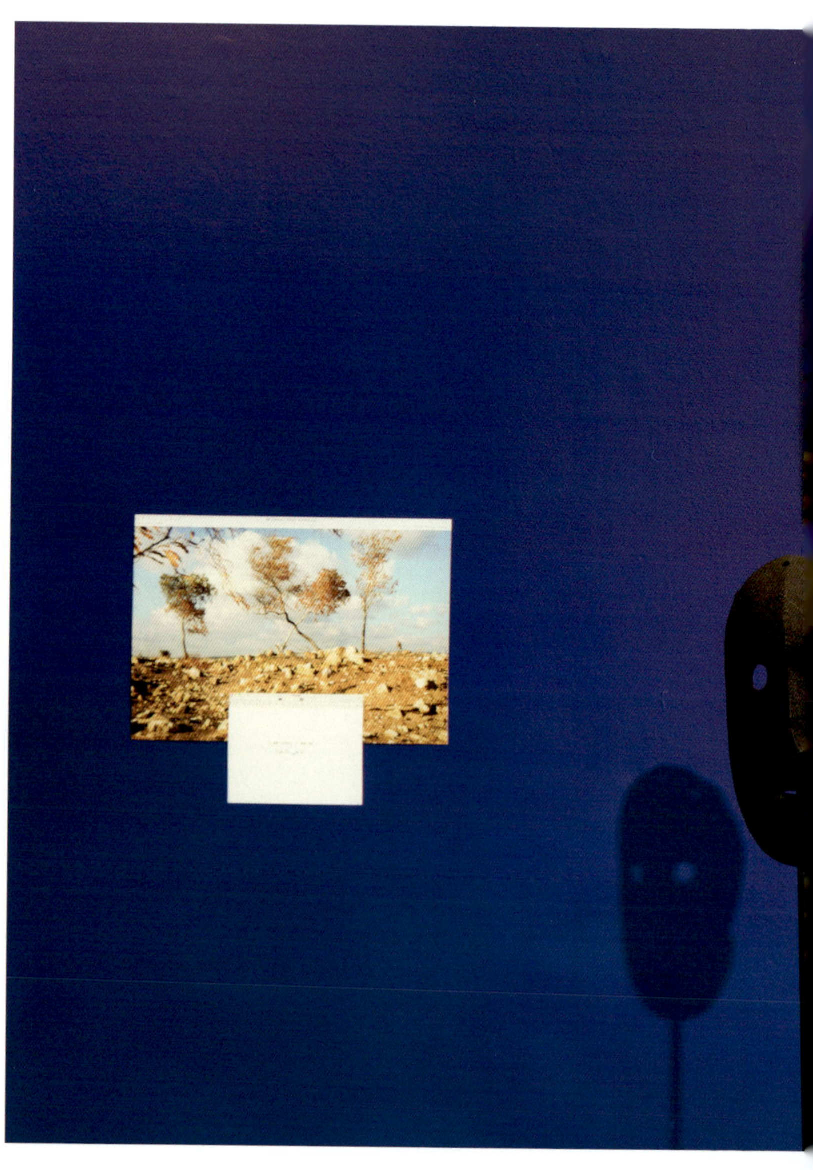

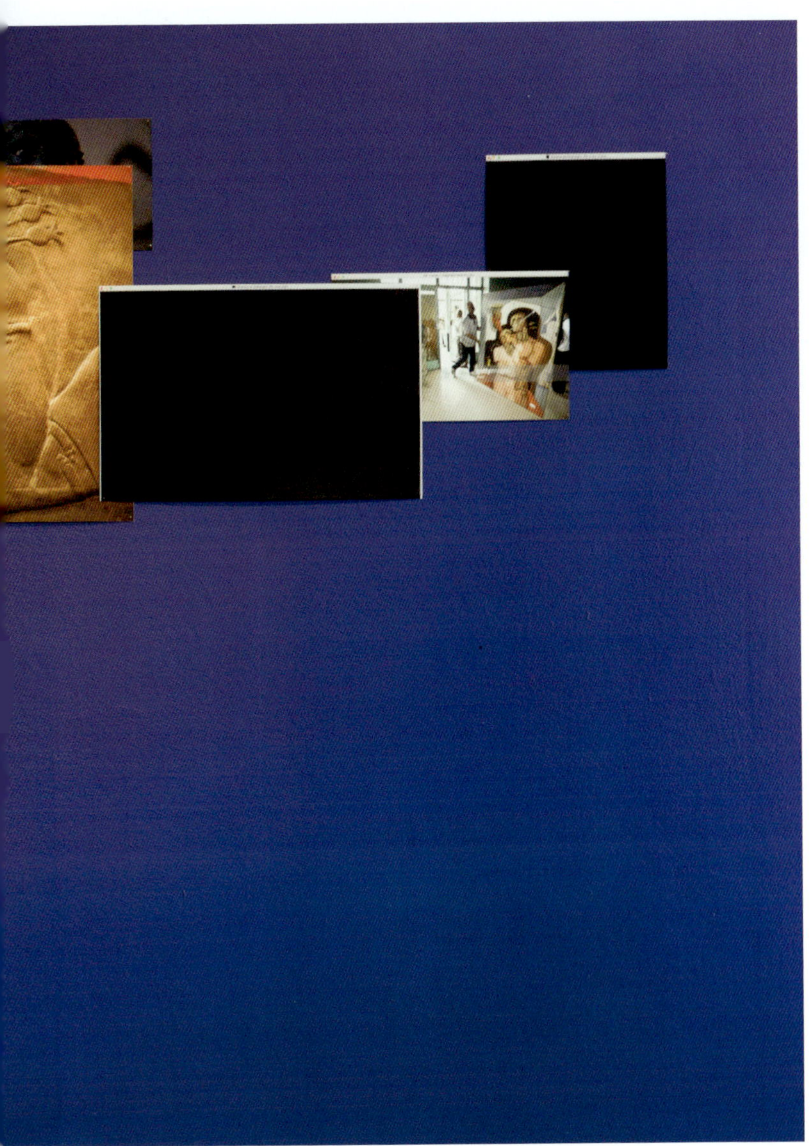

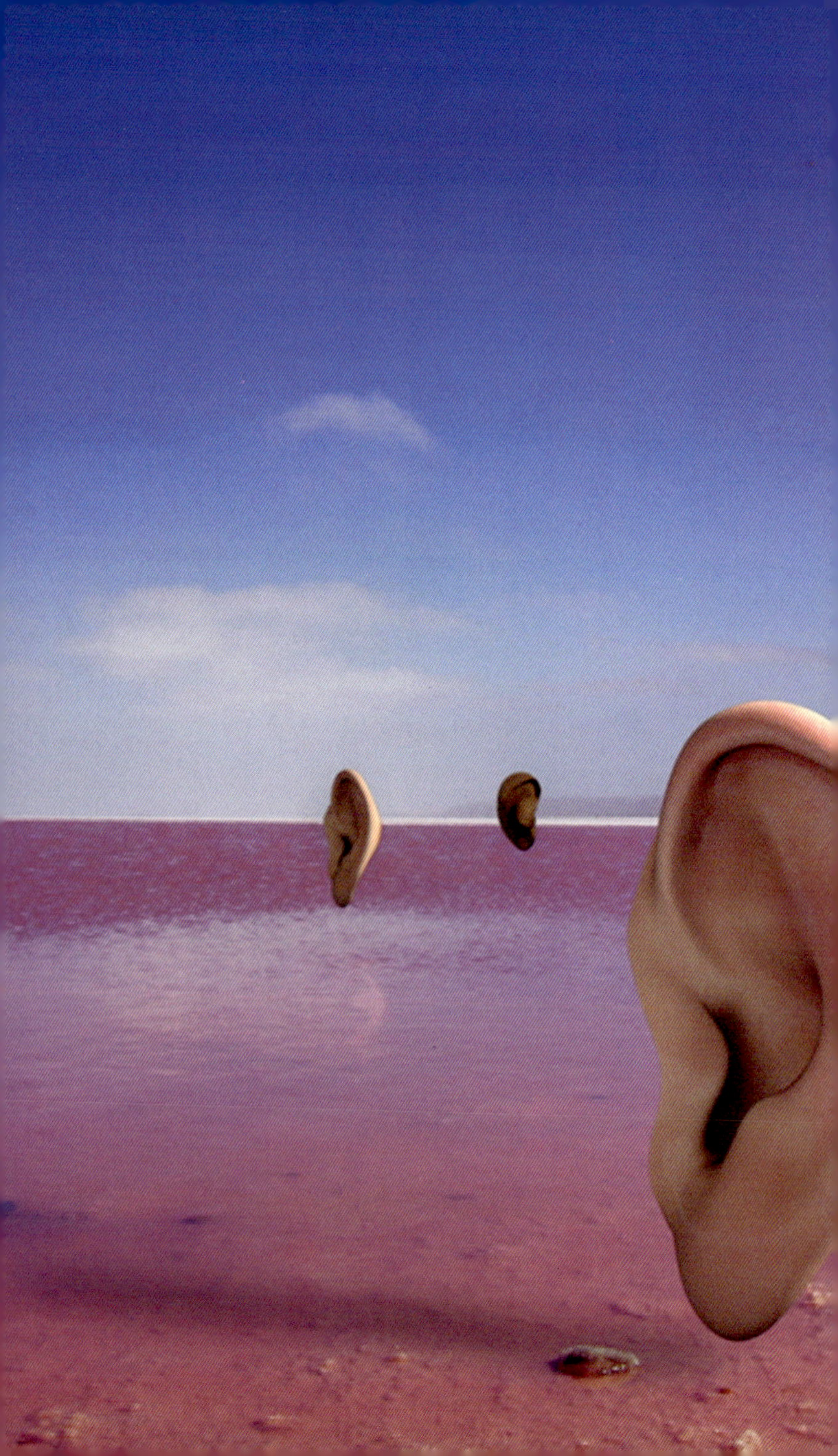

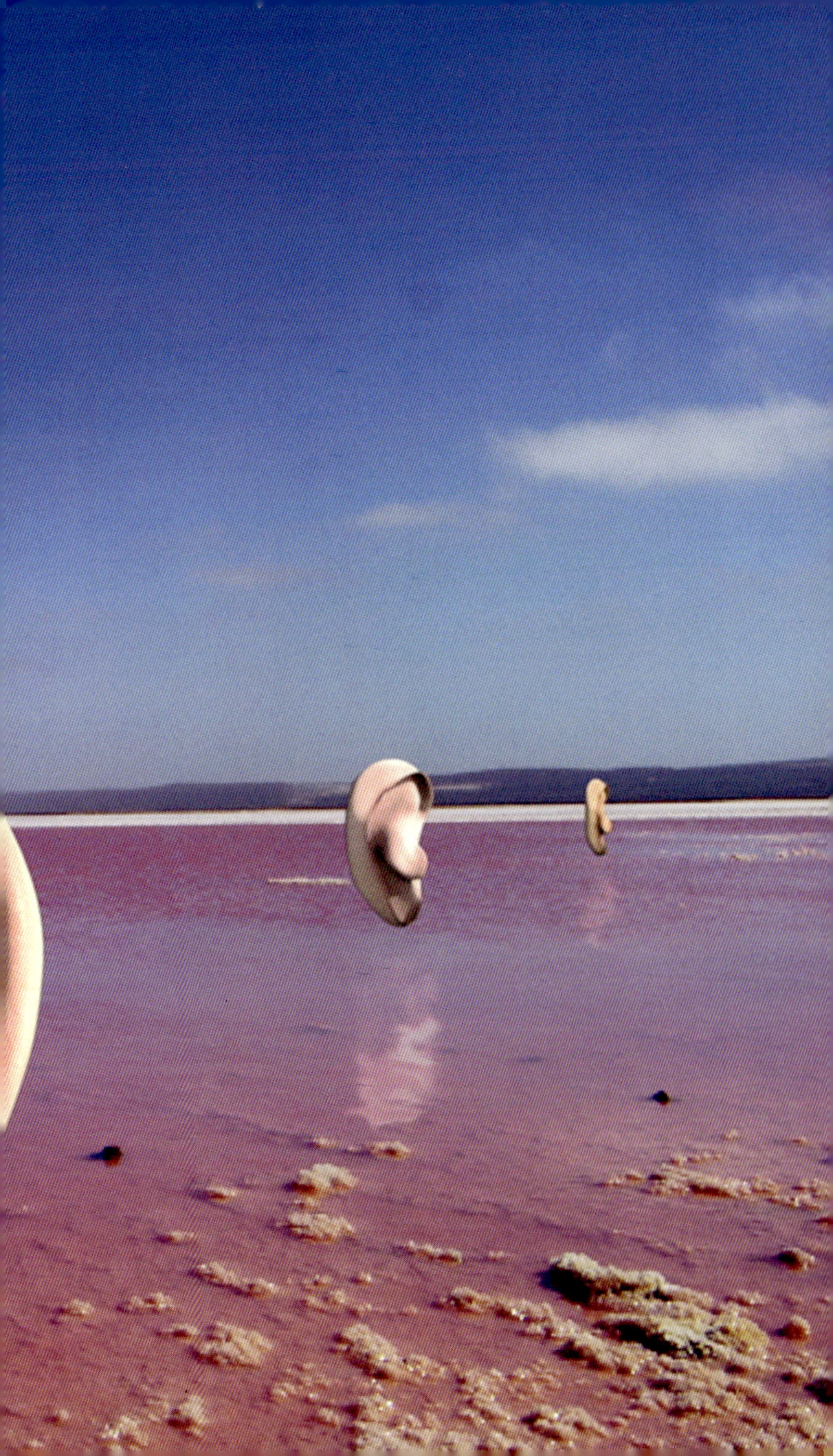

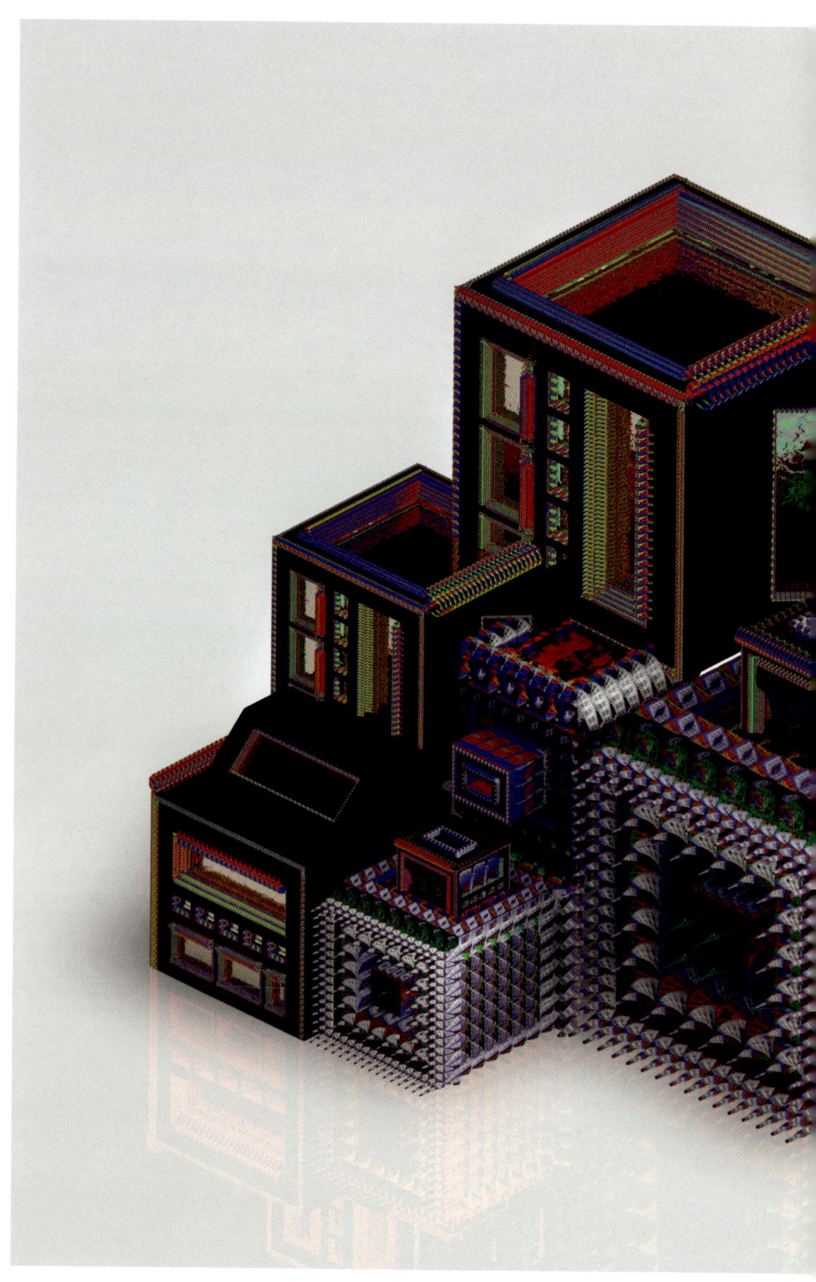

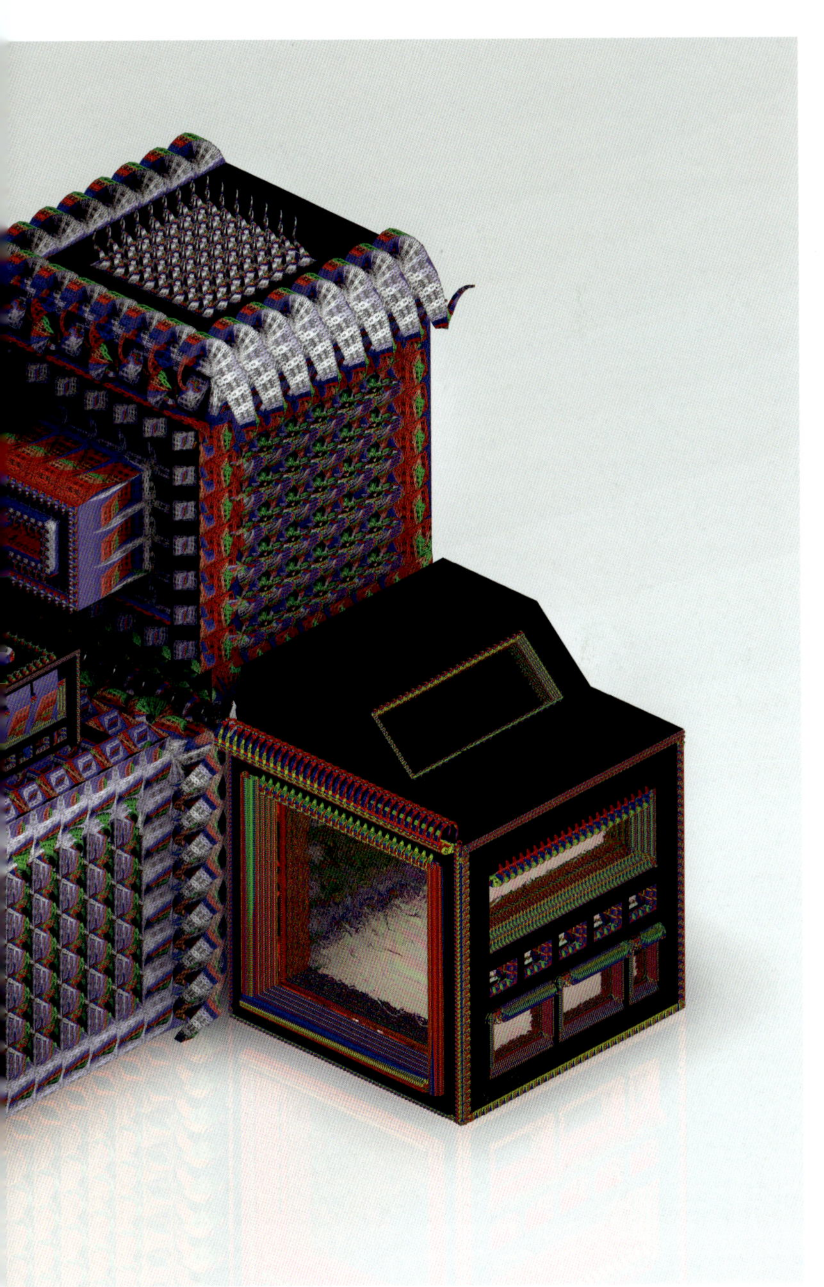

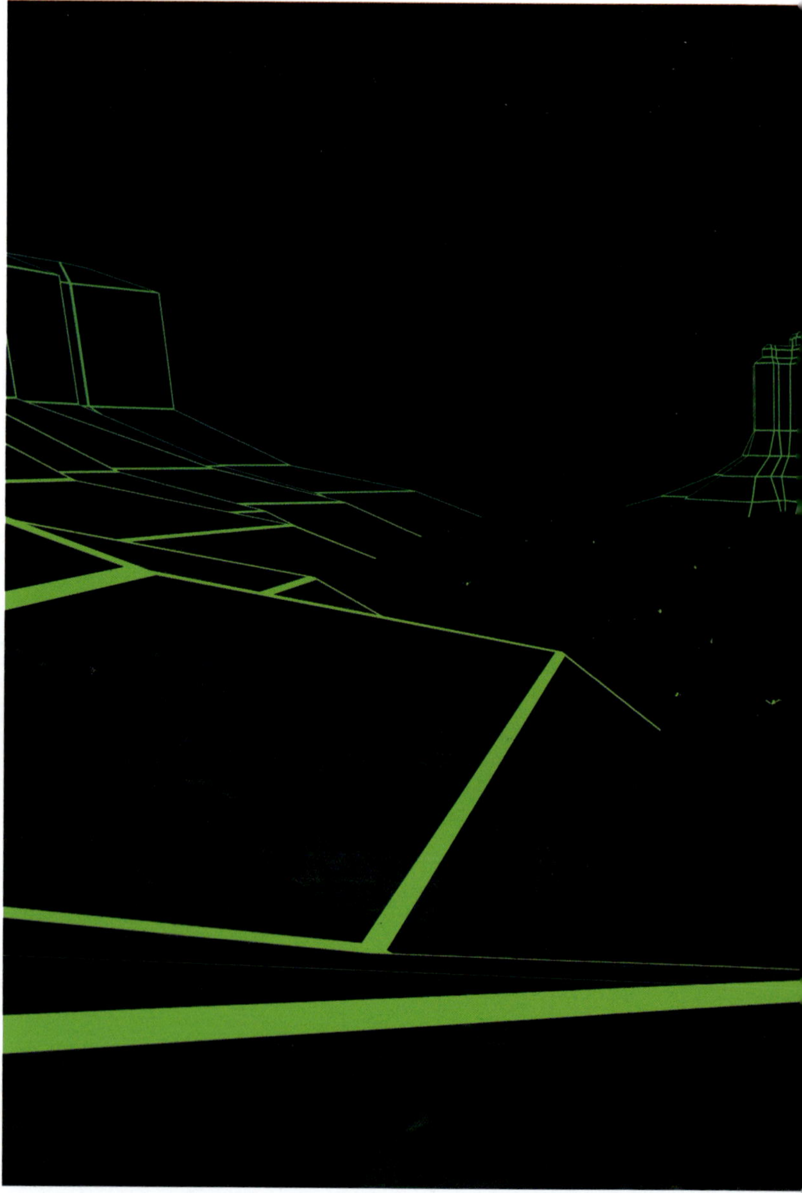

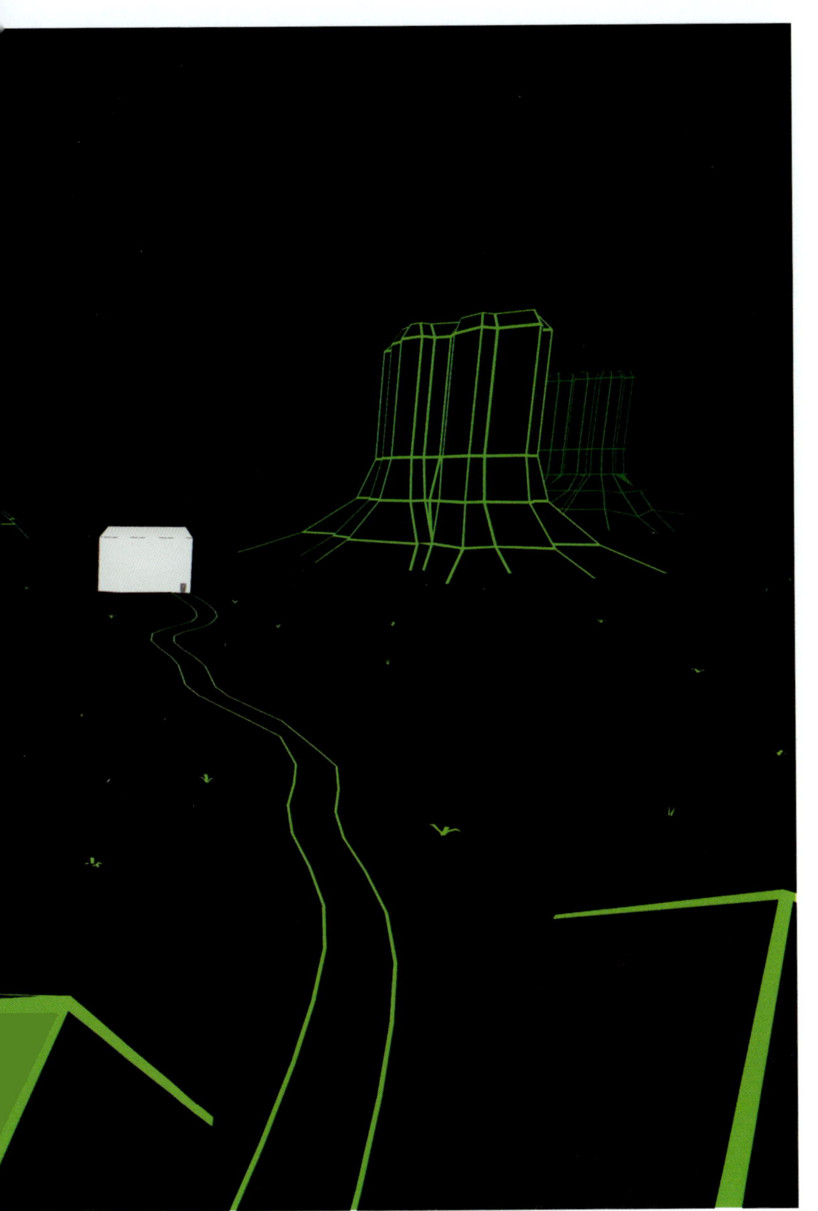

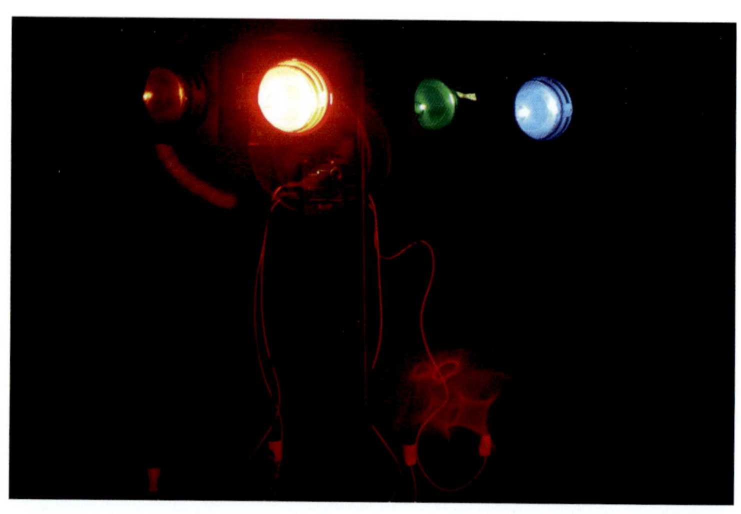

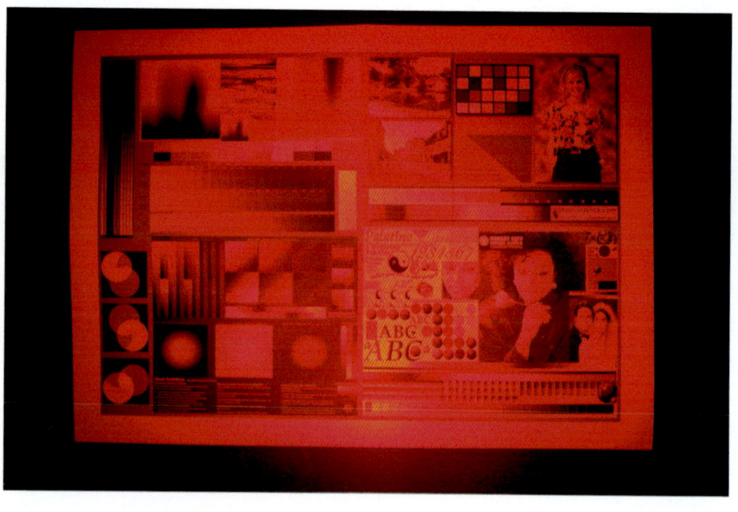
ABC
ABC

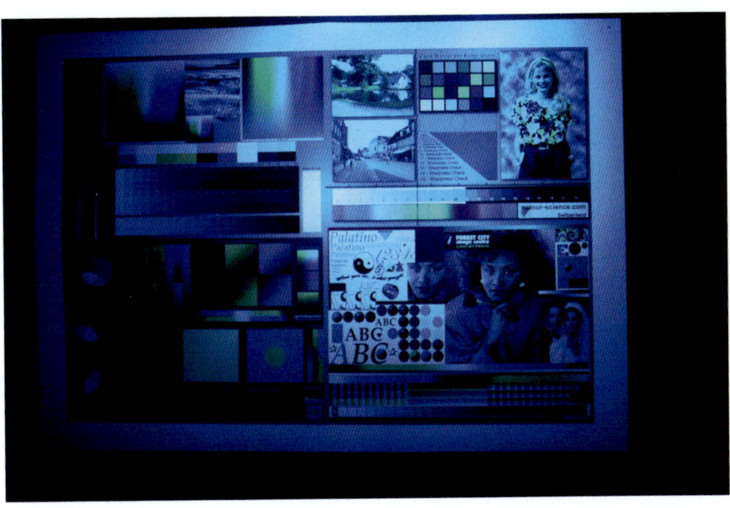
colour-science.com
Switzerland
Palatino
ABC

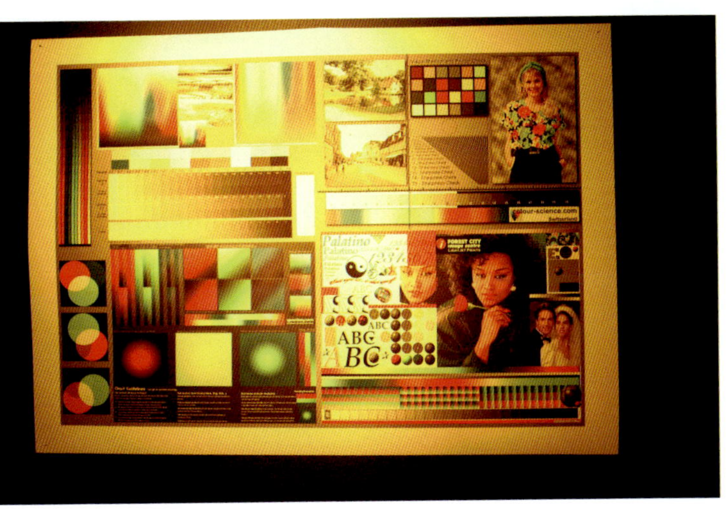
colour-science.com
Switzerland
Palatino
FOREST CITY
ABC

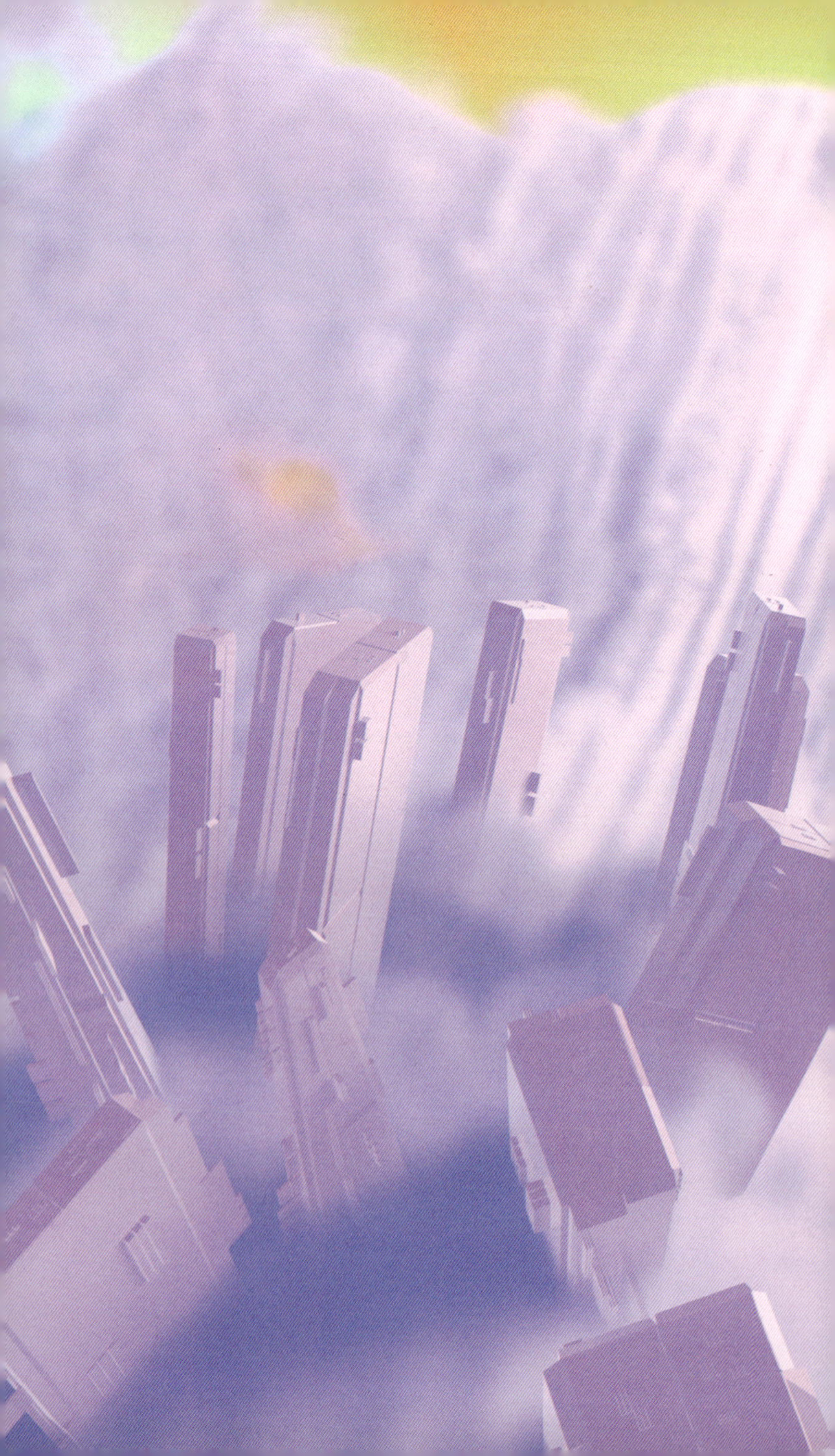

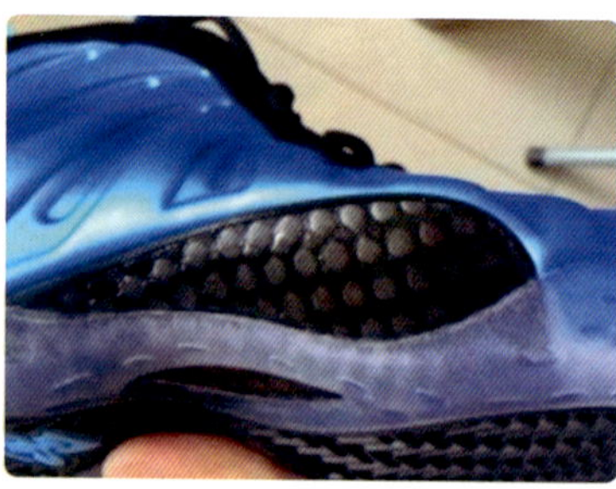

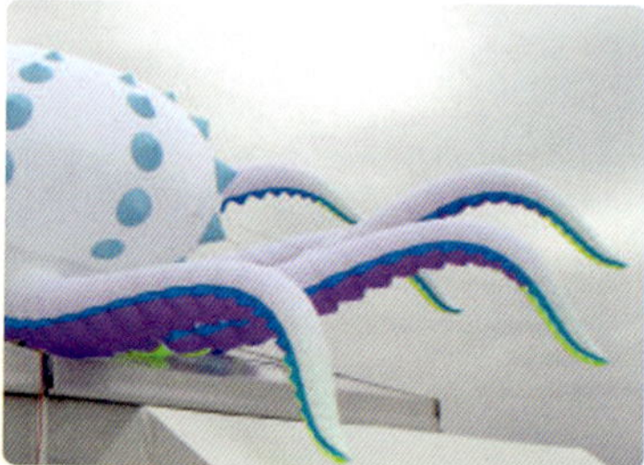

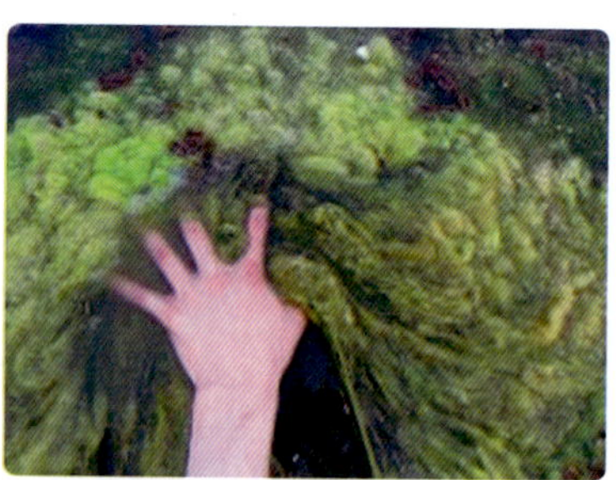

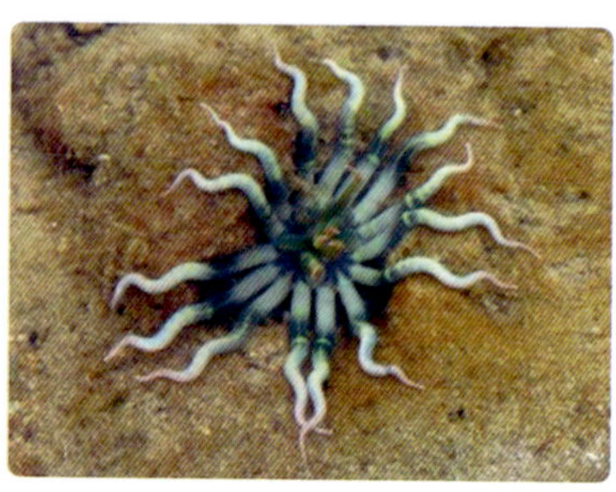

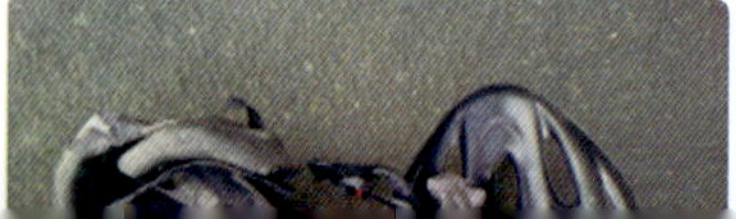

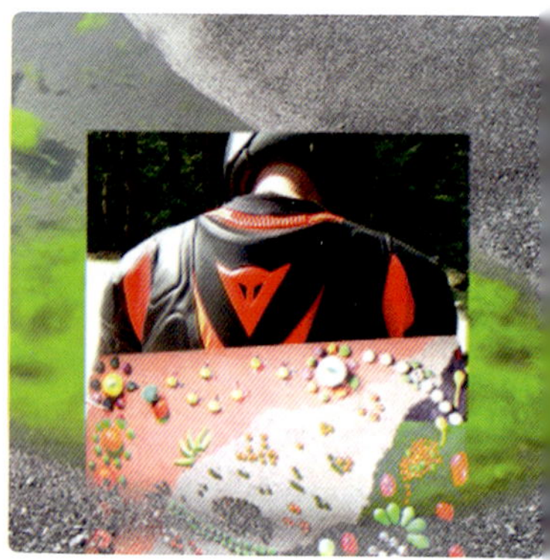

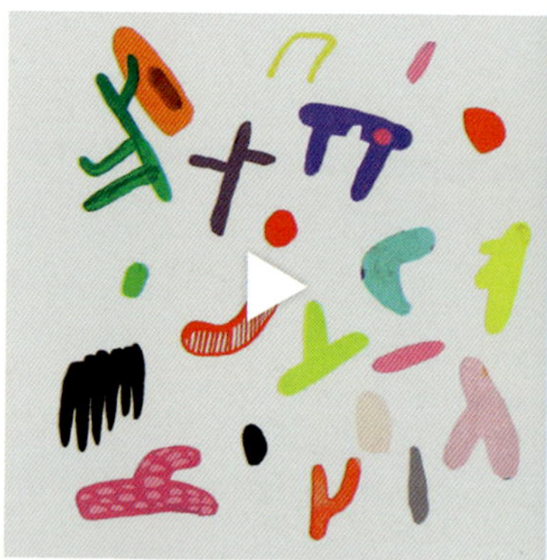

united-nations:

"I've had the privilege to make artwork for the United Nations, in efforts to help spread awareness about the World Humanitarian Summit this month. Doing what we can as individuals will create beautiful results as a whole." - Kindah Khalidy (www.instagram.com/kindahkhalidy)
In the lead up to the World Humanitarian Summit (@WHSummit), we asked artists from around the globe to create and donate a piece of art, symbolizing the "Agenda for Humanity", the Secretary-General's vision for the future of humanitarian action.
Learn more about the World Humanitarian Summit here: http://www.worldhumanitariansummit.or

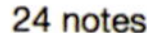

24 notes

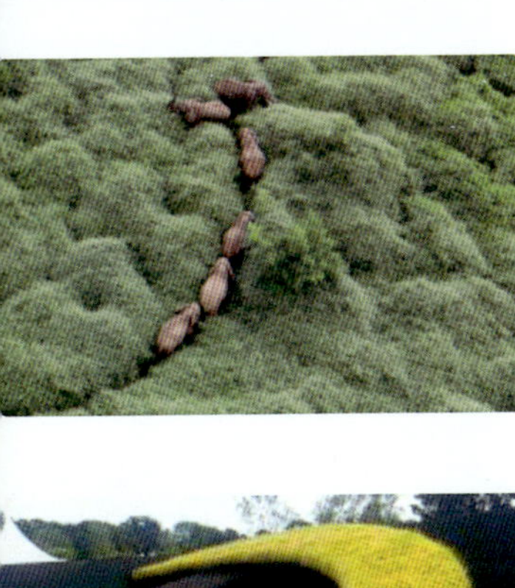

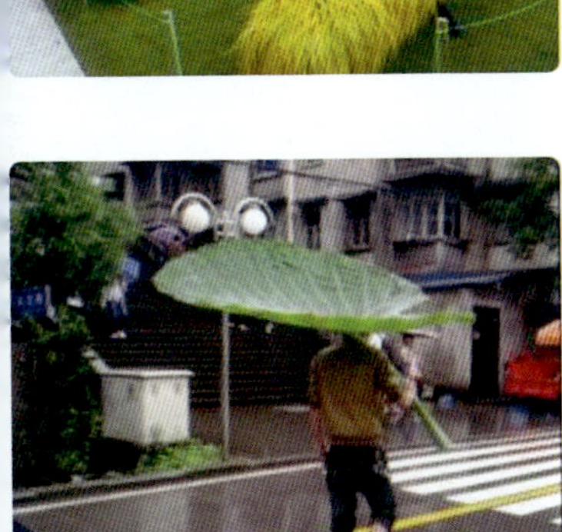

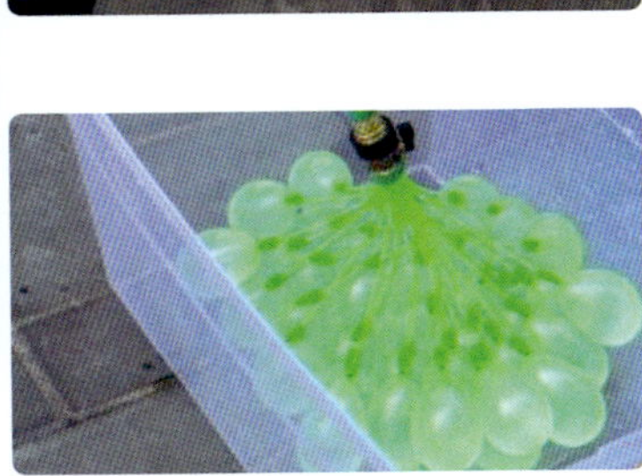

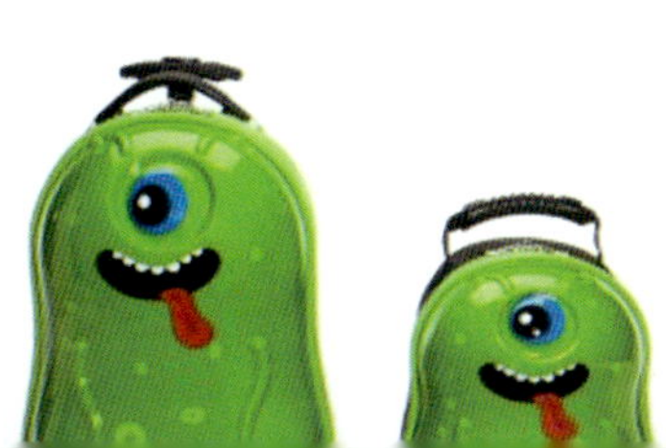

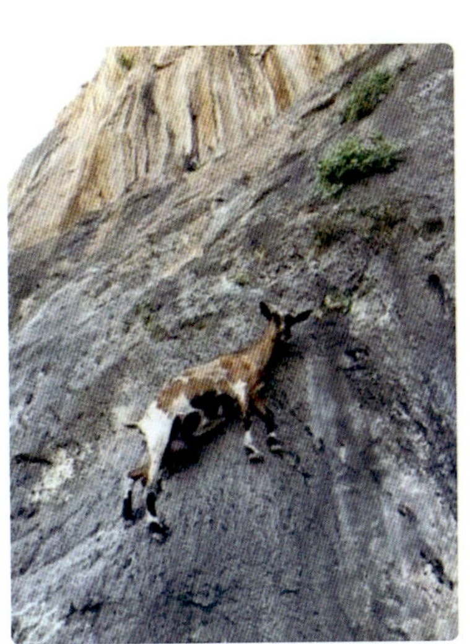

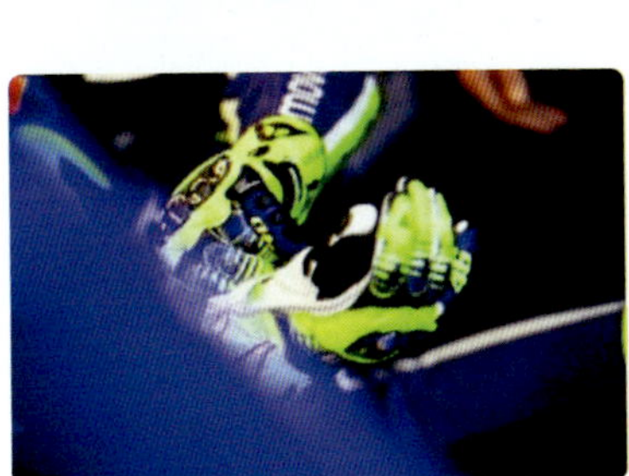

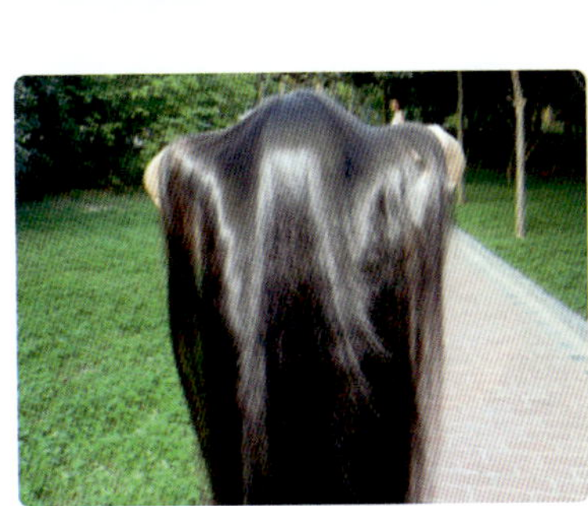

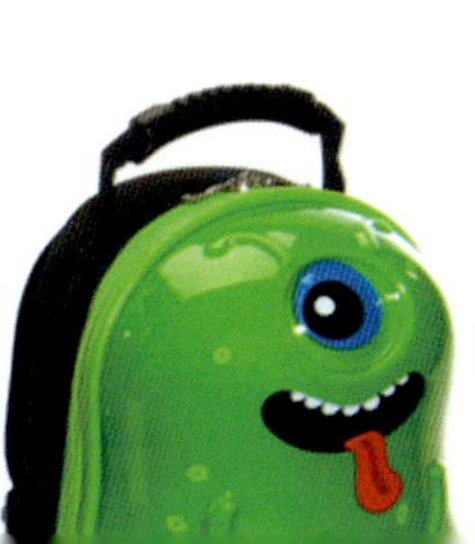

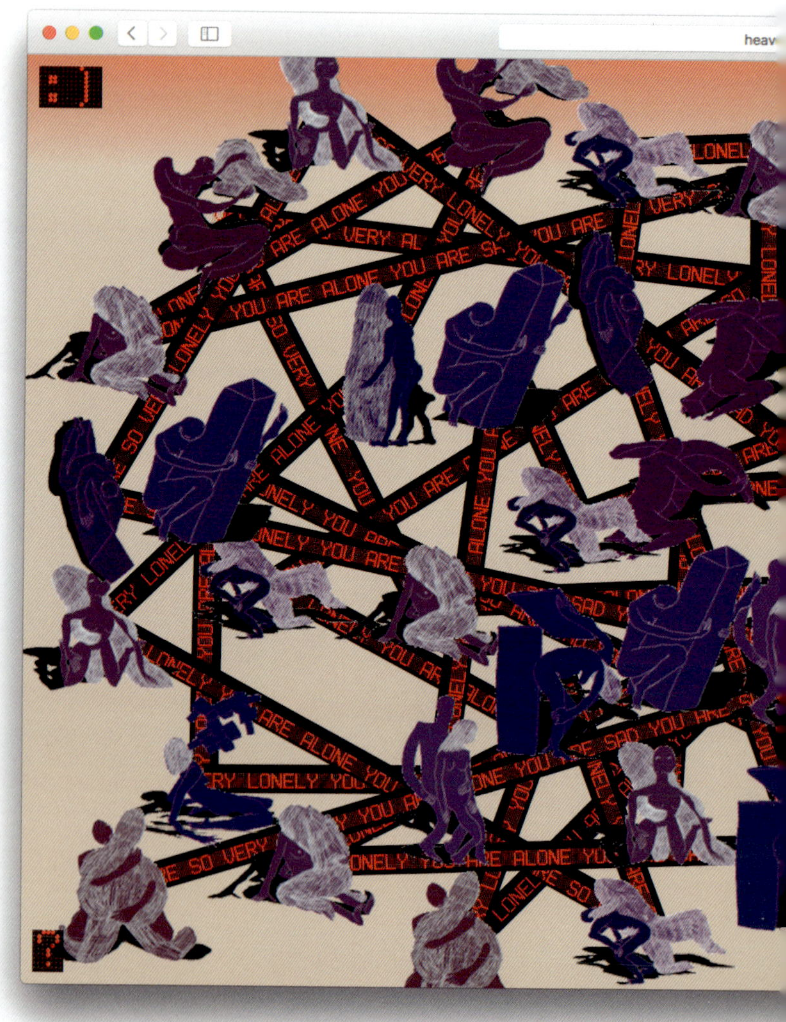

YOU ARE ALONE YOU
YOU ARE ALONE
VERY LONELY
YOU ARE SO VERY
RY LONELY YOU YOU
ARE ALONE
SAD YOU ARE

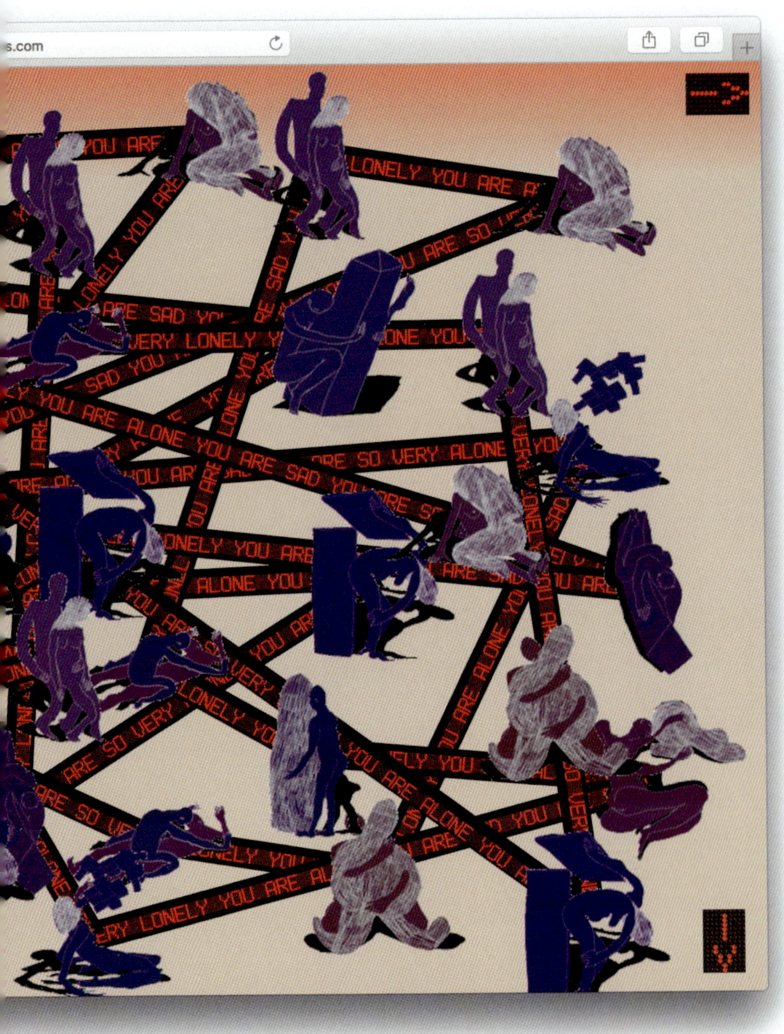
s.com
YOU ARE
LONELY YOU ARE A
ARE SO
ARE SAD YO
VERY LONELY Y
ONE YOU
SAD YOU
YOU ARE ALONE YOU ARE SAD YOU
ARE SO VERY ALONE
ONELY YOU ARE
ALONE YOU
ARE SO VERY
ELY YOU
YOU ARE ALONE
ARE SO VE
ERY LONELY YOU ARE AL

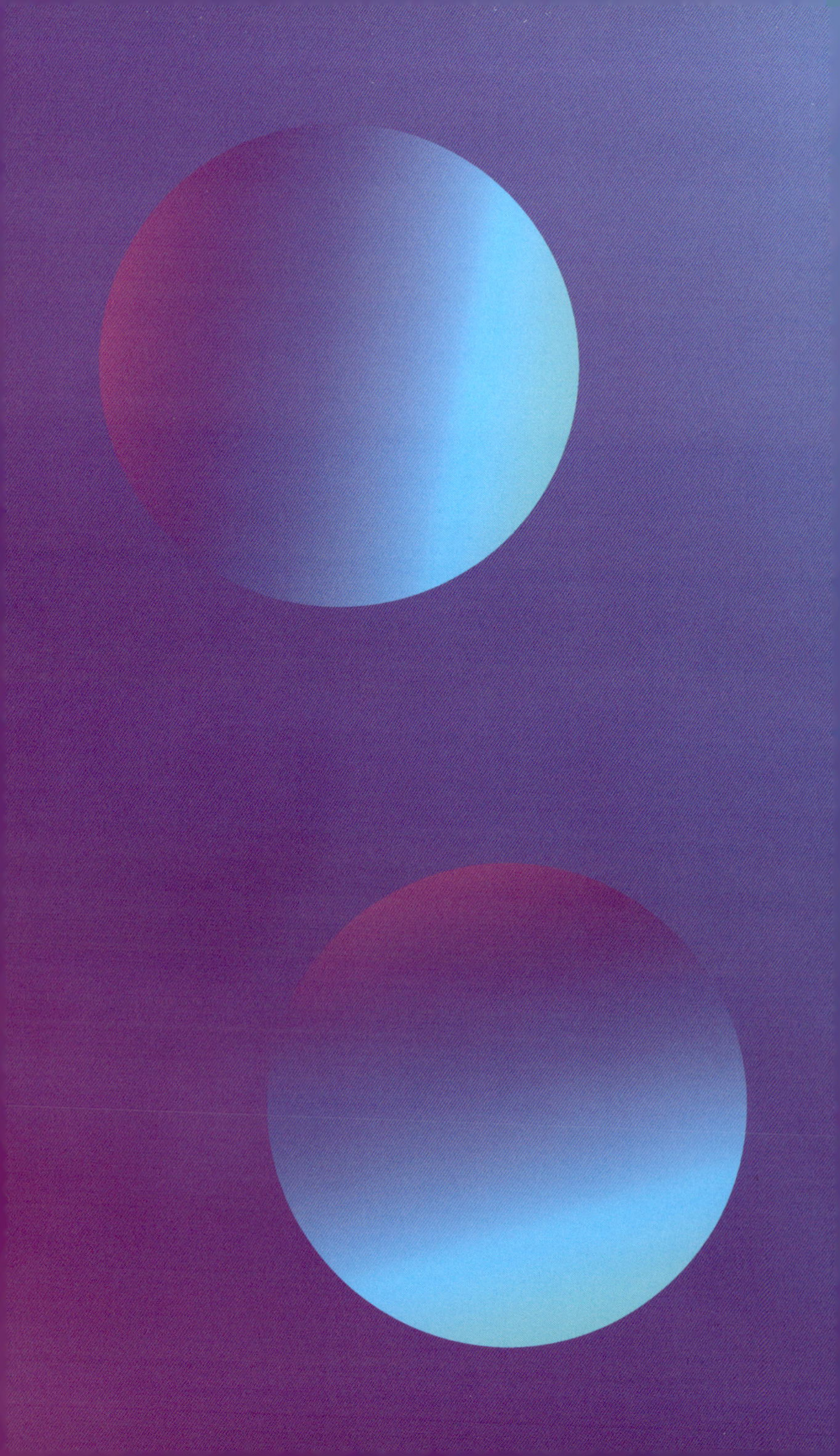

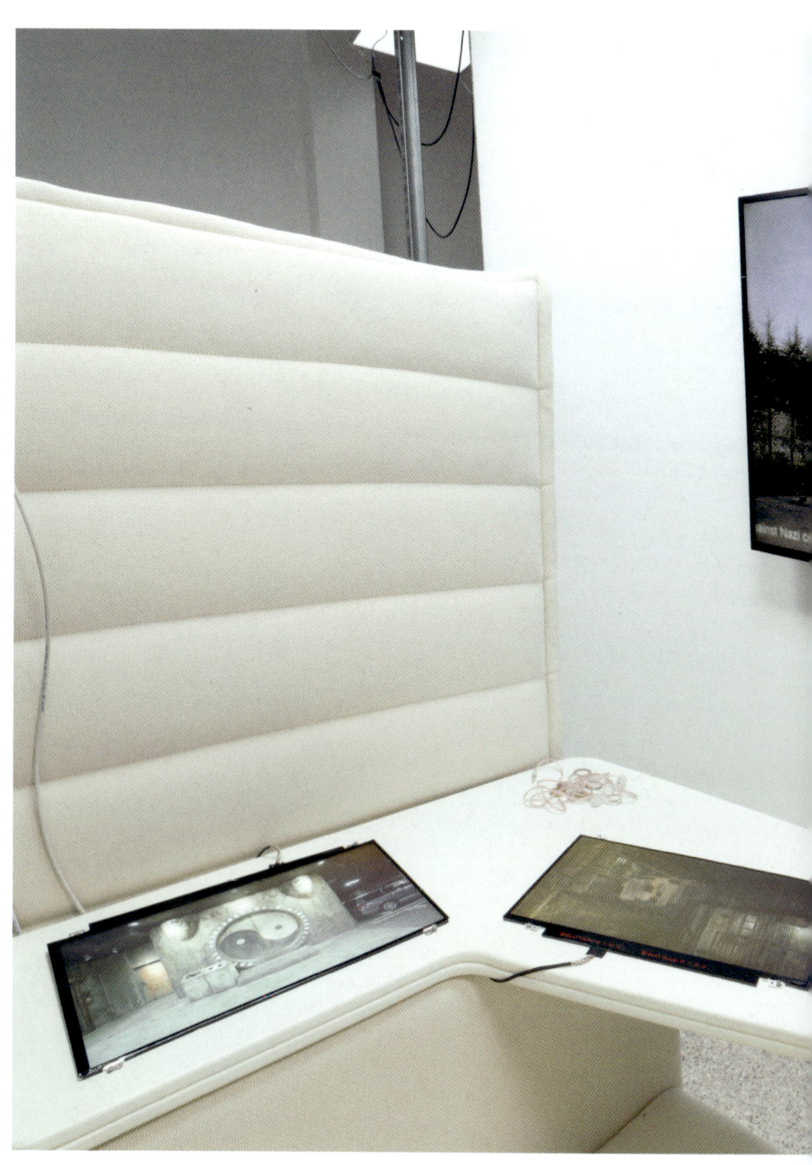

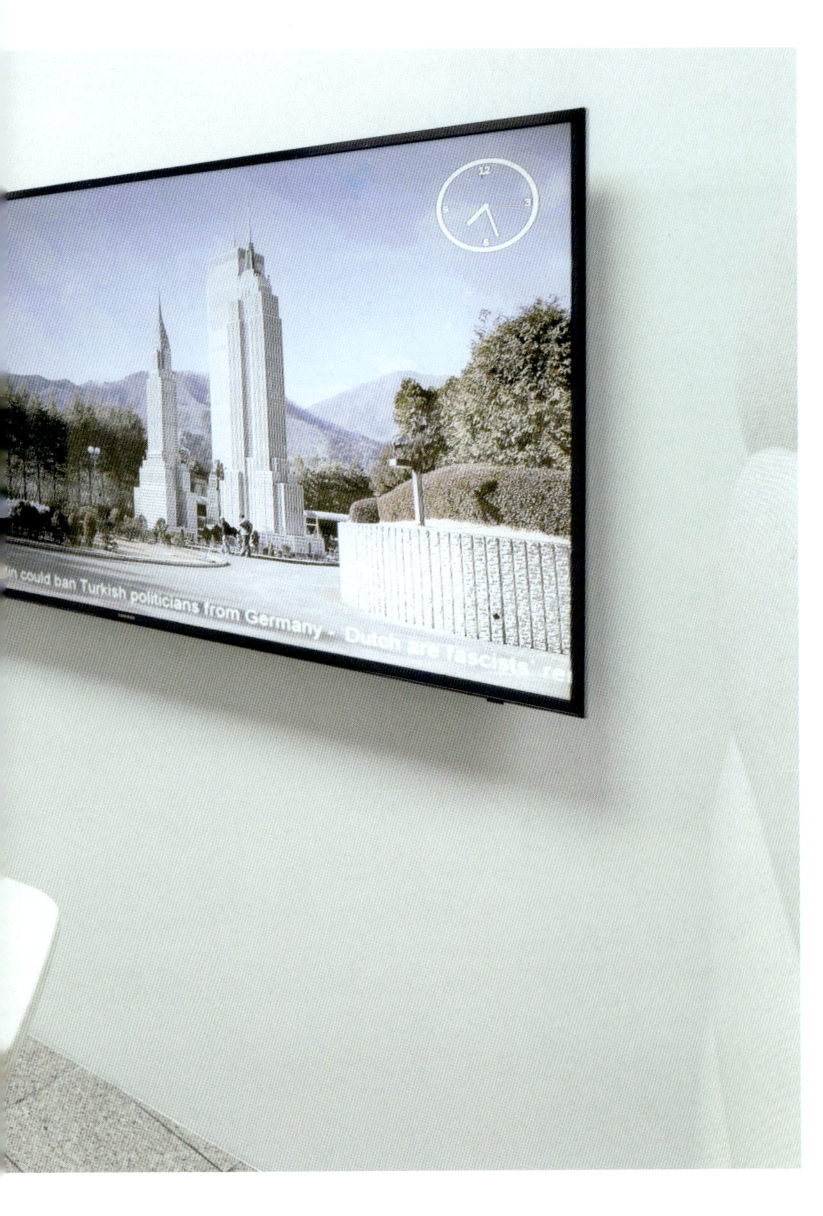
could ban Turkish politicians from Germany - Dutch are fascists

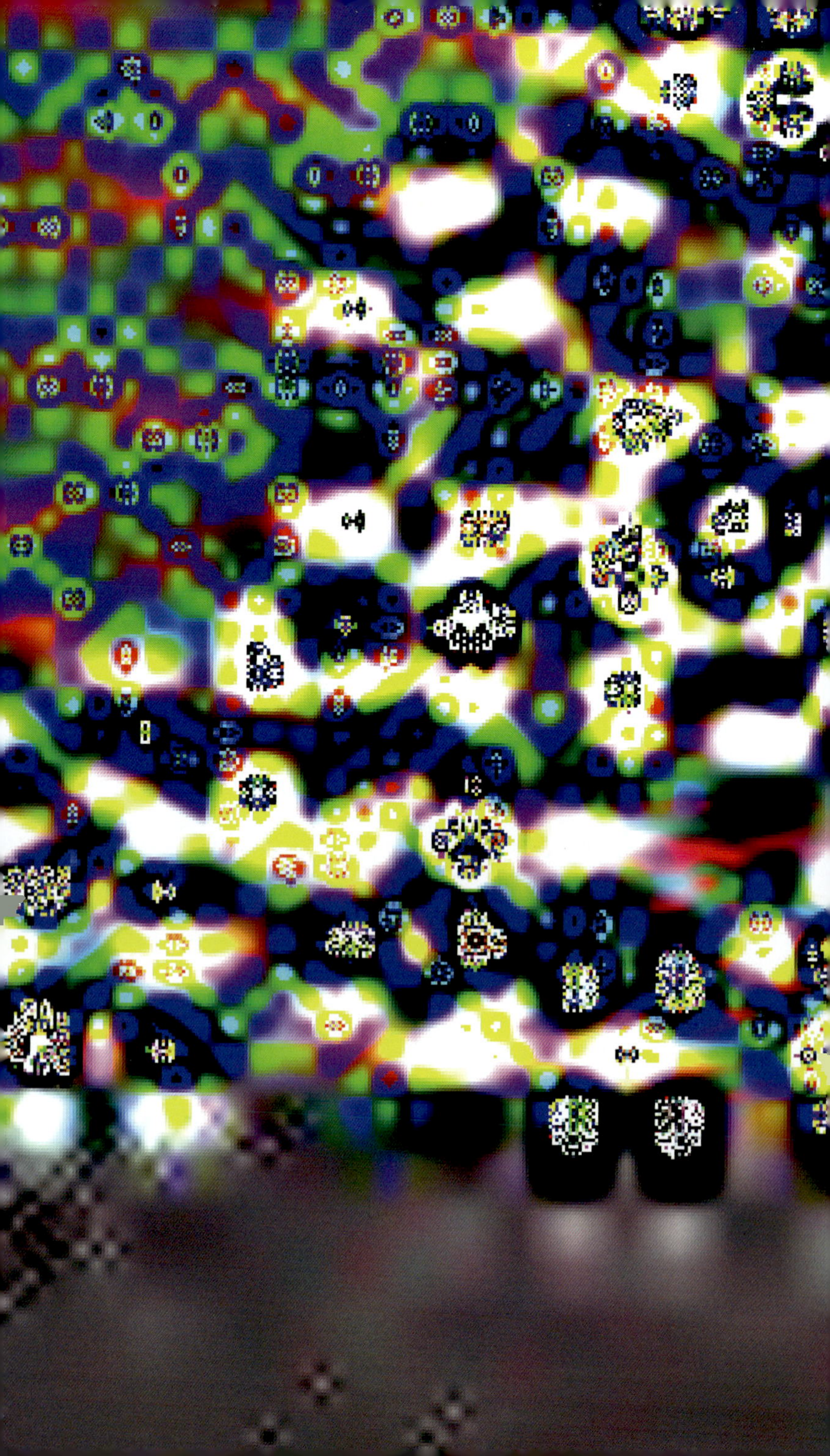

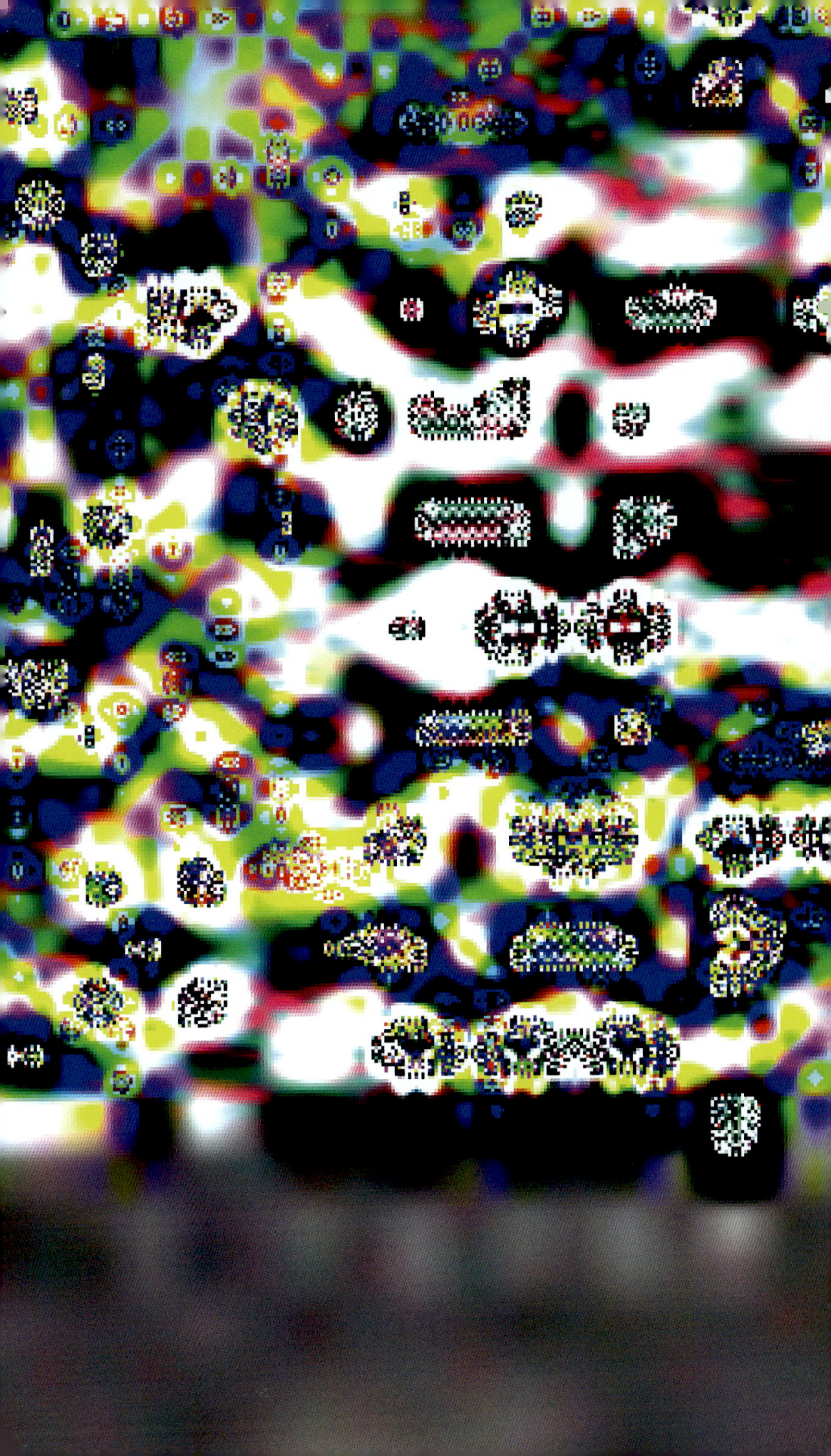

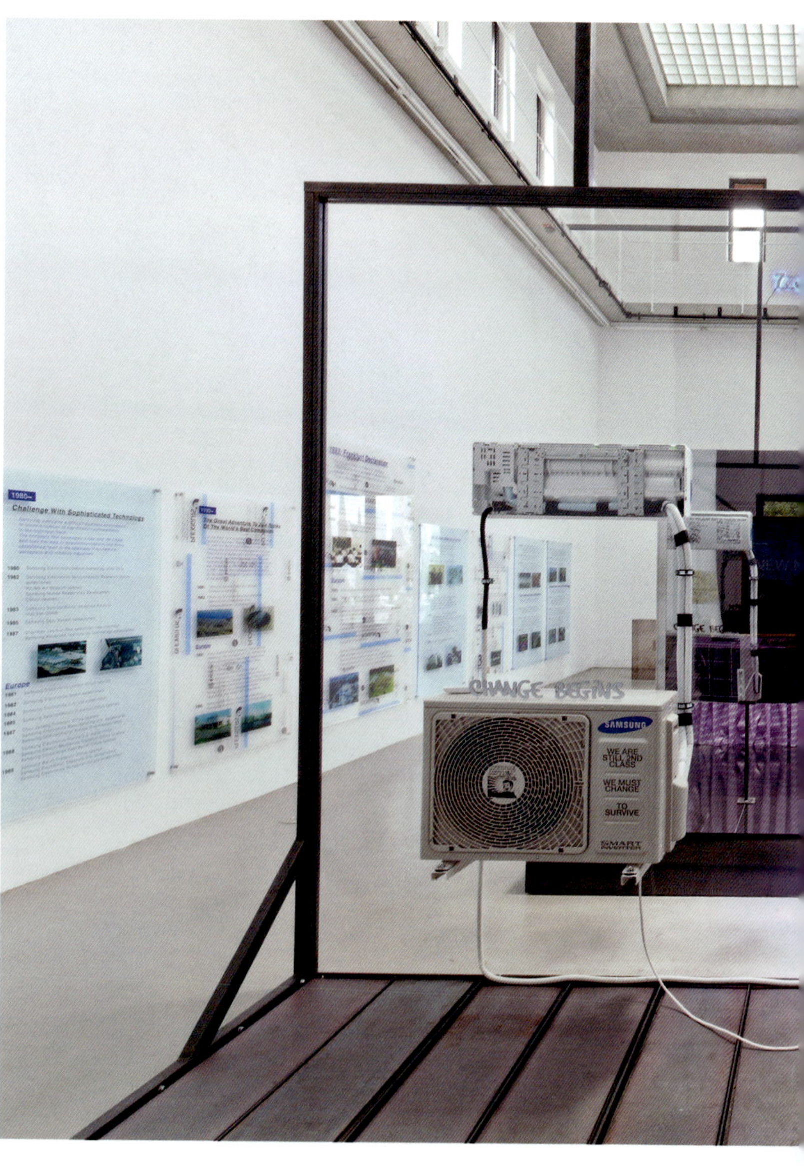
1980~
Challenge With Sophisticated Technology
Europe
CHANGE BEGINS
SAMSUNG
WE ARE STILL 2ND CLASS
WE MUST CHANGE
TO SURVIVE
SMART

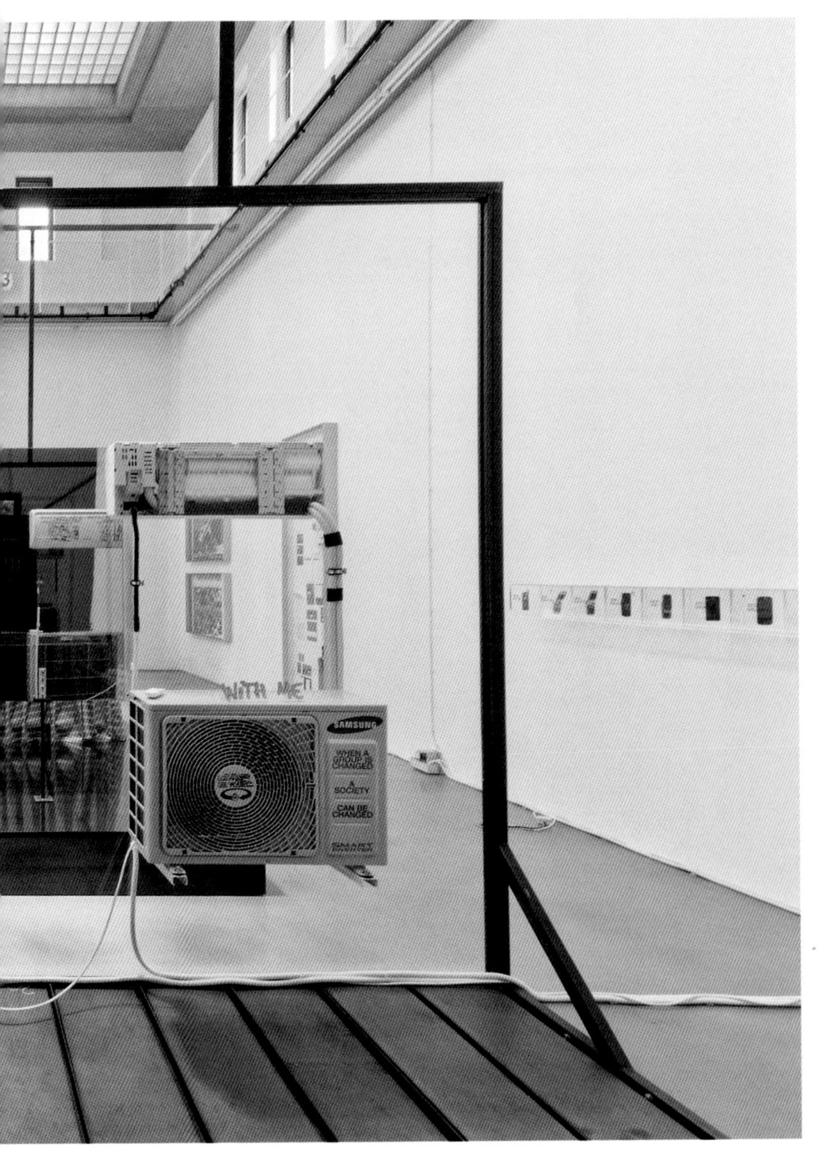
WITH ME
SAMSUNG
WHEN A GROUP IS CHANGED
A SOCIETY
CAN BE CHANGED

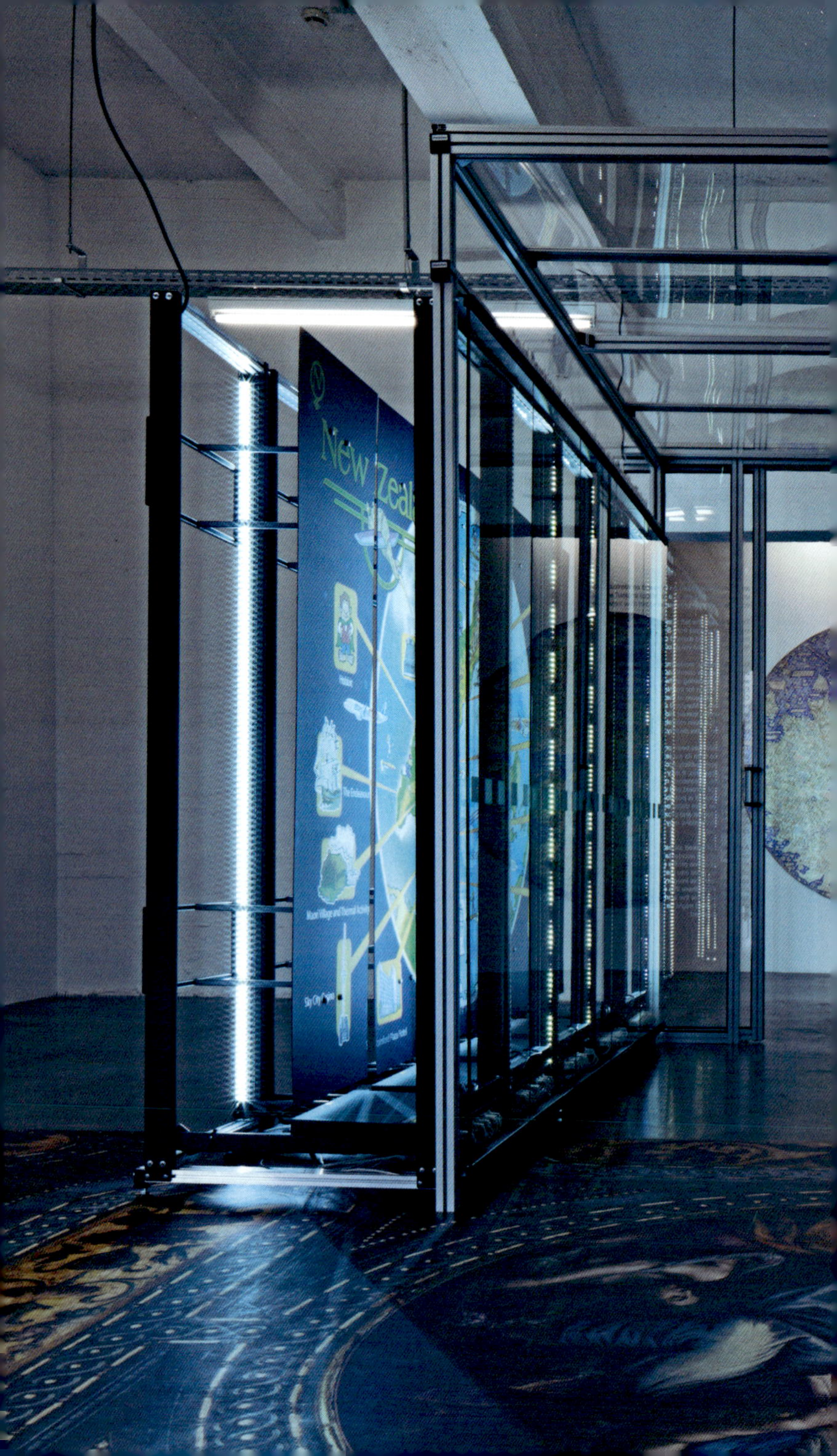
New

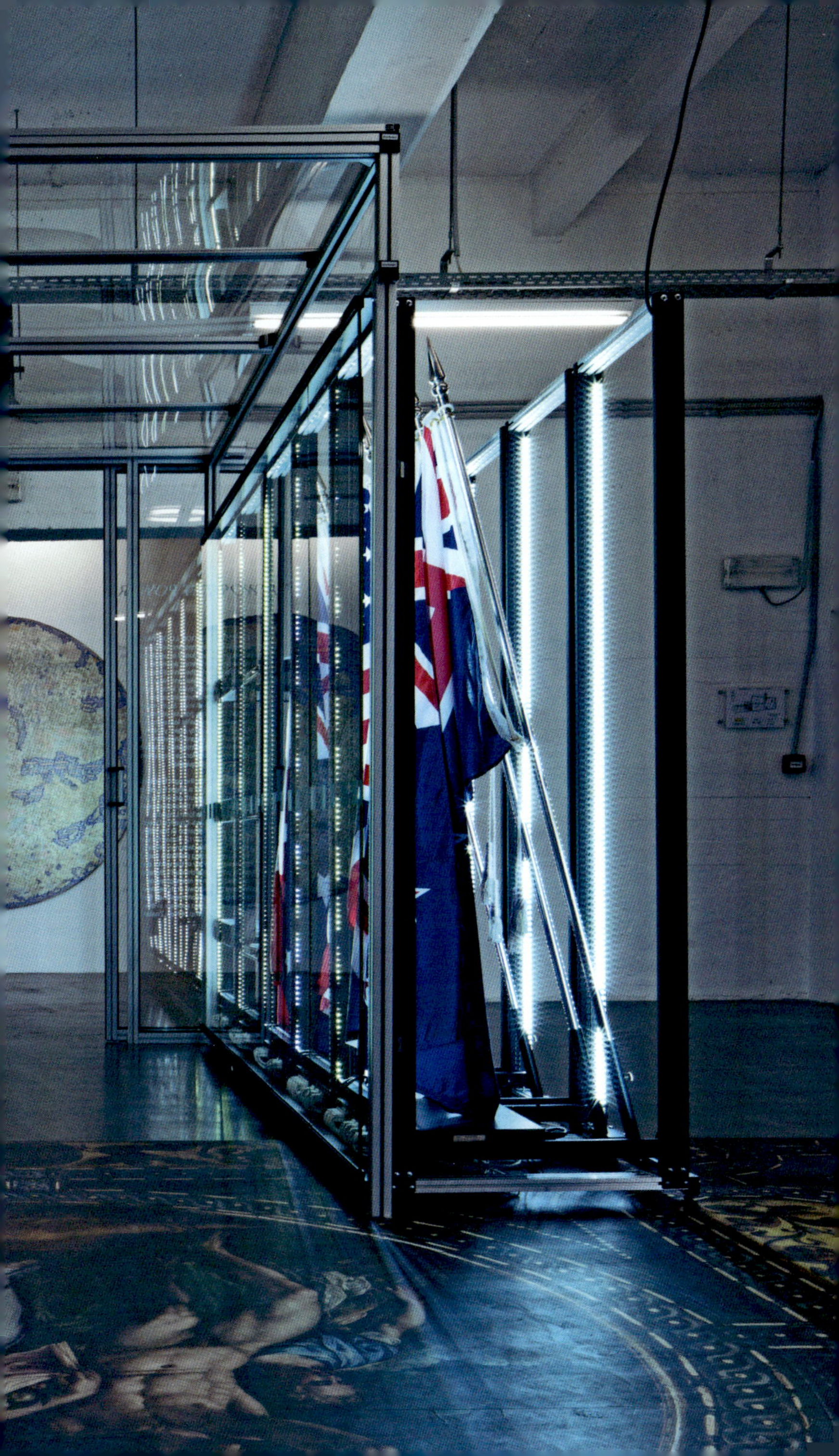

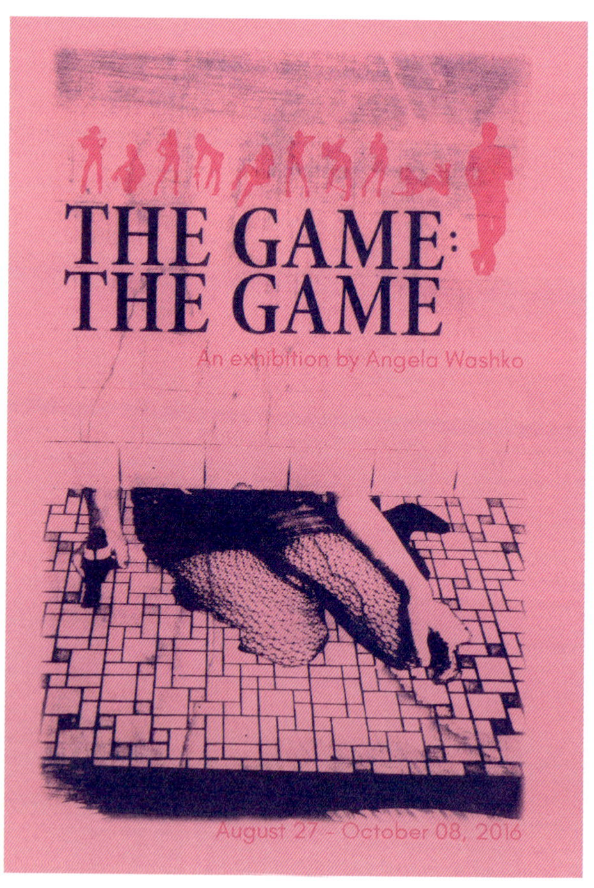
THE GAME:
THE GAME
An exhibition by Angela Washko
August 27 - October 08, 2016

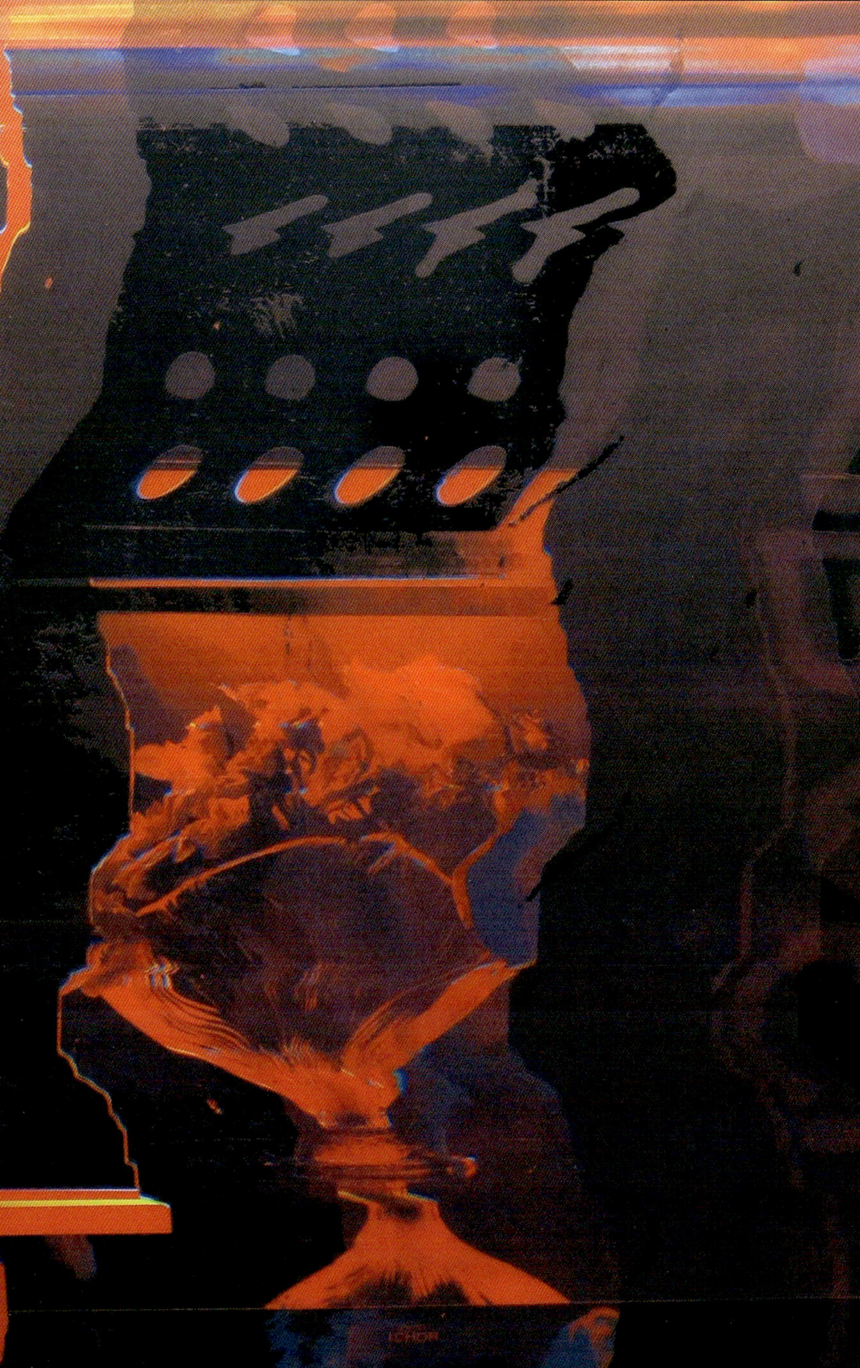

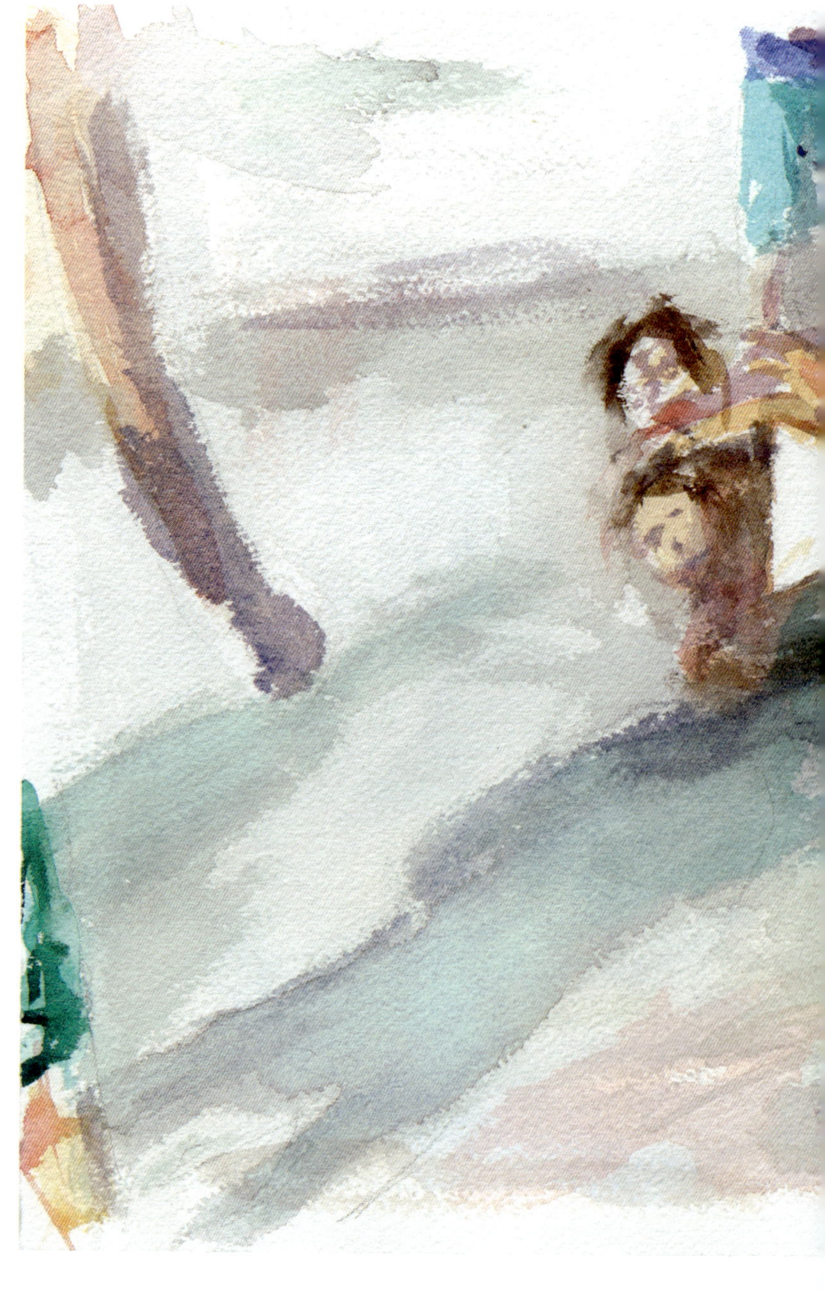

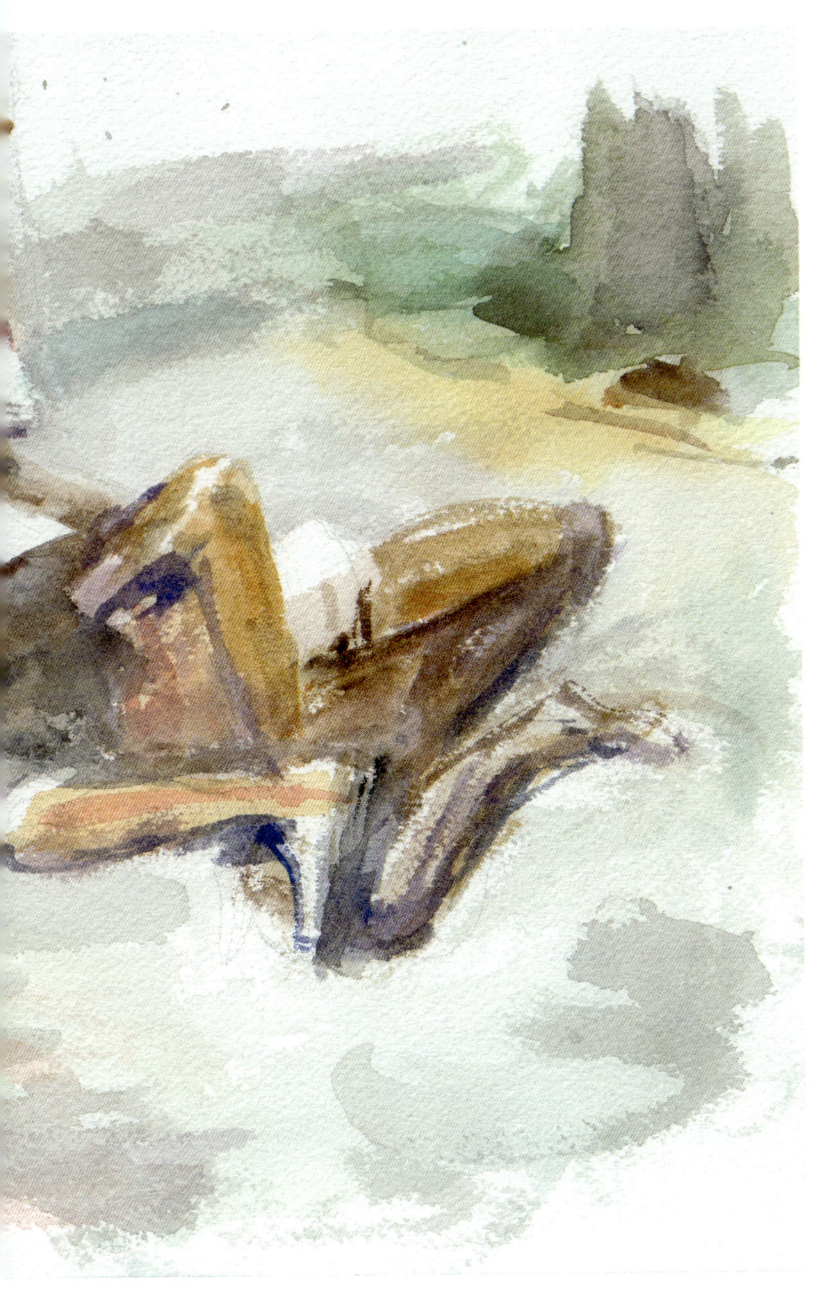

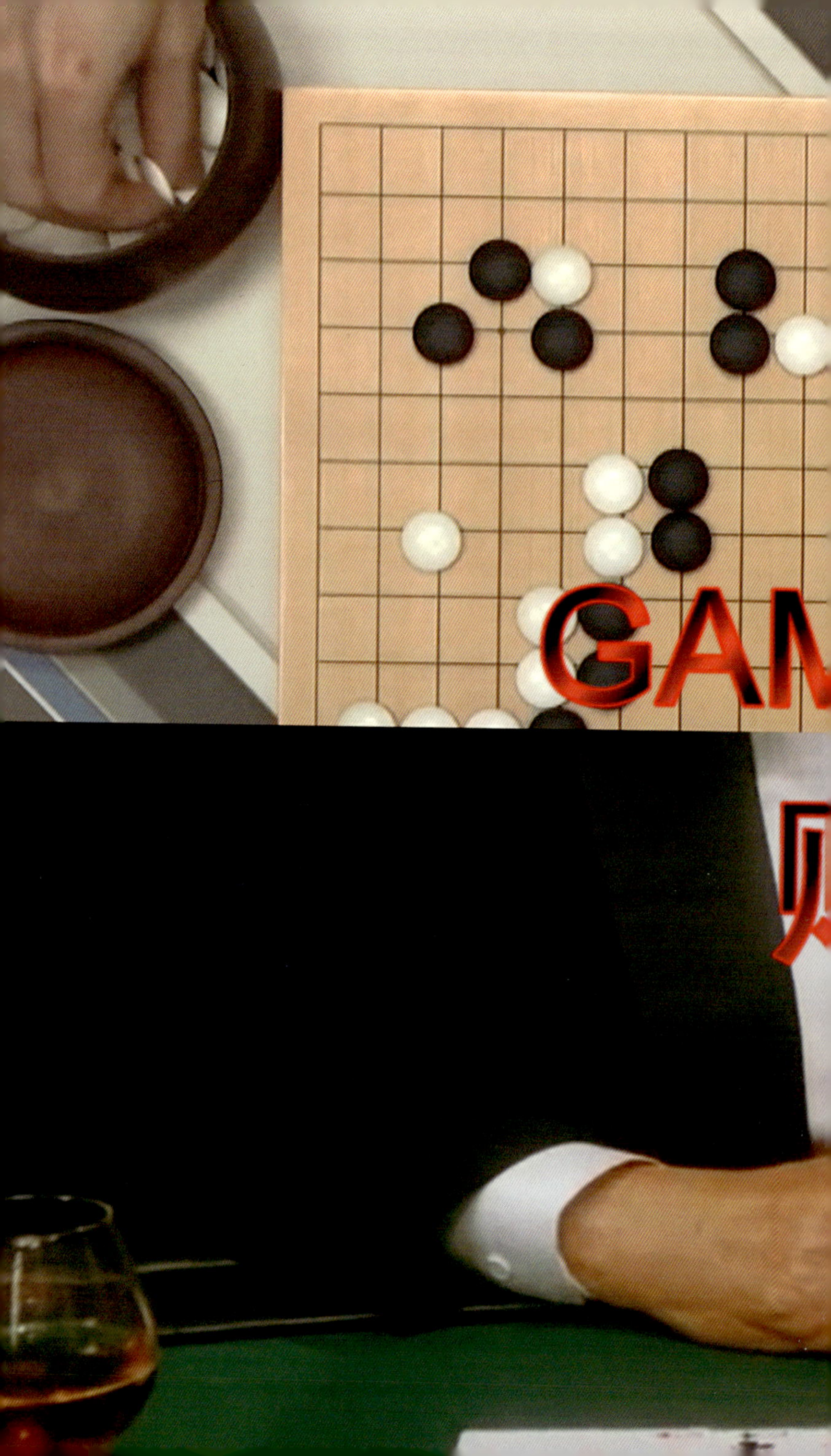

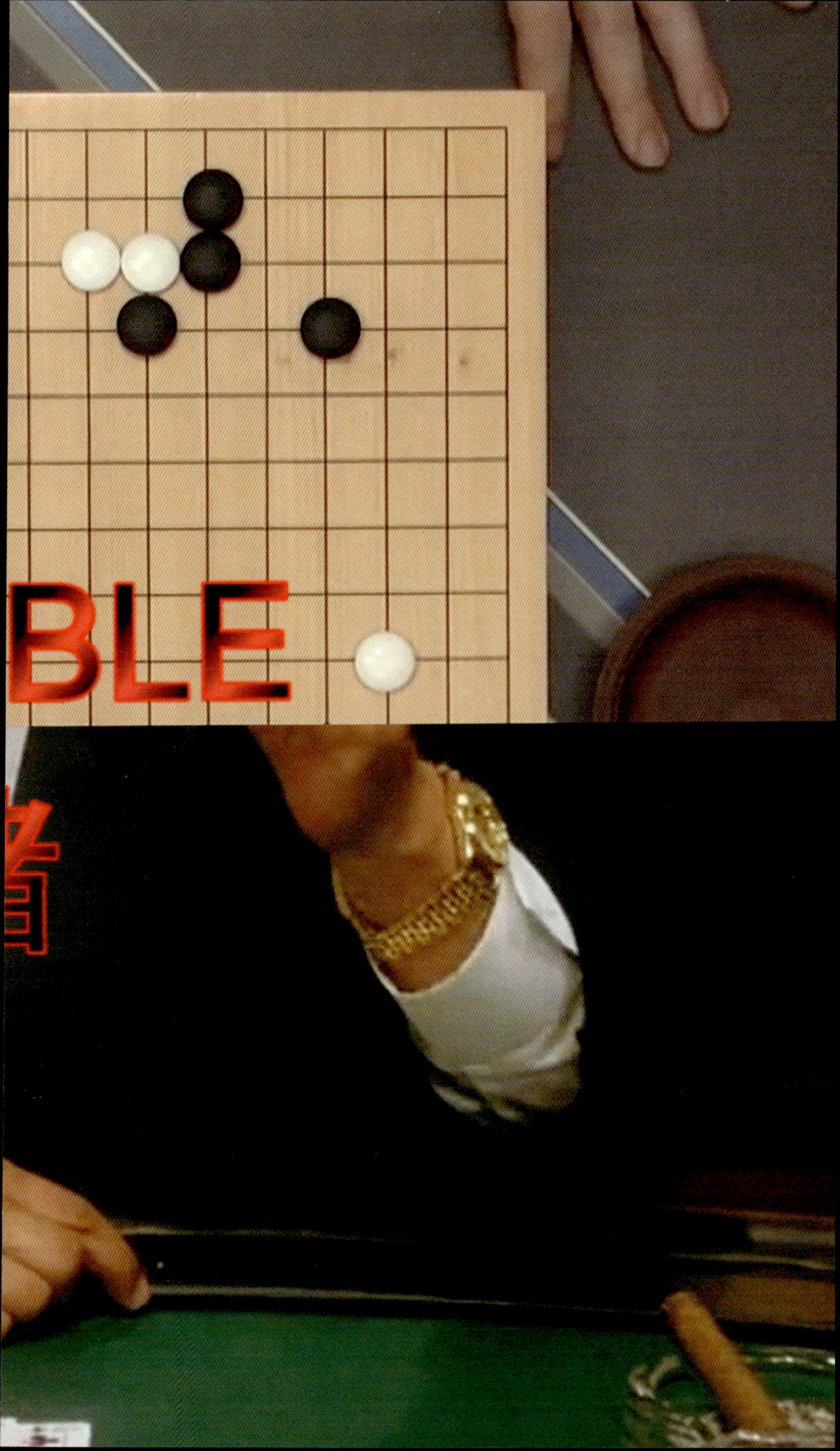
BLE

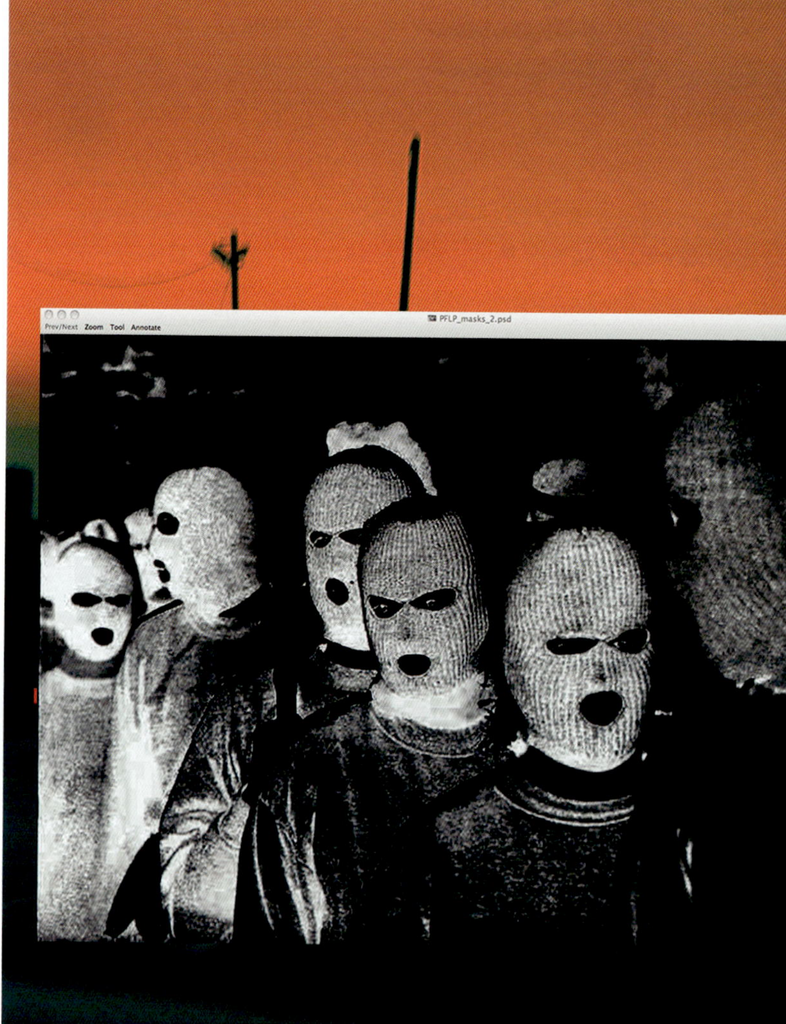
PFLP_masks_2.psd
Prev/Next Zoom Tool Annotate

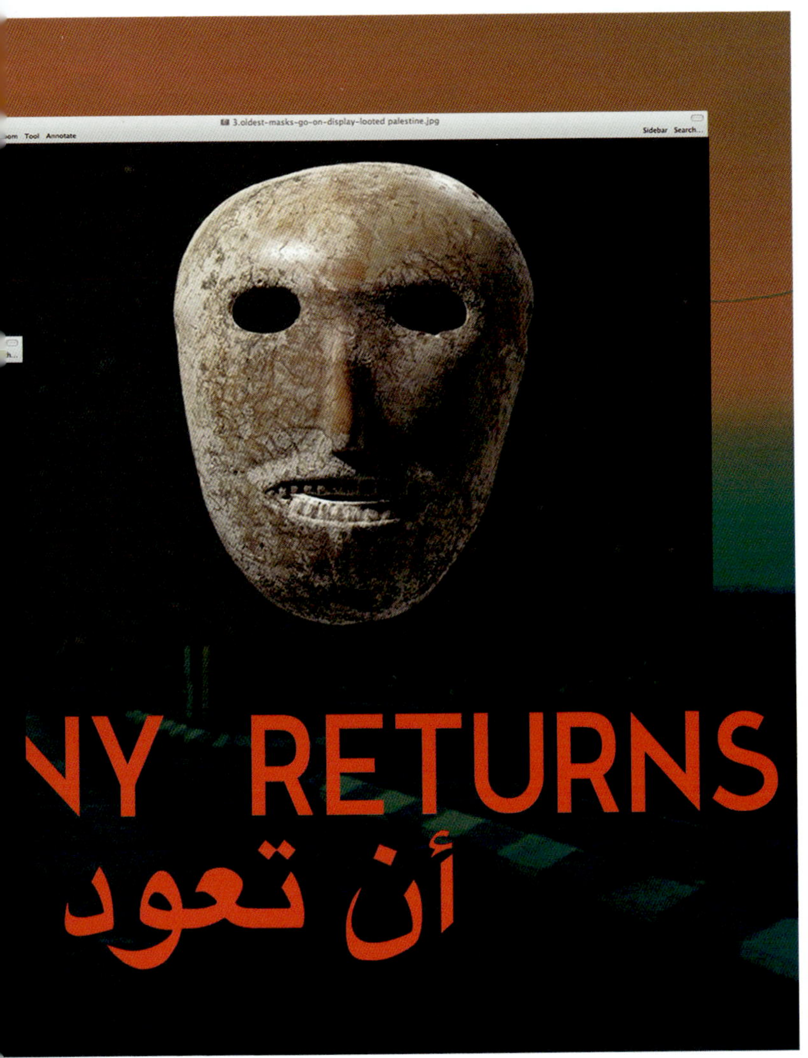
3.oldest-masks-go-on-display-looted palestine.jpg
Tool Annotate
Sidebar Search...
NY RETURNS
أن تعود

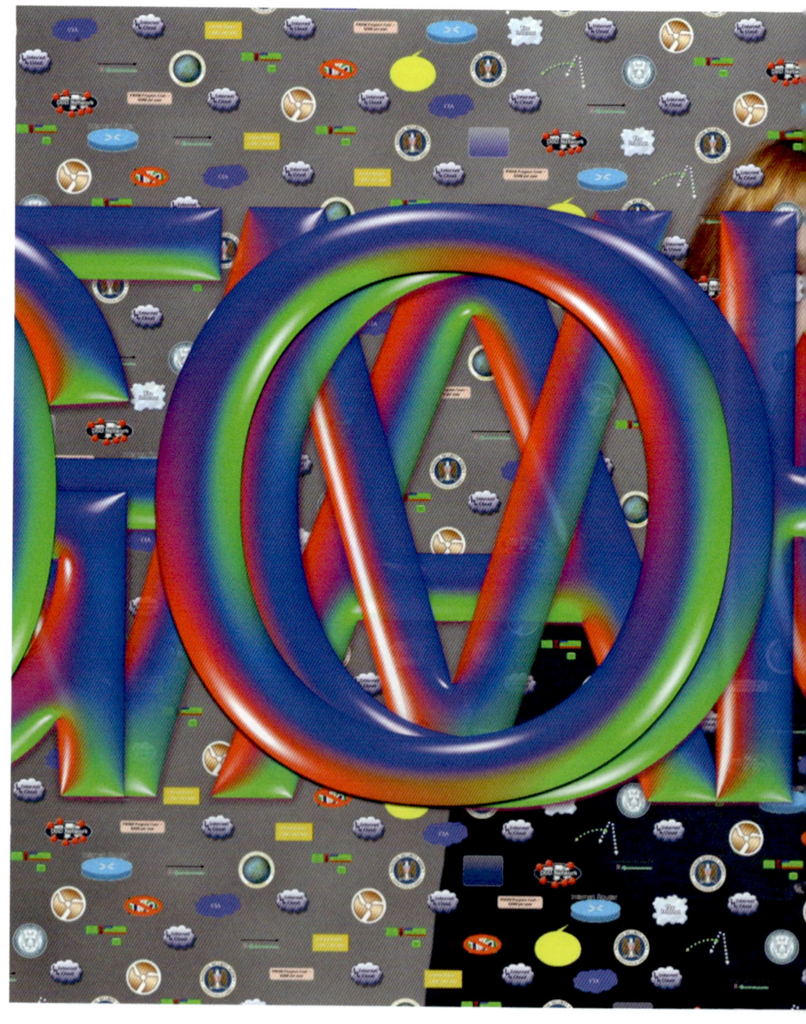

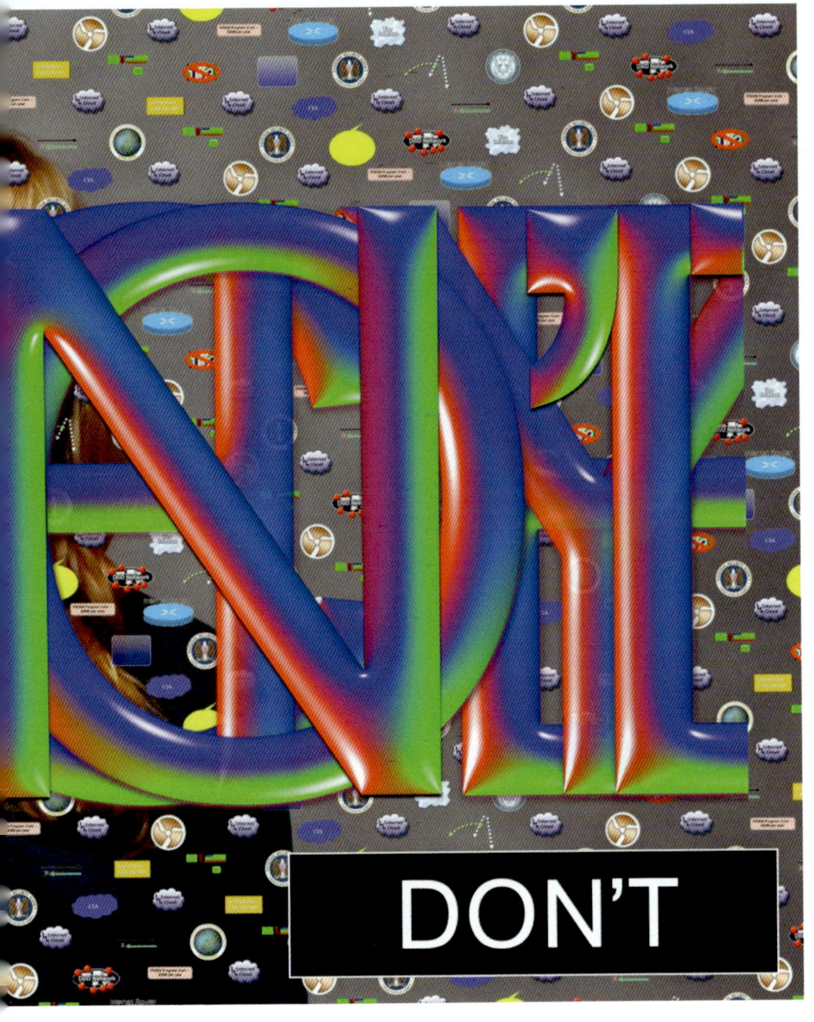
DON'T

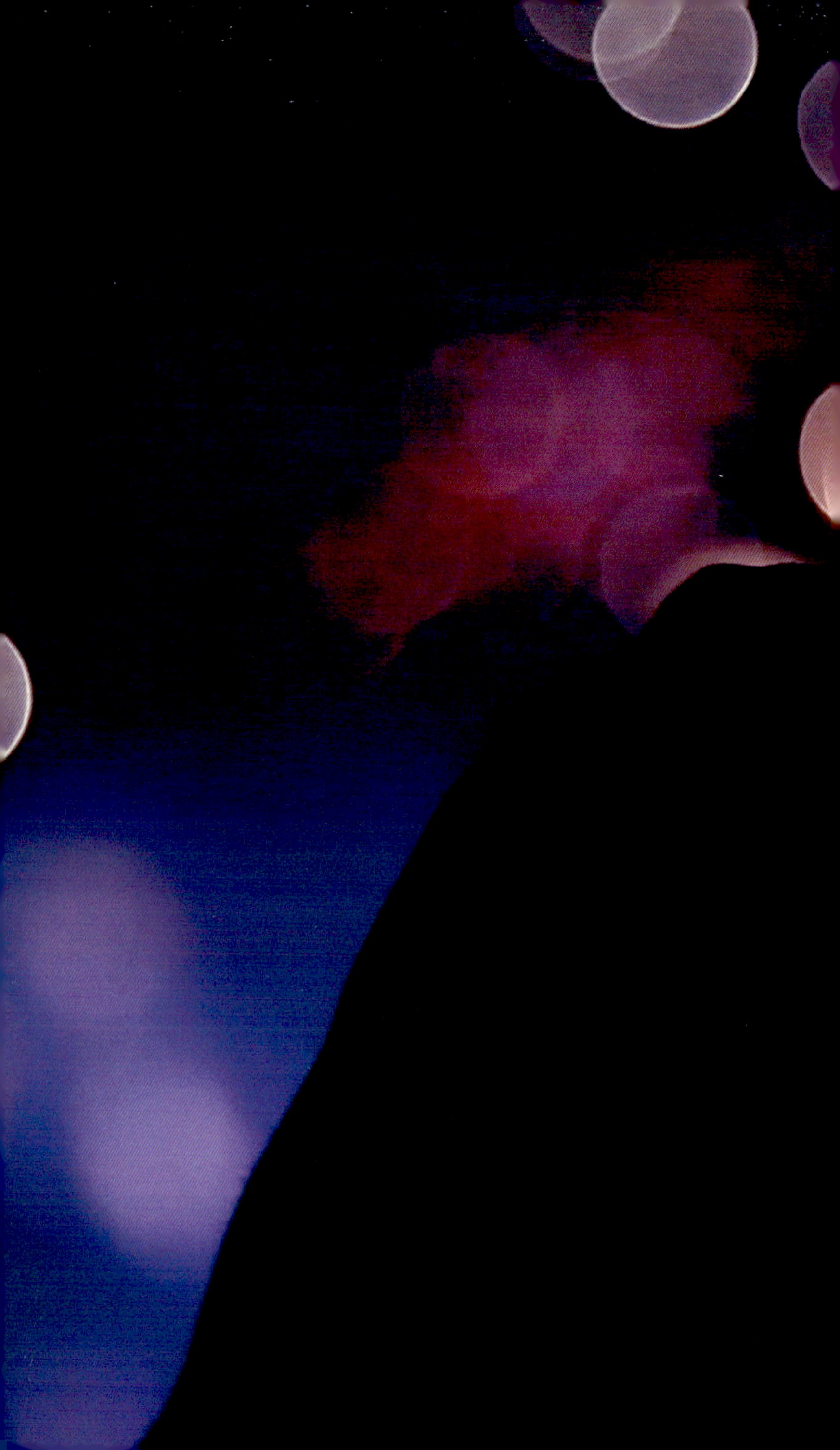

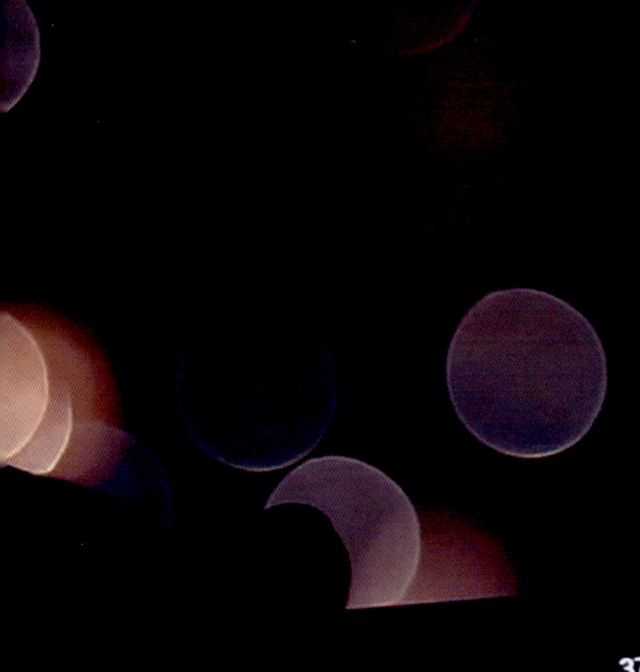

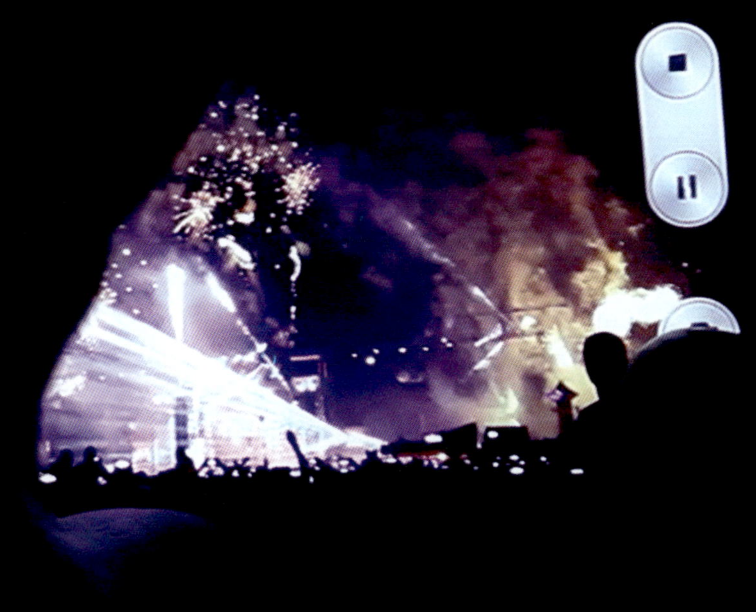
37114K

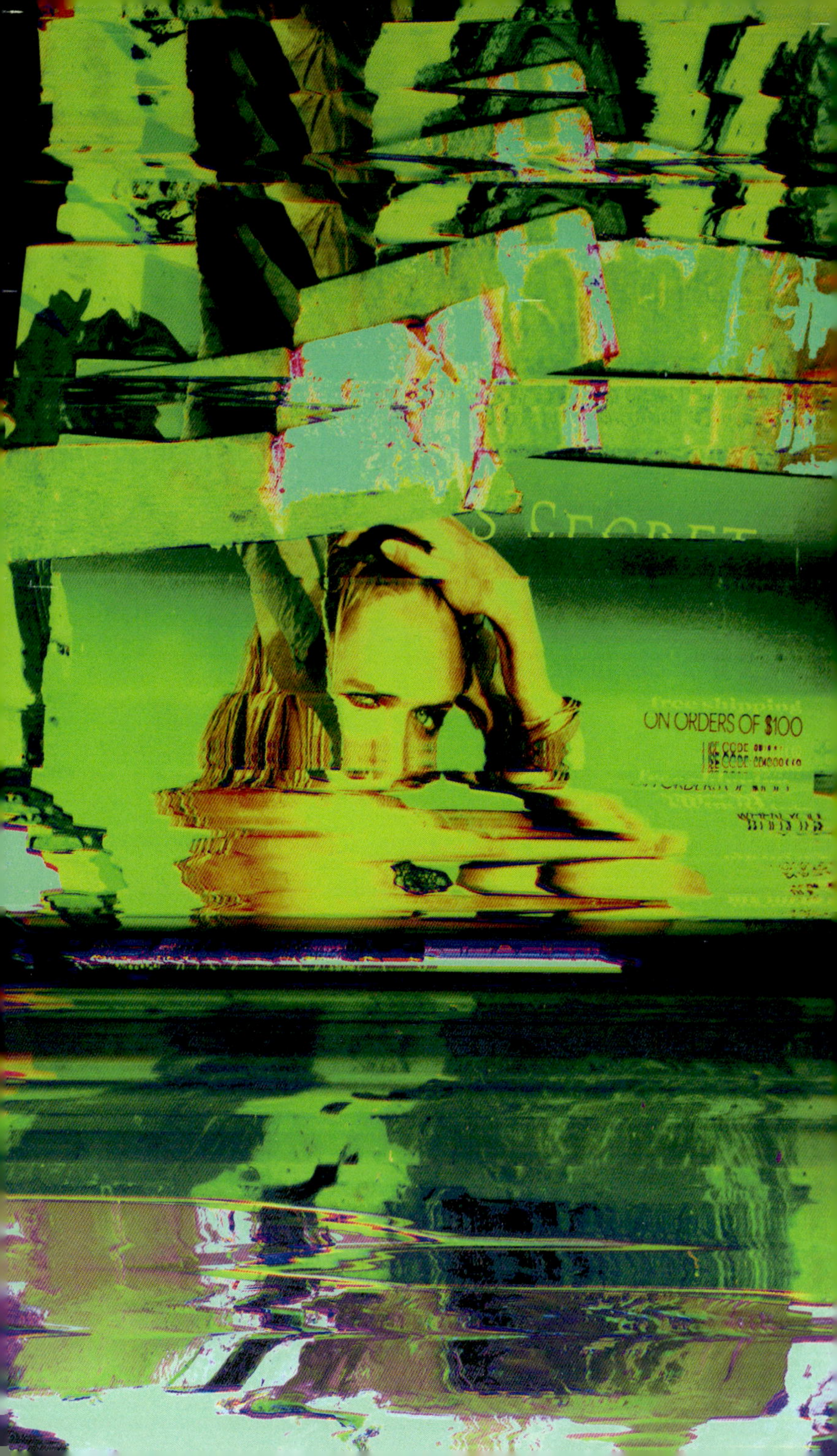

ON ORDERS OF $100

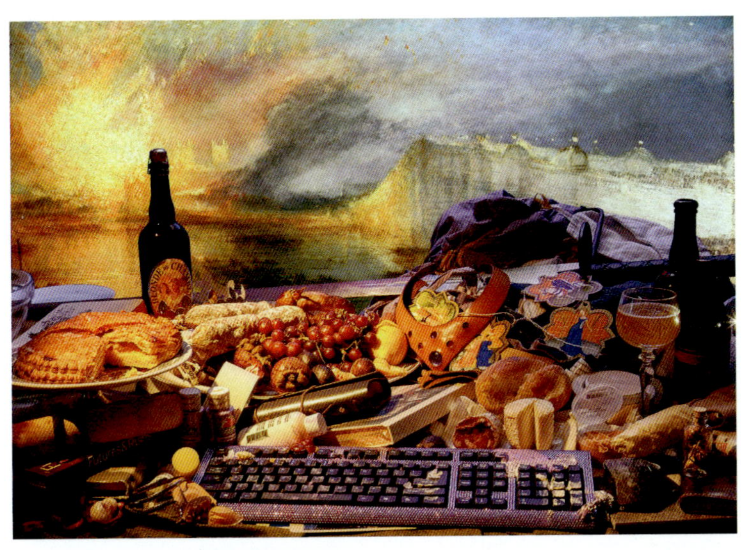

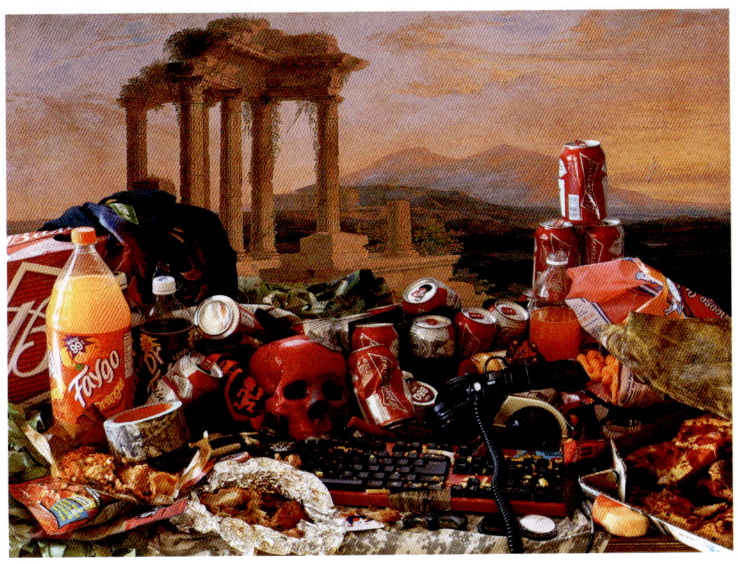
Faygo

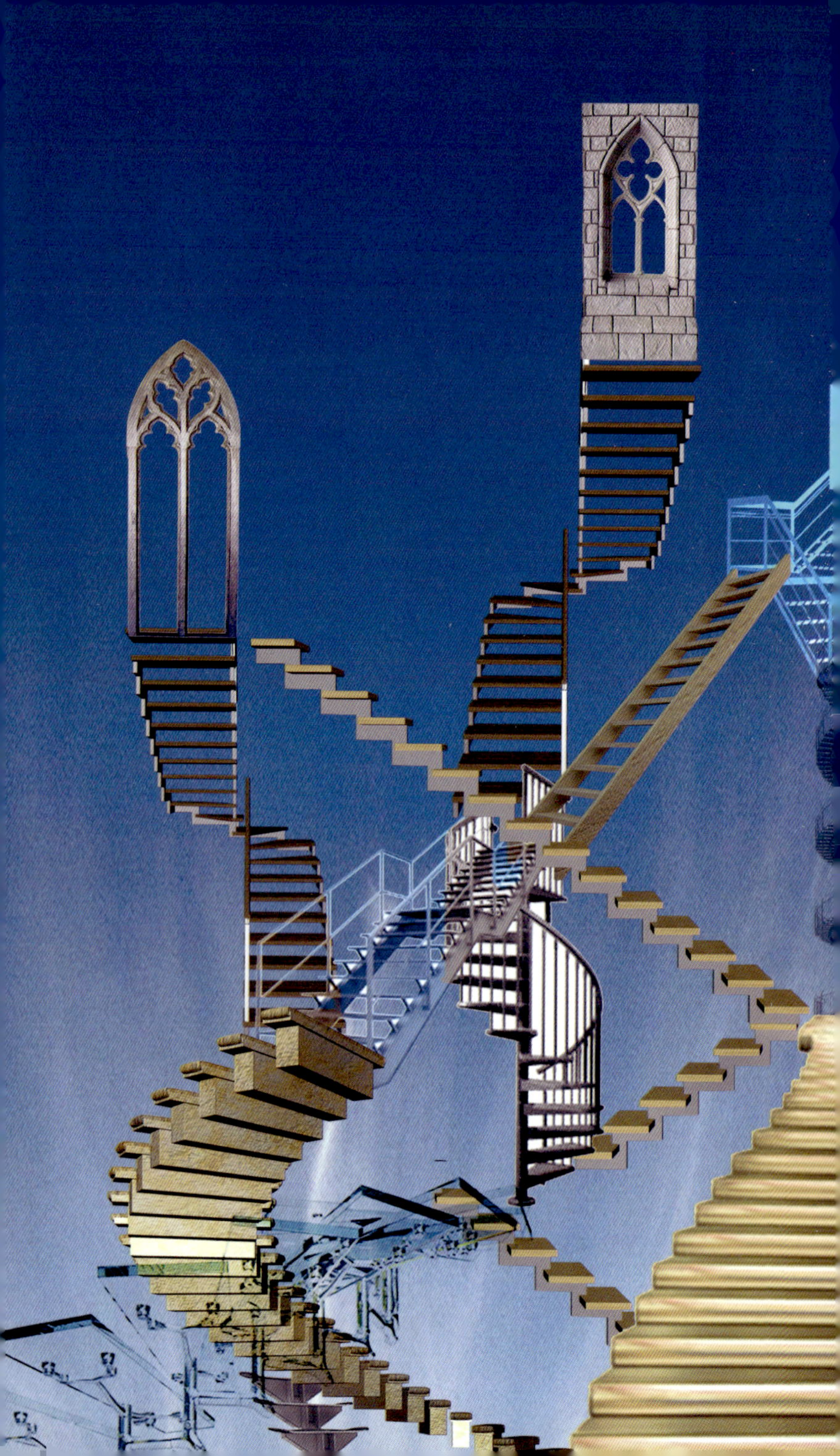

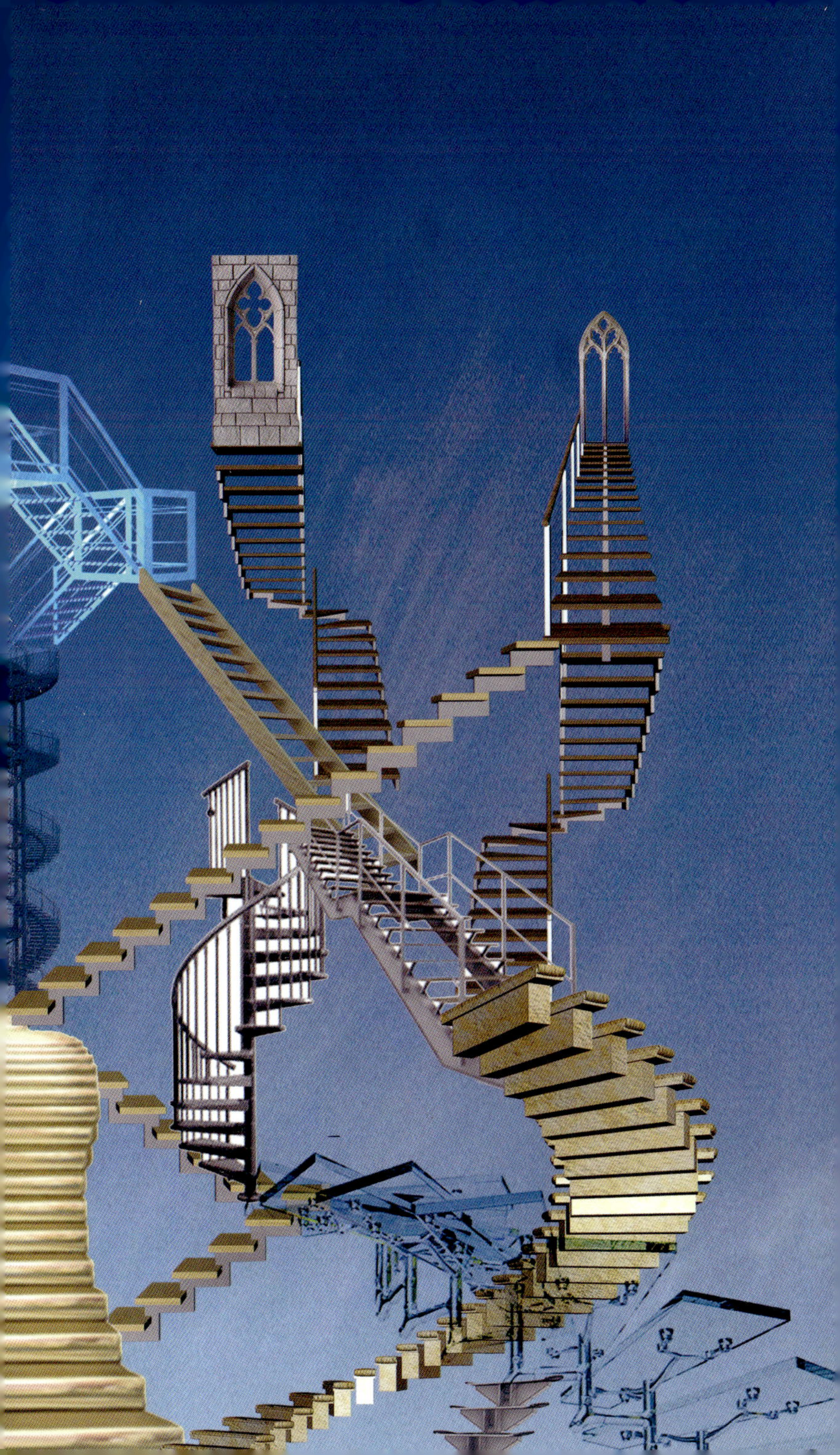

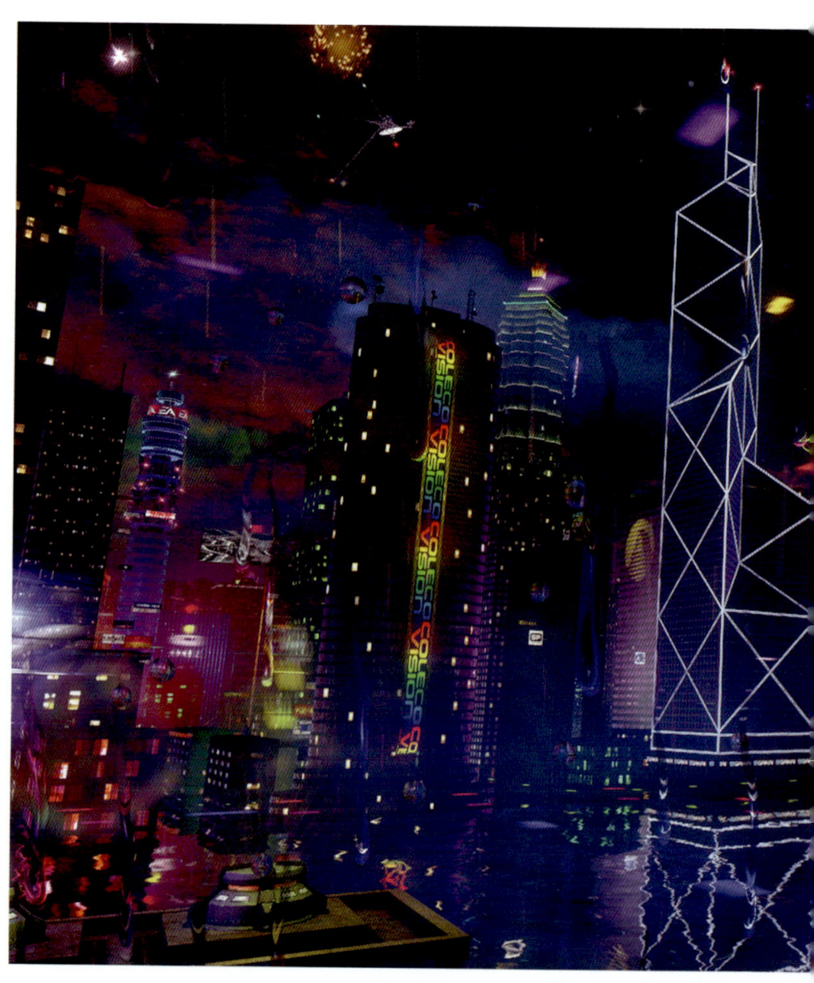
EA
COLECO COLECO COLECO
VISION VISION VISION

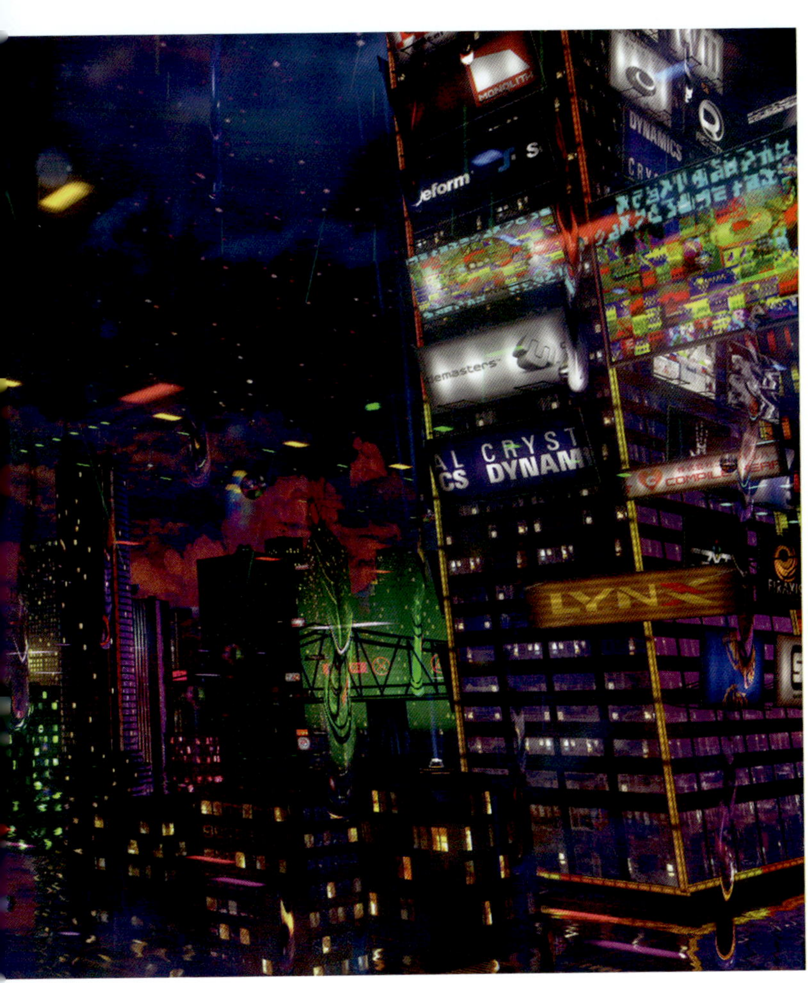
MONOLITH
DYNAMICS
LYNX

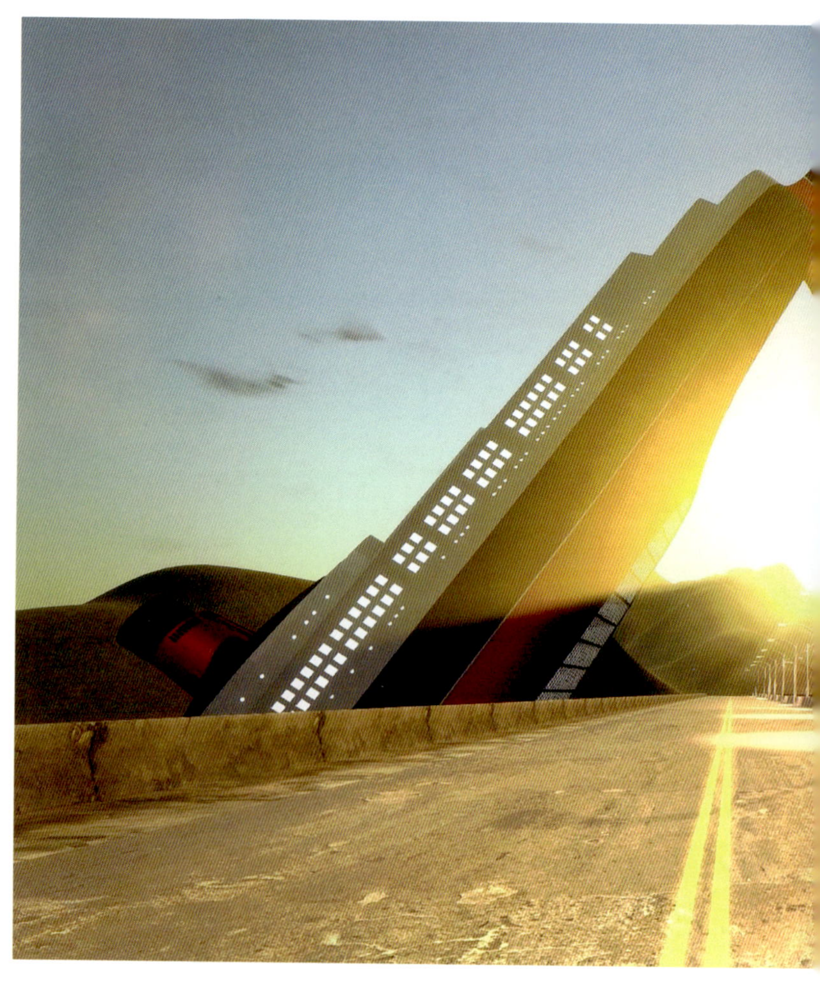

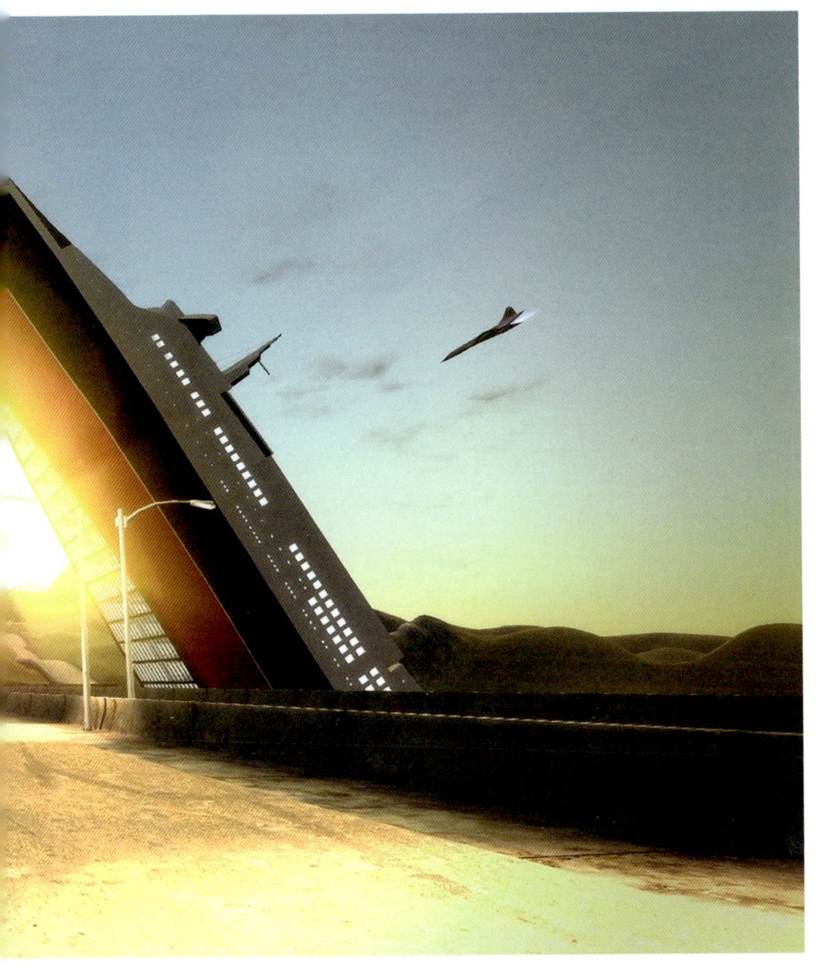

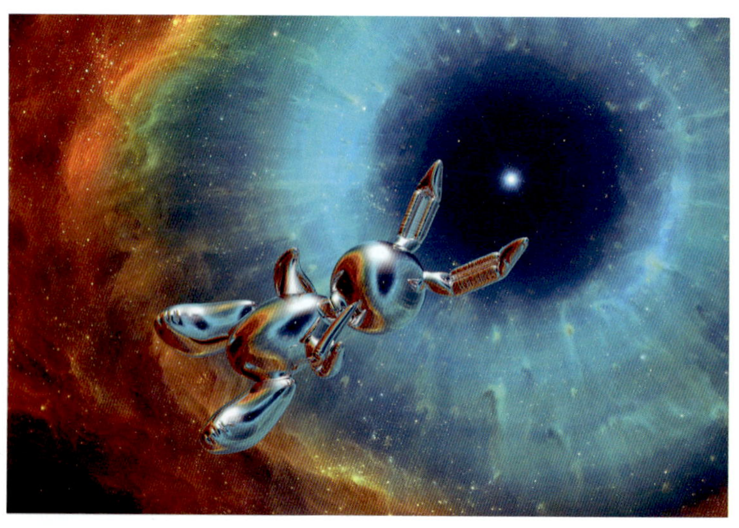

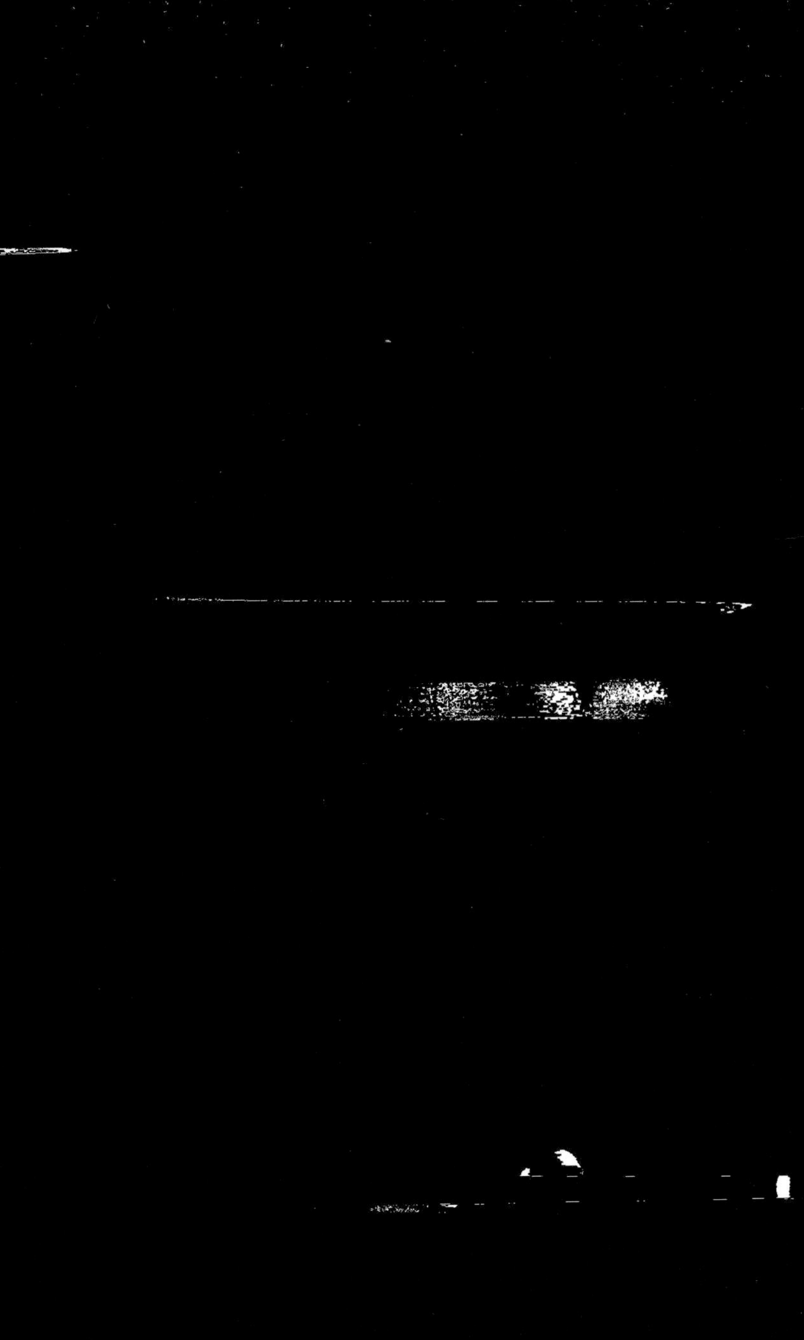

P 60
Cecile B Evans
Ref P 156–157

P 61
Ben Washington
Ref P 160–161

P 62
David Mullett
Ref P 164–165

P 65
Faith Holland
Ref P 145

P 66
Kari Altmann
Ref P 166–167

P 72
Lawrence Lek
Ref P 184–185

P 76
Ruanne Abou-Rahme
and Basel Abbas
Ref P 186–187

P 77
Anne de Vries
Ref P 190–191

P 84
John Kelsey
Ref P 182–183

P 88
Chris Dorland
Ref P 181

P 99
Samuel Fouracre
D.^^.$.®_Pony
2017

P 100–101
Carla Gannis
The Garden of Emoji Delights
2014
Courtesy of the Artist
and TRANSFER Gallery

P 102–103
Rafael Rozendaal
FloatBounce.com
2016
Courtesy of the Artist

P 104–105
Brenna Murphy
Earth Terrace
2015

P 106
Seana Gavin
Untilted
2016
Collage on card

P 107
Cory Arcangel
Photoshop CS: 86 by 60 inches, 300 DPI, RGB, square pixels, default gradient "Spectrum", mousedown y=25600 x=9200, mouseup y=1200 x=9200; tool "Wand", select y=1850 x=9200, tolerance=70, contiguous=off; default gradient "Spectrum", mousedown y=2000 x=1200, mouseup y=2000 x=1680
2015
Installation vides, Lisson Gallery, London, 2016
Photo: Jack Hems
Chromogenic print,
86 x 60 inches
Courtesy of the Artist
© Cory Arcangel

P 108
Laura Buckley
Maxwell flow
2016
Scanned James Clerk Maxwell colour wheels

P 109
Laura Buckley
Hands Holding On
2014
Scanned artist's personal photograph, digital print

P 110–111
Jeremy Shaw
Towards Universal Pattern Recognition (Copy. 9.23.91 Computers. Sep 23 1991)
2016
Archival press photo, kaleidoscopic acrylic, chrome
38.3 x 43.3 x 16 cm/15 x 17 x 6 1/3 inches
Photo: Trevor Good
Courtesy of the Artist and KÖNIG Galerie, Berlin

P 112–113
Metahaven
Interference (music video for Holly Herndon)
2015
Video still

P 114–115
Richard Mosse
Still frame from 'Incoming'
2017
Showing a young refugee holding an iPhone at the refugee shelter in the disused hangars of Tempelhof Airport in Berlin
Courtesy of the Artist and Jack Shainman Gallery

P 116–117
Nicolas Sassoon and Rick Silva
SIGNALS (interstitial)
2016
Single channel video
Courtesy of Nicolas Sassoon and Rick Silva

P 118–119
Nicolas Sassoon and Rick Silva
SIGNALS
2016
Multi-channel video projection, Wil Aballe Art Projects, Vancouver BC Canada
Courtesy of Wil Aballe Art Projects

P 120
Travess Smalley
2015-09-10_17-10-48
2015
Scripted digital image
11 x 8.5 inches

P 121
Travess Smalley
Capture Physical Presence #11
2011
Pigment print
46 x 34 inches

P 122
Giovanna Olmos
Francesca Gavin
2016
Portrait made with Procreate Pocket on iPhone 5c

P 123
Rachel Maclean
We Want Data!
2016
Digital Fabric Print Series
2.1m x 3m
Commissioned by
Artpace, San Antonio
and HOME, Manchester

P 124–125
Celia Hempton
Tony, Canada, 2nd November 2015
2015
Oil on polyester
25.5 x 30.5 cm
CH_PAI_406
SR-HEMP 1692
Courtesy of the Artist and
Southard Reid, London

P 126–127
Celia Hempton
Turkey, 22nd March 2017
2017
Oil on polyester
30 x 35 cm
CH_PAI_522
SR-HEMP 2073
Courtesy of the Artist and
Southard Reid, London

P 128–129
Artie Vierkant
Installation views from
series *Image Objects*
2013

P 130
James Hoff
Euphoria Headache
2016
Courtesy of the Artist and
Supportico Lopez

P 131
Douglas Coupland
I Miss My Pre-Internet Brain
2011
Courtesy of the Artist
and Daniel Faria Gallery,
Toronto

P 132–133
Ed Atkins
Even Pricks
2013
Video with surround sound
Courtesy of the Artist,
Cabinet, Isabella
Bortolozzi, Gavin Brown's
Enterprise, Dépendance

P 134–135
Ed Atkins
Even Pricks
2013
Video with surround sound
Courtesy of the Artist, Cabinet, Isabella Bortolozzi, Gavin Brown's Enterprise, Dépendance

P 136–137
Rachel Maclean
Still from 'It's What's Inside That Counts'
2016
30-min digital video
Commissioned HOME, University of Salford Art Collection, Tate, Zabludowicz Collection, Frieze Film and Channel 4

P 138
Marco Palmieri
Elide
2017
Courtesy of the Artist

P 139
Lynn Hershman Leeson
TV Legs
1988
From the series Phantom Limb
Gelatin Silver Print

P 140–141
Rafael Rozendaal
2015-timessquare
2015
Times Square, Midnight Moment, NYC
Photo: Michael Wells

P 142
Cory Arcangel
Photoshop CS: 86 by 60 inches, 300 DPI, RGB, square pixels, default gradient "Spectrum", mousedown y=25600 x=9200, mouseup y=1200 x=9200; tool "Wand", select y=1850 x=9200, tolerance=70, contiguous=off; default gradient "Spectrum", mousedown y=2000 x=1200, mouseup y=2000 x=1680
2015
Installation view, Lisson Gallery, London, 2016
Photo: Jack Hems

Chromogenic print
86 x 60 inches
Courtesy of the Artist
© Cory Arcangel

P 143
Antoine Catala
Feel Images (Distant)
2015
Photo: Bryan Conley
Courtesy of the Artist,
47 Canal, New York
and Carnegie Museum
of Art, Pittsburgh

P 144
Lynn Hershman Leeson
Tempt Fate
1979–1983
From Lorna, the first inter-active laser disc art piece
Chromogenic Print

P 145
Faith Holland
Skin Scroll
2016
Still from an animated GiF

P 146–147
Angelo Plessas
Faunamagica.com
2016
Courtesy of The Breeder,
Athens

P 148
Adham Faramawy
SXC N00DZ
2014
Video, 6 min 30 sec

P 149
Adham Faramawy
There's this thing, this feeling…
2017
Naughton Gallery, Belfast

P 150
Aram Bartholl
Point Of View,
Babycastles NYC,
Feb 2015
Photo: Aram Bartholl
Courtesy of Babycastles
Gallery, NY

P 151
Antoine Catala
Distant Feel
2015
Photo: Joerg Lohse
Courtesy of the Artist, 47 Canal, New York and New Museum, New York

P 152–153
Ruanne Abou-Rahme and Basel Abbas
Only the beloved keeps our secrets
2016
Video still
Courtesy of the Artists and Abraaj Art Prize

P 154–155
Ruanne Abou-Rahme and Basel Abbas
And yet my mask is powerful 2
2016
Installation view at Carroll / Fletcher, London
Courtesy of the Artists and Carroll / Fletcher, London

P 156–157
Cecile B Evans
What the Heart Wants
2016
HD video
Courtesy of the Artist and Emanuel Layr Galerie, Vienna

P 158–159
Brenna Murphy
HyperCubeArray
2015
Courtesy of the Artist and Pleasure Editions

P 160–161
Ben Washington
Geometric Figuring
2013
Screen grab of explorable digital environment

P 162–163
Constant Dullaart
Celebrate, Calibrate!
2009
DMX controller, stage lights, appropriated test print collage
Courtesy of the Artist and Future Gallery Berlin

P 164–165
David Mullett and Duncan Ransom
A Flash of Colour
2015
Immersive stereoscopic MP4 viewed in GearVR
Courtesy of the Artists

P 166–167
Kari Altmann
Still from *Softmobility.com*
Captured 2017

P 168–169
Margot Bowman
Heavenisforquitters.com
2016
Website
Music FaltyDL
Development Edvin Canon

P 170–171
Rafael Rozendaal
SlickQuick.com
2014
Dimensions Variable, Duration Infinite
Courtesy of the Artist

P 172–173
Yuri Pattison
Vitra Alcove (kowloon walled city kawasaki warehouse redux)
2017 (detail)
Photo: Citizen's of Nowhere, Kevin Space, Vienna 2017 / Georg Petermichl
Courtesy of the Artist, mother's tankstation, Dublin, Labor, Mexico City

P 174–175
Rosa Menkman
Myopia
2015

P 176–177
Simon Denny
Business Insider, Wiels, Brussels
2016
Photo: Jens Ziehe
Courtesy of the Artist and Wiels, Brussels

P 178–179
Simon Denny
New Mangement
2014
Installation View,
Portikus, Frankfurt (Main)
Photo: Helena Schlichting
Courtesy of the Artist
and
Galerie Buchholz, Berlin/
Cologne/New York

P 180
Angela Washko with
risograph printing
by Jimmy Riordan
Catalogue cover from
exhibition at TRANSFER
Gallery, NYC

P 181
Chris Dorland
Untitled (silicon violence)
2017
UV ink on Alumacore
46 x 32 inches

P 182–183
John Kelsey
Dans la rue, 4
2016
Watercolour on arches
paper
22.7 x 31 cm (framed:
30 x 38 x 3 cm)
Courtesy of the Artist and
Galerie Buchholz, Berlin/
Cologne/New York

P 184–185
Lawrence Lek
QE3
2016
Full HD Video Simulation,
20 min 16 sec
Glasgow International
2016, Director's
Programme curated
by Sarah McCrory,
Tramway, Glasgow, UK
Courtesy of the Artist

P 186–187
Ruanne Abou-Rahme
and Basel Abbas
Screenshot 2015-07-14
17.51.08
2015
Courtesy of the Artists and
Carroll / Fletcher, London

P 188–189
Metahaven
Home (music video for
Holly Herndon)
2014
Video still

P 190–191
Anne De Vries
Critical Mass: Pure Immanence
2015
Still from the video: 11 min

P 192
Chris Dorland
Untitled (corporate cannibal)
2017
UV ink on Alumacore
94 x 46 inches

P 193
Jon Rafman
You Are Standing in an Open Field (Fire)
2017
Archival pigment print and resin, on aluminium
Unique
59 x 79 inches (159 x 200.6 cm)

P 193
Jon Rafman
You Are Standing in an Open Field (Ruins)
2017
Archival pigment print and resin, on aluminium
Unique
59 x 79 inches (159 x 200.6 cm)

P 194–195
Jasmin Werner
Detail of digital collage as announcement for the exhibition *Status Faux* at Gillmeier Rech, Berlin
2016

P 196–197
Tabor Robak
20XX
2013
Courtesy of the Artist and team (gallery, inc.)

P 198–199
Lawrence Lek
QE3
2016
Full HD Video Simulation, 20 min 16 sec
Glasgow International 2016, Director's Programme curated by Sarah McCrory,Tramway, Glasgow, UK
Courtesy of the Artist

P 200
Tom Ireland
The Heavens_eye-nebula2560x1440.2017
2017
Still taken from the work
The Heavens
2015-ongoing

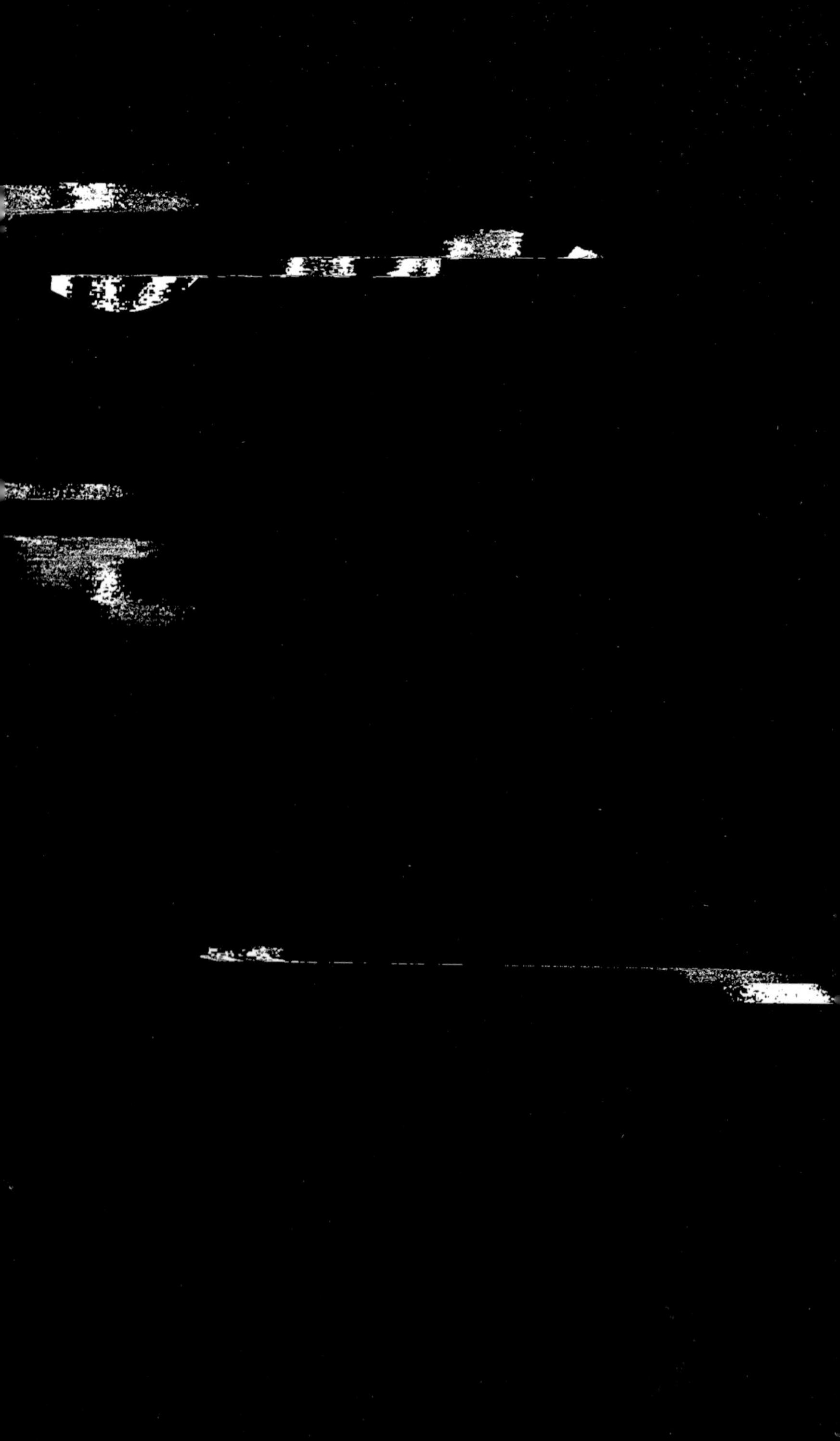

EDITORIAL ASSISTANTS

This book would not have been possible without the help of Emily Chancey, Bee Brittany Smith and Thomas Rackowe-Cork.

ACKNOWLEDGEMENTS

Angelique Spaninks, for inviting me to write the lecture-essay for the STRP festival that inspired this book; Luke Powell and Jody Hudson-Powell for approaching me to take things further; Pentagram's Margherita Papini for her exceptional talent and hard work; Mat Hill for his truly inventive approach to typography; Fenton Smith and all at Boss Print; Ashley Johnson for her eagle eyes; the family Gavin, especially Paola, my role model and dream editor; to all the artists who contributed their work and inspired me in so many ways; to Apple, Sony, Nokia, and Samsung, without whom I might just be reading books…

ABOUT THE AUTHOR

Francesca Gavin is a writer and curator based in London. She was the co-curator of the Historical Exhibition of Manifesta11. She is an editor at large at *Kaleidoscope*, contributing editor at *Twin*, *Art Papers*, *Good Trouble* and *semaine*. She has contributed to publications including the *Financial Times*, *Newsweek*, *Vogue*, *wallpaper**, *Artsy*, *Mousse* and *Cura*. She has a monthly radio show, *Rough Version*, on NTS.live. francescagavin.com

WATCH THIS SPACE
Francesca Gavin

BOOK DESIGN
Pentagram

DESIGN TEAM
Luke Powell
Jody Hudson-Powell
Margherita Papini

PRINT
Szaransky Print Company

Set in Arial Narrow

The Arial family was released by Monotype in 1982. The font is packaged with all versions of Microsoft Windows and is estimated to be installed on 1.5 billion computers worldwide.

ISBN
978-1-5272-3612-7

This is the second paperback edition of this book. Some images have been amended to fit the format. This book has been produced in a limited edition of 500.

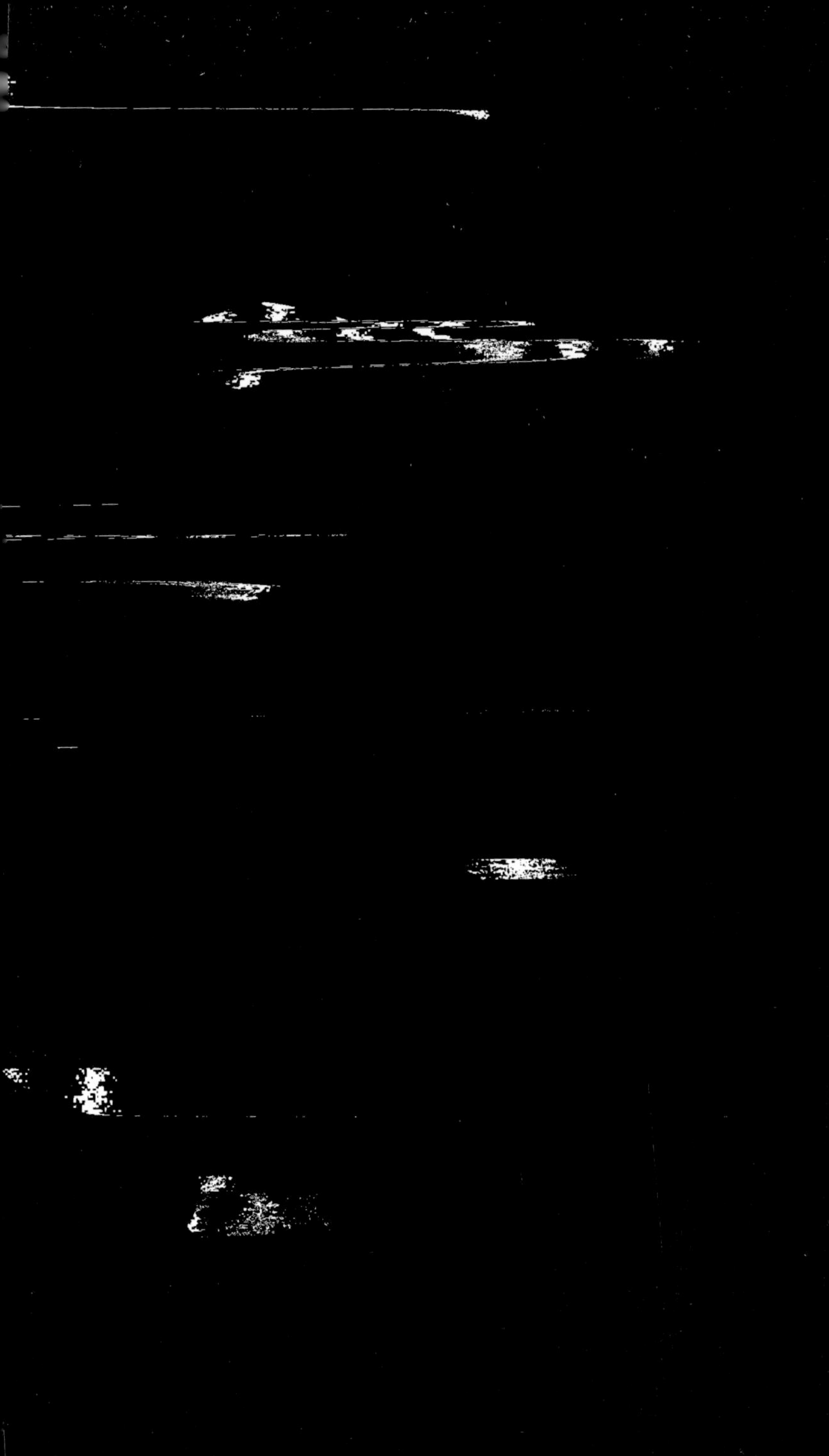

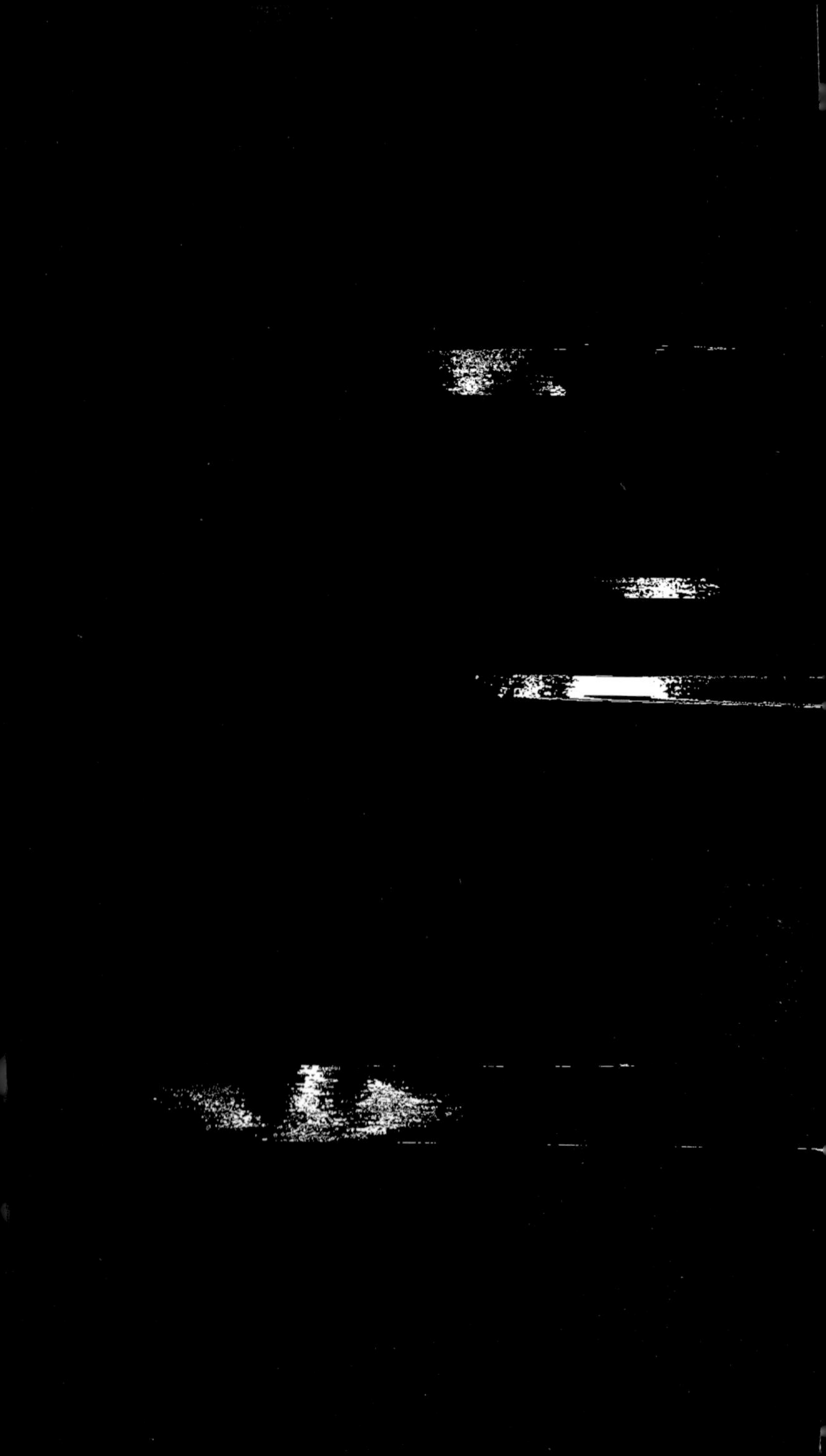